The Doctor From The East

The Doctor From The East

Asif Javed

Copyright © 2020 by Asif Javed.

Library of Congress Control Number: 2020908837
ISBN: Hardcover 978-1-9845-7937-9
Softcover 978-1-9845-7936-2
eBook 978-1-9845-7935-5

All rights reserved. No part of this book may be reproduced or transmitted in any form or by any means, electronic or mechanical, including photocopying, recording, or by any information storage and retrieval system, without permission in writing from the copyright owner.

Any people depicted in stock imagery provided by Getty Images are models, and such images are being used for illustrative purposes only.
Certain stock imagery © Getty Images.

Print information available on the last page.

Rev. date: 05/15/2020

To order additional copies of this book, contact:
Xlibris
1-888-795-4274
www.Xlibris.com
Orders@Xlibris.com
811454

Foreword

Asif Javed is among the few in the U.S.-based Pakistan expatriate community who has been able to straddle both the East and the West.

Born sixty-three years ago in a village near Mandi Bahauddin, Asif came from a Gondal Jat background. His early school education was done seated on tats (mats). His father, a lawyer, was a graduate of Aligarh University. He was an upstanding, old-fashioned gentleman attired in a suit and well respected in the community and would play tennis and read English-language newspapers while also being a quietly observant Muslim. So from an early age, Asif learned how the East and the West could be made complementary without compromising on quintessential Muslim values.

Asif was the youngest of eight siblings, and his primary education was in the village school until grade 8. After matriculation in Mandi Bahauddin, he joined the prestigious Government College Lahore as an FSC student (sophomore). From there, he transitioned into the elite King Edward Medical College Lahore, from where he secured his bachelor of medicine and bachelor of surgery.

His initial medical training was in England, where for six years he was in London, the Midlands, Wales, and York. In 1991, he came to America and stayed for six years in Pittsburgh where he did internal medicine residency under the late doctor Usman Ahmad, to whom he remains indebted. In 1997, he shifted to central Pennsylvania and has stayed to date in the town of Williamsport, which is 190 miles from Baltimore and 80 miles from Harrisburg. It is the birthplace and headquarters of Little League Baseball.

Asif Javed's passions are reading and traveling. He has been to Egypt, Morocco, Spain, Greece, Turkey, Peru, Chile, and most countries in Western Europe. From the beginning, Asif had an acute awareness of limitations that could hold him back and developed the drive to surmount them. That enabled him to ceaselessly strive for excellence.

Through determined grit, he was able to gain fluency and facility in the English language. I, for one, have benefited from his prolific pen. Sitting in the United States, he has been able to take a long view of his homeland, along with a keen perspective of the West. Medicine consumes much of his waking hours, but during the remains of the day, he has somehow managed to allocate space for daily reading on a broad range of subjects.

Today Asif, I can venture to assert, is one of the most fluent and readable purveyors of the English language in the community. His writings have ranged from Punjab politics to postpartition Indian cinema to English literature to the Tsarist wars in Dagestan. All the time, he manages to convey seemingly dense subjects in a seamless, flowing style, making his writings a treat to read.

It is my particular privilege to be asked to write the foreword to Asif Javed's book, which I strongly recommend in these days of turmoil to grasp what Pakistan is all about and what makes it relevant to the Western experience. In doing so, the "Doctor of the East" has built a bridge to the West.

Mowahid Hussain Shah
Washington, DC

Preface

This book is a collection of articles, all of which, except one, have been published in *Pakistan Link*, a weekly newspaper published from Anaheim, California. What has made me consider publishing this book? The short answer is Prof. Alaf Khan, a retired professor of medicine from Peshawar who writes almost flawless English. I consider him a far better writer than myself and therefore have tremendous respect for his opinion. He has read some of these articles, and it is his urging that has made me proceed.

Why have I written these articles? I am a fairly busy practicing physician, but my passion has always been history and, to a lesser extent, literature. As I started to read in my teenage years, one thing often intrigued me about the writers: while their stories and novels are often interesting, their personal lives are even more fascinating. Saadat Hasan Manto, Leo Tolstoy, Josh Malihabadi, Sahir Ludhianvi, Kipling, the Brontë sisters, and many others have had unusual, exciting, often tragic lives with better stories of their own than the ones that have come out of their pen. These deserve to be told. I have made an attempt.

As the readers may notice, many of the articles are about people connected to movies and music. Dilip Kumar, Madhubala, Balraj Sahni, Suraiya, K. L. Saigal, Mukesh, Talat Mahmood, Khurshid Anwar, and Salim Raza have their lives explored in the limited space available. There are three articles on freedom fighters: Bhagat Singh, Dada Amir Haider, and Hadji-Murad. While Bhagat Singh's life story is well known, the other two's is not, hence the articles. There are better writers than me to write about the social issues. But I could not resist the temptation to address a few; "Being Alcoholic," "What Is Wrong with Us" and "The Arrogant Ones" fall in this category.

A lot has been written about the life of Z. A. Bhutto. My article about him has generated more controversy than I have anticipated. It has generated praise as well as severe criticism. I am not surprised, for Z. A. Bhutto had been, and continues to be, a very polarizing political figure. The flood of e-mails that I have received about this article have come from sources as diverse as a sitting ambassador of Pakistan, a relative of Z. A. Bhutto, a Pakistan Air Force (PAF) pilot who used to fly Z. A. Bhutto, and some people who have personally suffered during his regime. Nawab of Kalabagh, Yahya Khan, and Iskander Mirza have all played important roles in the history of Pakistan; and therefore, their sketches may be of interest to some readers too.

My father has influenced my life more than anyone else. Usman Ahmad, a Pakistani physician in Pittsburgh, was my teacher, mentor, and later friend. He had introduced me to *Pakistan Link* way back in the midnineties. Prof. Nasrullah Malik was my maternal uncle. He had introduced me to literature. They have already gone to their final abode. I have fond memories of all three. Their obituaries are included.

Akhtar Faruqui, the editor of *Pakistan Link*, has been wonderful over the years. He has read and, at times, corrected the errors and at least twice changed the titles of my articles—for the better, I must admit. Mowahid Hussain Shah, the lead writer of *Pakistan Link*, with his vast knowledge, has been my guiding light and mentor. Both have my gratitude for having written the foreword and introduction to this book. My nephews Tahir and Amir Ijaz, both civil servants in Pakistan, have accompanied me to several places mentioned in the book. Abu Turab, another nephew in the UK, made an extraordinary effort to locate the final resting place of Ch. Rahmat Ali in Cambridge. They all have my love and thanks.

Last but not the least, Shazia, my wife. While it is customary to thank one's spouse, in this case, it is certainly well deserved. With all the hundreds of hours spent writing that have been taken away from my family, not once has she complained. It is only with her help that I have learned to negotiate the computer and all the gadgets associated with it. Thanks also to all the guidance and technical support from the excellent staff at Xlibris, my publisher.

In writing these articles, I may have partially succeeded in one goal: I have been educating myself. I remain uncertain about the response to this publication. The culture of book reading is dying in Pakistan and in the Pakistani community in the USA. I hope this effort has been worthwhile. Any commemts or corrections are welcome at <u>asifjaved@comcast.net</u>. Happy reading and God bless.

Asif Javed
Williamsport, PA, 2020

Introduction

As a starry-eyed college student enamored of Shafiq-ur-Rahman's Shaffoo Bhai and Jane Austen's Elizabeth Bennet, I carried vivid memories of the supreme sacrifice of James Dillingham Young and his wife, Della, principal characters of O. Henry's *The Gift of the Magi*, who parted with their most cherished possession to buy a present for the other. The story formed part of our English curriculum at the D. J. Sindh Government Science College in Karachi, Pakistan. Almost half a century later, I read the story again and found it equally riveting. Now transformed into an infirm oldie in his twilight years, I could still summon empathy and adoration for the couple as readily as the dreamy youngster of yesteryear. This time, it was my grandson—a student at the Cypress High School, California—who shared the privations of James and Della with me. *The Gift of the Magi* was part of his grade 11 English course.

Good writings defy time and immediate surroundings to sustain their appeal. The entrancing aura of a well-knit article or story is lasting. Surely, Hardy's rustic Tess or Jude couldn't be out of sync in the year 2020 for technology-savvy readers obsessed with Instagram, Twitter, Facebook, and accompanying high-tech spin-offs.

Without being extravagant with words, I dare say that the same is true of Dr. Asif Javed's writings in *Pakistan Link*. Insightful and instructive, they are studded with revealing facts that are well documented to testify to the innate truth. The gifted writer tells us of the life and time of the Brontë sisters, Ibn Battuta, Leo Tolstoy, Nawab of Kalabagh, Rudyard Kipling, Zulfikar Ali Bhutto, et al. In more ways than one, the articles remind the reader of Dale Carnegie's *Little Known Facts about Well-Known People*. No wonder Dr. Javed enjoys immense popularity among *Link* readers and his articles are read and reread. Even stray readers mention him.

Pakistan Link derives its strength from distinguished writers like Dr. Asif Javed. I am happy his work is being published in a single volume—to be preserved and remembered.

Akhtar Mahmud Faruqui
Editor, *Pakistan Link*
Anaheim, California
March 6, 2020

A Tale of Two Countries

Once upon a time, there was a country. Its vast territories encompassed three continents. It also had a mighty army. In the year 1326, it was ruled by Orkhan. He was the son of Osman, the founder of this legendary Ottoman Empire. Orkhan was a wise ruler, and he came up with a novel idea. He "recruited in to his army from among Christians a picked and disciplined infantry force to serve the Sultan in person," writes Lord Kinross in *The Ottoman Centuries*. "This was the corps of Janissaries . . . they were now developed by Murad [the third Ottoman sultan] in to a militia . . . handpicked for their virility, physique, and intelligence, inflexibly trained, strictly disciplined, and inured to all forms of hardship, they were like monks . . . their lives became dedicated to military service under the Sultan's direction."

Little did Orkhan and Murad realize that the Janissaries were to influence the destiny of their nation for centuries. The Janissaries soon developed a reputation to be invincible. In 1402, when Amir Timur threatened Bayezid, the Ottoman sultan's reply to the invader from Central Asia showed his confidence in the Janissaries:

> Thy armies are innumerable; be they so; but what are the arrows of the flying Tartar against the scimitars and battle-axes of my firm and invincible Janissaries.

The Janissaries were to lead the Ottoman Empire to countless glorious victories, including the capture of Constantinople in 1453. Ironically, they were also to be one of the reasons for its downfall.

The Ottoman Empire's slow decline began in 1566 after the death of Süleyman the Magnificent. Over the following three and a half centuries, it went through numerous upheavals: frequent wars with its hostile neighbors, incompetent sultans and grand viziers, rampant corruption, and intrigues of the harm among many others. By the sixteenth century, as Europe came out of medieval darkness and started to go through Renaissance, the Ottoman Empire started to fall behind. "Their military development had failed to keep pace with that of the West," writes Kinross. There were some sultans and grand viziers here and there who recognized this and wanted to reform the army. They were aware that, to the north, Peter the Great had modernized the Russian army and navy and made no secret of his hostility toward Ottomans. There were wars also off and on with Habsburg Austria to the west and with Safavid Persia to the east. Most such attempts at reformation failed, however, because of the Janissaries. Their "rebellious inclinations had been noted for years . . . They had lost their discipline and zeal for war," notes Kinross. But they continued to resist reform:

> From the last decade of 16th century onward, they became, as their masters the Sultans grew weaker, progressively more turbulent and exacting in their demands . . . In 1589, they gave serious trouble to Murad . . . For the first time in history, they stormed their way into the Seraglio [palace], where the Divan was in session, and demanded the heads of the ministers . . . Rather than face the insurgent troops in person, the Sultan bowed the knee to their superior force by sanctioning the executions. Twice more during the next three years, they drove home their advantage, demanding and securing the deposition of two successive Grand-Vazirs. . . . The Janissaries had indeed begun to present a serious threat to the Empire. For centuries the strong arm of the Ottoman forces in their imperial conquests, they were now in their greed and indiscipline deteriorating as a warlike force abroad and developing in to a subversive force at home . . . In the capital, as one inadequate Sultan followed another, they came to be a dominant power and a focus of sedition. . . .

> The eighteen-year-old Sultan Osman, stung to indignation by the stigma of becoming "subject to his own slaves" devised an elaborate scheme to counter this threat to his sovereignty.

Unfortunately, the young sultan's plan for the suppression of the Janissaries—which needed topmost secrecy—was leaked with disastrous results: the Janissaries stormed his palace and tore the grand vizier to pieces. As far the unfortunate sultan Osman, he was humiliated in public, deposed, imprisoned, and then executed. Thus ended the first serious attempt by an Ottoman ruler to control the Janissaries.

After this tragic failure, the Ottoman Empire once again "relapsed in to anarchy whereby meek Sultans were too scared of confronting Janissaries." In 1730, the Janissaries had yet another mutiny on some flimsy ground and forced Sultan Ahmad III to hand over to them the grand vizier, the chief admiral, and another senior official; all three were strangled to death. A terrified sultan was asked to abdicate. Fearful for life, he promptly obliged. The Janissaries' reign of terror continued.

Two centuries passed. In 1826, another eighteen-year-old—Sultan Mahmud II—was on the throne. Mahmud finally showed the resolve to deal with the menace of the Janissaries. Aware of the risks involved and the tragic fate of his ancestor, Sultan Osman, Mahmud made his move with utmost prudence. Here is Lord Kinross's narration from *The Ottoman Centuries*:

> The way thus now lay open for the elimination of the most powerful enemy within the Ottoman state, the corps of Janissaries . . . the chief source of the rot at the core . . . For his coup against the Janissaries, the Sultan had prepared his own troops in advance, foreseeing fierce conflict in the streets and thus concentrated on the enlargement and improvement of his force of artillery, which alone could ensure their destruction. . . . He entrusted its command to officers picked for their loyalty, under a general so ruthless as to earn in the ensuing slaughter the name of "Black Hell." . . . As the Sultan had anticipated, the Janissaries refused to accept this provision

(reforms policy). Once more they overturned their camp kettles in the traditional gesture of revolt . . . bent on massacre, they advanced on the Sultan's palace, crying for the heads of his chief ministers . . . But this time, Sultan was prepared for them. His troops and artillery were ready for action . . . As the mob of Janissaries pressed through the narrow streets towards Seraglio, the guns opened fire from its walls, cutting swaths through their columns as they fell helpless against an unrelenting blast of grapeshot . . . they retreated to within the walls of their barracks, to barricade themselves against an expected assault. . . . But no assault came. . . . Instead, Sultan's heavy artillery thundered shells in to the barracks, setting them on fire and soon laying them in ruins, while four thousand of the mutineers perished. Such, within little more than half an hour, was the extermination by modern arms of the nucleus of a military force five centuries old . . . It was completed with unremitting severity, by the slaughter throughout the provinces of thousands more. On the same day the Sultan abolished, by proclamation, the corps of the Janissaries; their name was proscribed and their standards destroyed.

And so it came to pass that, in the blessed year of 1826, with one bold stroke of Mahmud II, the Janissaries were eliminated once for all. What had become a clear and present danger to the state, and to the very person of the sultan, was no more. "They were liquidated to the very last man," notes Kinross.

And that brings our tale to the other country, Pakistan. Our Islamic republic has its own version of Janissaries to deal with. The Ottoman Janissaries passed into oblivion two hundred years ago, but their successors have recently emerged in Pakistan. They are not hard to identify. Just juxtapose the pictures of the original Janissaries with those of Khadim Rizvi, Abdul Aziz (Lal Masjid fame), et al., and there you have it. The current PM has been to Oxford. History may not have been his subject at the illustrious place of learning. He may not have heard of the Janissaries.

But as these lines are being written, a group of mullahs is being shown on TV. Ferocious in their looks and ignorant to the core in their beliefs, they are asking for the head of the chief justice of the highest court in the land. Their audacity is there for all to see. At their command is a hysterical mob blocking a major road and threatening to wreak vengeance on the innocent citizens. Quaid's Pakistan, the sixth largest country in the world with a professional army and an atomic power, has been allowed to become hostage to a few. The nation finds itself utterly at the mercy of a few zealots. Z. A. Bhutto's unwise decision, in 1973, to yield to religious fanatics, followed by their appeasement by the cunning Zia-ul-Haq, has brought our nation to the brink of anarchy. The current government has the support of judiciary and military. Vast majority of the people are fed up with the religious bigots.

"It was the best of times; it was, also, the worst of times," writes Charles Dickens in *The Tale of Two Cities*. Dickens had been writing of the reign of terror that had taken over Paris during the French Revolution. But the great storyteller might as well have been referring to Pakistan. But a well-planned, properly executed action, like the one by Sultan Mahmud II two hundred years ago, may still change the worst of our times to the best of times.

Reference: *The Ottoman Centuries* by Lord Kinross

The Greatness of Al-Andalus: Myth or Reality

Legend had it that Abu Abdullah—the last Muslim ruler of Granada—stood at a vantage point outside Granada before finally leaving the land of his proud ancestors for good on his way to Africa. Tears in his eyes were noticed by his mother, who scolded him, "If you were unable to defend your kingdom like a man, at least do not shed tears like a woman." Hours earlier, he had tamely surrendered his kingdom to the joint Christian forces of Ferdinand and Isabella, finally bringing to an end the Islamic rule in the Iberian Peninsula.

Some seven centuries earlier, an expedition had moved in the opposite direction in 711, having crossed the strait that divides southern Europe from North Africa. It was led by a Berber by the name of Tariq ibn Ziyad. Under his command was a force of seven thousand men, mostly Berbers, although the overall command remained in the hands of Musa ibn Nusayr, who was the Umayyad governor of northwest Africa, a province of the Umayyad caliphate based in Damascus. Victory after victory followed, and in a little over five years, most—but not all—of the Iberian Peninsula was securely in the hands of Muslims. Tariq was joined by Musa himself the following year before the later was recalled to Damascus. Musa was never to return. There are various legends about his ill treatment by the caliph and his difficult last days spent in extreme poverty or captivity. Not much was known of Tariq after his military mission was accomplished.

In 732, the Muslim army moved farther north and kept going until it was finally defeated in the Battle of Tours in central France. The Battle of Tours was one of the most decisive battles in history since it represented the high-water mark of the Muslim invasion of Europe. Never before or since had they gone so far into western Europe. Perhaps this defeat was merely a reflection of the fact that Muslims were far from their base, and the man power may have been stretched to the very limit; the setback at Tours was the end of advance into Europe.

The Islamic rule in Spain—renamed Al-Andalus by the Muslims—continued in one shape or form from 711 to 1492, but unlike the other long dynasties—for instance, the Ottoman Turks or Moguls—it was far from a single dynasty. For the first forty years or so, Al-Andalus was a province of the Umayyad caliphate based in Damascus. In 750, there was a violent overthrow of Umayyads by Abbasids, who moved the capital to Baghdad. The male Umayyads were massacred, all but one. The lone survivor was a young man of twenty who fled to Morocco—in disguise—to his mother's family. His name was Abd ar-Rahman, who was to found one of the great dynasties of its time a few years later. As was expected, the passing of the caliphate to Abbasids merely changed the loyalty of the governor of Al-Andalus; it continued to be a province of the caliphate as before.

In 756, Abd ar-Rahman moved north across the Strait of Gibraltar, defeated the Abbasid governor of Al-Andalus in a battle, and established the independent emirate of Al-Andalus. This started the second phase of Islamic rule in the Iberian Peninsula. Over the following 250 years, Abd ar-Rahman and his able successors made Al-Andalus the envy of Europe. The Islamic Spain was wealthy and culturally diverse and had an efficient government and a strong professional army. The population was a mixture of men of Iberian stock, Berbers and Arabs. The Umayyad Spain seemed to have reached its zenith in the tenth century. At the time, its prestige was such that many Christian states up north were its vassals, and its influence extended even into northern Morocco.

The decline of Umayyad Spain was relatively sudden and unexpected. From the height of its glory, it fell into a civil war and, by 1031, had thirty independent city-states competing and fighting with one another. The Umayyad caliphate was effectively over. The reasons were many and beyond the scope of this article. This period of anarchy was referred to as the "era of party kings."

The hostile Christian states in the north were watching the disintegration of Al-Andalus and made some threatening moves. At this juncture, Muslims looked to the south for help from a fellow Muslim. The powerful ruler of Morocco and Algeria of the Almoravid Dynasty was happy to oblige. His name was Yusuf ibn Tashufin. Yusuf came to Spain in 1086, inflicted a crushing defeat to the Christians in the Battle of al-Zallaqah, and so began the next phase of Islamic rule in Spain known as the Almoravid period. This was the first Berber dynasty to rule Spain that lasted almost fifty years. In this, Al-Andalus was effectively a province of the Almoravid Empire based in North Africa. In 1170, Almoravids were replaced by Almohads in Africa, and Al-Andalus became a province of their empire.

By this time, however, the Christian forces were on the march and had started the Reconquista. There was a decisive victory for the Christians over Almohads at Las Navas de Tolosa in 1212 that effectively restored Christian rule of the Iberian Peninsula. There was one exception to this in the southeast of Spain, a small Muslim state that measured 240 by 70 miles. This was to last almost 250 years and was the kingdom of Granada; this was the very last phase of Muslim rule in Spain.

Founded in the year 1231 by ibn Nasr, an Arab from Medina, Granada managed to survive that long despite heavy odds due to its mountainous terrain, proximity to Muslim Morocco, and careful diplomacy that made it become a vassal state of the Christian north at times. It was a prosperous kingdom with limited military resources that eventually became weak due to infighting, mostly quarrels of succession, among the ruling elite. It surrendered to the joint forces of Castile and Aragon in 1492.

Despite the end of Muslim rule in 1492, there were hundreds of thousands of Muslims in Spain who continued to live under the Christian rule. Initially, they were treated well; but by 1499, intolerance had set in. Muslims as well as Jews were given the option of baptism or forced exile. Historians reported that close to half a million moved to North Africa, where to this day there were small enclaves of Al-Andalus.

What is the legacy of Islamic Spain? It is ironic that most of the great cultural achievements belong to the latter part of the Islamic rule when its political power has been in the decline. There is Alhambra, a fortress-cum-palace in Granada, constructed in the fourteenth century. The great mosque of Cordova and the palace city of Madinat al-Zahra, recently excavated and partially restored, are other good examples of Umayyad architecture.

Ibn Zaydun's poetry in the eleventh century has been outstanding, as has been Ibn Hazm's book on sects, widely believed to be the first ever work on the comparative religion. There are many other scholars with significant contributions to the cultural greatness of Al-Andalus, but one that towers above everybody else, undoubtedly, is Ibn-Rushd (1126–98), known as Averroës to the West. Ibn-Rushd has been an outstanding jurist, and his name is frequently mentioned among the greatest philosophers of all time. He was an Aristotelian scholar par excellence and, with his deep penetration into the thought of Aristotle, wrote commentaries on his works, which were subsequently translated into many European languages. Maimonides, Ibn al-Khatib, Ibn Bajjah, Ibn Tufayl, and many others have been all scholars of merit. Ibn-Khaldūn, the author of that remarkable historical work *Muqaddimah*, though born and based in Tunis, had come from an Arab family of Spain and spent years in Granada. Some critics believe that there is a major Andalusian influence in his work. Ibn Juzzay, who helped Ibn Battuta with the writing and editing of his travel book *Rihlah*, had also come from Granada. The list goes on and on.

Montgomery Watt, in his excellent book *A History of Islamic Spain*, quotes an economic historian: "If the north wanted best in science, medicine, agriculture, industry or civilized living, it must go to Spain to learn." In the same book, he reports a Christian writer who complained that fellow Christians were so taken with the Arabic language and its literature as to neglect and even express contempt for Latin texts. And what did the Christians see when they retook Seville in 1248? Here are the words of Americo Castro: "Those victorious armies could not repress their astonishment upon beholding the grandeur of Seville; the Christians had never possessed anything similar in art, economic splendor, civil organization, technology and scientific and literary productivity." The intrinsic greatness of Al-Andalus is perhaps expressed best by that great Islamic scholar, the late Montgomery Watt, who wrote: "The life of Al-Andalus is indeed a noble facet of total experience of mankind."

Reference: *A History of Islamic Spain* by Montgomery Watt

Atatürk: The Nation Builder

As a young army officer, Mustafa Kemal (MK) once told a friend, "I am going to make you PM of our country one day."

"And what will you be?" asked his surprised friend.

"The one who appoints PM," Mustafa Kemal said.

Enver Pasa, one of the founders of Young Turks, was his superior in the army. While approving Kemal for promotion, he remarked, "Once he is a general, he will like to be sultan; once a sultan, he will like to be God."

The above two incidents should leave no doubt in the reader's mind that the founder of modern Turkey was ambitious and did not hesitate to proclaim his greatness.

Born in Thessaloníki—now in northern Greece—MK's family was precariously middle class. His paternal grandfather may have been of Albanian origin. His father, Ali Riza, was a junior civil servant who died when MK was seven or eight. Years later, when shown a picture of his father, MK remarked, "This is not my father." His mother, Zubaida, remarried while MK continued his education.

Two years before MK's birth, the Russian army was encamped just a few miles from Istanbul while, only two hundred years earlier, the Ottomans had laid siege to Vienna; this was how far the once invincible Ottoman Empire had declined. By the time MK got his commission in the army, the First World War was raging. The Turks were under attack from multiple hostile neighbors. It was after defeat in the war, followed by the flight of the leaders of Young Turks, that MK emerged as a leader who is now remembered as a radical modernizer and nation builder.

In April 1915, three-quarters of a million soldiers were crammed into the Gallipoli Peninsula; the sole objective of the Allies was the Ottoman capital, Istanbul. There are only a few times in the life of individuals as well as nations that make or break them; for MK, Gallipoli was that moment, and he seized it. There is a statement attributed to MK that has become part of the folklore of the Turkish war of independence: MK issued an order to his regiment that he wanted them to die for him. In the ensuing furious hand-to-hand fighting, most of his regiment was wiped out, but the Turkish line held, until reinforcement arrived to save the day. The Allies had to withdraw, much to the chagrin of a young Winston Churchill, then a young lord of the Admiralty. In 2010, while visiting Gallipoli, this writer came upon the graves of three Indian soldiers—Imam Din, Allah Ditta, and Hussain Khan—who were made to fight against their fellow Muslims by the British Indian Army. It is interesting to note that, in the fog of war, MK's exploits at Gallipoli remained largely unnoticed until an interview that he gave almost three years later; it was only then that he was rightfully acknowledged as the victor of Gallipoli and savior of Istanbul.

By all accounts, MK was handsome; he was of fair color and had piercing blue eyes. He liked women and had had numerous affairs. Even later in life, he was not always discreet about it. He liked to smoke, drank alcohol, and frequented nightclubs. Once at a ball, he danced with the beautiful daughter of the French ambassador and, under the influence of alcohol, started to kiss her while in full view of guests. MK hated signs of oriental life; he disliked baggy trousers and was fluent in French but could hardly speak Arabic. He was obsessed with order, good clothes, and cleanliness.

MK's nationalist fervor had become a legend; once, he overheard a Turkish officer admonishing a junior fellow officer who was upset with an Arab soldier. Having heard a statement that Arabs were a race to be respected and were superior to Turks, MK was furious and made one of his most celebrated statements, saying, "The Arabs may be a noble race, but Turks are even nobler."

MK's personal life was a disaster. He married twenty-four-year-old Latife, the beautiful daughter of a wealthy merchant from Izmir. It was a failed marriage and, in many ways, reminiscent of Quaid's marriage to

Rutti. Both wives were young, beautiful, and from high-profile families while their much older husbands were preoccupied with the national struggle. The marriage was strained also by a long-term affair that MK had with the niece of his stepfather. This attractive young woman named Fikriye, who was totally devoted to MK, continued to pursue him even after he was married; depressed after MK's refusal to see her, she shot and killed herself.

MK was convinced from the beginning that only he could lead Turkey in the right direction. Many of his original companions, among those Gen. Ali Fuat and Karabekir, fell by the wayside while he continued his relentless pursuit of radical reforms and modernization. He was lucky to have found a superb subordinate in the person of Colonel Ismet, later known as Ismet İnönü. Ismet, who gained fame by his brilliant defeat of the Greek army at İnönü, turned out to be a perfect complement for MK. The two men were very different in their lifestyle: MK was very Westernized and secular—he once declared that he had no religion—while Ismet was a practicing Muslim—he was known to carry a miniature Koran in his pocket—and a shrewd politician. But they both shared the vision for their homeland and, despite their differences, managed to work together. MK had enormous respect for İnönü; aware that Ismet was hard pressed financially, MK left a portion of his will for the education of Ismet's children.

MK had been born into a multiethnic, multilingual, predominantly Muslim Ottoman Empire. But while serving in the First World War, he convinced himself that Islam alone would not keep the country together. His bitter experience in the Middle East, where the Arabs changed sides immediately after the defeat of the Turkish army, coupled with rebellion in Hejaz by Sharif Ḥusayn, showed him that religion can only keep people together while their interest went with it—a sad lesson learned by Pakistan in 1971. Ironically, the Jewish population of Anatolia, by and large, remained loyal to the Ottoman Empire.

In November 1918, MK arrived at Haydarpaşa train station in the Asian part of Istanbul, which was then occupied by the victorious Allies. He looked at the harbor and, having noticed fifty or so Allied warships, said to his ADC, "They will leave as they have come"—prophetic words. While the Turkish war of independence was to come, MK was already determined to fight it and lead it. On another occasion, while the peace negotiations were delicately poised in Lausanne, Ismet—who was representing nationalist Turkey—asked for advice. MK's reply was blunt—Turkey would not cede an inch of territory. This was not empty rhetoric; later events were to prove Turkish resolve.

MK lived at a time of enormous change in his part of the world: the communist revolution in Russia, Reza Shah's secularization of Iran, as well as Amanullah's reforms in Afghanistan. Of these, only MK's reforms in Turkey have survived the test of time. The rest either failed or have been reversed.

MK left Turkey fully independent and a respected member of the international community. There was internal order, and despite a one-party system, he did leave behind the basic framework of democracy that had flourished. He did not allow his party to dominate the state like Nazis in Germany, fascists in Italy, or communists in USSR. He was financially clean as was İnönü.

He could be eccentric and, at times, made decisions on impulse. Once while dancing in a nightclub in Istanbul, the band stopped playing because of a call to prayer from a neighboring mosque; he seemed irritated and remarked, "The places of worship should not be in proximity to the entertainment areas." The next day, the minaret of the mosque was pulled down. On another occasion, he was approached by the owner of a nightclub who wanted a loan application approved from the bank while unable to provide a collateral; MK wrote a letter of approval there and then while under the influence of alcohol. The following day, wiser counsel prevailed and per regulation, the loan was denied.

MK became the leader of nationalist Turkey at a time when the Ottoman Empire had been defeated in the WWI, Istanbul was occupied by the Allies, and the Greek army had invaded the heartland of Anatolia, coming almost two hundred miles inland from the western Turkish border. At his death, he could rightfully claim to have left behind an independent, stable country, a respected member of the community of civilized nations. Along the way, he had single-handedly ushered in—by the sheer force of his conviction—drastic reforms that radically changed the face of Turkey.

MK had his faults. He did not take insubordination lightly. Once, Dr. Galip—a rather emotional young member of his party—criticized the education minister rather harshly in MK's presence. MK was visibly annoyed and asked him to apologize to the minister. To everybody's shock, Galip refused. MK was furious and asked him to leave the table; Galip refused again, saying, "The table belongs to the nation and is not your personal property." MK was impressed and got Galip appointed as education minister. Sometime later, MK invited him to his house. (Galip had lost his ministry by then.) At MK's instructions, which were given beforehand, Galip's chair was lifted in the air by two guards and then put back in its place. "This is how we elevate people and then bring them back where they rightfully belong," MK scornfully remarked. MK's detractors also pointed out that he did not always practice at home what he preached in public; his reforms gave Turkish women equal rights, but at home, his wife was lonely, unhappy, and bitter while he continued late nights with his friends. She was eventually divorced.

MK was not immune to flattery either. A telegram to MK by Celal Bayar, the future president of Turkey, read, "I will work as your idealistic laborer on the radiant road opened by your great genius which comprehends better than anyone the needs of the people and the country." Sometime later, a newspaper editor went way overboard in his description of MK's family background; his father was written as a senior civil servant and a very successful businessman while his mother from a rich and famous family—neither was true. MK's humble origins were widely known. This only reinforced the view that MK wanted to create his own cult.

"Atatürk was a competent commander," wrote his biographer, Andrew Mango. "He was a shrewd politician—British PM Lloyd George's fall from power being partly due to MK's tactics—and a statesman of supreme realism. But above all, he was a man of enlightenment; and the enlightenment was not made by saints."

MK was not an idealist; he was a practical man who chose his options carefully. He once remarked that he won the Turkish war of independence by the use of telegraph wire. Resources were limited, and at a critical moment in the war, peasant Turkish women used ox carts to move critical war material to the front against the Greek army.

He was a superb organizer and knew how to delegate—a critical trait lacking in some leaders. During delicate negotiations in the Turkish war of independence, he proved his political skills by using the Bolsheviks against the West, Bulgarians against the Greeks, and France against Britain.

He worked late into the night while consuming endless cups of Turkish coffee and alcohol and chain-smoking. Years later, when he developed liver cirrhosis as a result of heavy drinking, he found it hard to stop alcohol despite warnings from his physician. The strict disciplinarian in public had failed himself in private. He was fifty-eight at the time of death in 1938 in Dolmabahce Palace, once abode of the mighty Ottoman sultans. Ironically, the last words of the man with no religion were "Wa-alaikum-as-salaam."

Reference: *Ataturk* by Andrew Mango

Balraj Sahni: The Gentleman Actor

Back in the '40s, Balraj Sahni (BS) was struggling to make his mark in the film world when he was given a good role by Zia Sarhadi, who was directing *Hum Log*. BS had a mighty struggle playing that role. One day he got really frustrated, walked up to Zia, and asked to be replaced by someone who could do justice to the role. "Balraj," said Zia, "We will sink or swim together." *Hum Log* was a success and launched BS's film career.

Success came to BS late. He was well in his forties when *Hum Log* was released. He was in poor health and way past the age for a typical hero by the time his career took off. In his early days, he had an intense fear of camera too and would spend hours watching Dilip Kumar and Meena Kumari, trying to learn their craft.

After *Hum Log*, he worked in many movies. But the movie that really made him a star was Bimal Roy's *Do Bigha Zamin*. In this movie, BS played the role of a rickshaw puller in Calcutta. BS put his heart and soul in that role. His brother and biographer, Bhisham Sahni, noted that BS actually spent time with a rickshaw puller to study him. This was a tour de force performance. *Do Bigha Zamin* has become a cult classic. To his last day, BS remained proud of his performance in that movie.

BS was a misfit in the film world. There were many reasons for that. He was highly educated (a master's in English literature from Government College (GC) Lahore, where he had been a student of Professor Sondhi and Patras Bokhari, both of whom were involved in the GC Dramatic Club. Also, he was an idealist. Early on, he had tried his hand in journalism in Lahore. Having failed, he had a teaching stint in Tagore's Shantiniketan. He then went up to Wardha, where he worked with Gandhi. Those who knew him then saw a certain restlessness about him. He then proceeded to England, where he worked as broadcaster at BBC for four years. Now this was not the profile of a typical actor in Bombay back then. No wonder he was a misfit.

In personal life, he went through many setbacks. His first wife, an actress, died young. BS remarried, this time a first cousin, against Hindu custom. One of his daughters went through years of marital difficulties, developed depression, and attempted suicide. Having survived that, she died of stroke that was misdiagnosed. Through all that adversity, a heartbroken BS kept himself busy to distract himself.

And then along came *Garm Hava*, a movie about the plight of Indian Muslims after 1947. BS was given the role of a Muslim shopkeeper of Agra who suffered numerous difficulties postpartition. There was a scene in *Garm Hava* when BS opened the door of his daughter's bedroom and found her dead body after her suicide. BS's portrayal of a visibly shocked and then grieving father looked so real that it brought tears to one's eyes. Not many realized that BS was not merely acting the scene. Having gone through the same tragedy in real life just a few months before, he was simply reliving the trauma. Unbeknownst to him, *Garm Hava* turned out to be his swan song. It was released to critical acclaim after his death.

Despite his professional success, BS was unhappy in Bombay. A sensitive man with strong moral values and political convictions, he had decided to retire to his beloved Punjab to Prem Nagar, a town near Amratsar that used to attract writers and poets. That was not to be. Just weeks before his planned move to Prem Nagar, he died.

BS felt very nostalgic about Punjab. He had been born at Rawalpindi, but his ancestral town was Bhera, the sleepy ancient town near Sargodha that had also given Neelo, Shireen, and Ali Baksh (Meena Kumari's father) to the film world. In 1962, BS visited Pakistan. Among the places he visited was Heer's mausoleum in Jhang. In Rawalpindi, he went to see his old house. As he approached his ancestral house, a marriage party (baraat) was being received by the now occupants of the house, who were also refugees from East Punjab. Unperturbed, BS quietly introduced himself to the host family and joined them in serving food to the guests. Most of the guests remained unaware of his identity. Such was his humility.

BS was a writer too. The books that he wrote—all in Punjabi—included two travelogues, two books of reminiscences, an unfinished novel, one full-length play, two pamphlets, and many articles. This was considerable output for a full-time actor who worked in 135 movies. After *Do Bigha Zamin*, BS was seen by many as someone who represented the downtrodden. He was once approached by a postal worker at Delhi railway station. The postal worker, who had obviously seen this movie, looked at BS and asked, "When will you make a movie about us?"

There was yet another aspect of BS's multitalented personality. He had developed Marxist tendencies and was an active member of Indian People's Theatre Association (IPTA). In association with like-minded people like K. A. Abbas, he participated in plays and movies that represented the poor. *Dharti Ke Lal* was one such movie, directed by K. A. Abbas. IPTA also staged plays like Gogol's *Inspector General* and George Bernard Shaw's *Pygmalion*.

A modest man by nature, BS shunned publicity. He was offered membership of Rajya Sabha, the upper house of Indian Parliament, which he politely declined. He was being considered for the post of principal of Poona Film Institute when he died. However, one invitation that he gladly accepted was to be the chief guest at the convocation of Jawaharlal Nehru University. Many were surprised at this. There was some resentment too that an actor had been invited to a prestigious university convocation. But those who heard his speech realized that the speaker was not just an actor; he was also a sensitive educated man who really cared for the society that he lived in.

BS died in April 1973. As he was being rushed to the hospital with a heart attack, he dictated a note to the doctor in the elevator: "I have lived a good life. I have no regrets." This scribe was then a student at Government College Lahore. I read the news of his death and, in my youthful ignorance, did not pay much attention. Decades later, I visited my alma mater, only to discover BS's name on the college wall. Just look at the other names on that wall: Iqbal, N. M. Rashid, Abdus Salam, Patras Bokhari, Faiz, Bano Qudsia, Khurshid Anwar, Khushwant Singh, Sir Ganga Ram, Sir Zafrulla Khan, and the like. BS, I thought, was in elite company; he was a lot more than just a good actor.

Reference: *Balraj My Brother* by Bhisham Sahni

Being Alcoholic

Many years ago, a friend asked me to bring whiskey for him during my annual visits to Pakistan. I obliged. A few years later, his wife told me in confidence to stop that practice. When asked why, she reported that he had been falling around after drinking and that she had had enough of that embarrassment in front of their daughter-in-law. Naturally, I stopped. There was more to the episode, but we would return to this later.

Drinking alcohol and being alcoholic is not synonymous. Alcoholism refers to uncontrolled drinking and preoccupation with alcohol. For unclear reasons, there have been disproportionate number of writers and poets who have succumbed to alcoholism. Possibly no other self-inflicted ailment has destroyed so many careers in literature.

One of the most famous, and tragic, was of Manto, one of the greatest short story writers of Urdu. In his last days, he had become an embarrassment to himself. He started asking for money from anybody who would oblige. Once, as he was seen approaching Pak Tea House, two of his friends rushed to the toilet to avoid him. On another occasion, he was manhandled by a salesman of Edelji, a wineshop in Lahore. Apparently, Manto had failed to pay for alcohol that he had been buying on credit. This shocking incident was witnessed by many of Manto's friends, who did come to his rescue.

And then there was Asrar ul Haq Majaz, a precocious and talented poet. Back in the '30s, one of his verses—later immortalized by Talat Mahmood in *Thokar*—had touched the hearts of youth all over India:

Ae gham-e-dil kya karoon
Ae whasht-e-dil kya karoon

Majaz, whose nephew Javed Akhtar is a popular poet and writer in India, unfortunately became alcoholic. A concerned friend once made a suggestion to him: Majaz should time himself with a *gharee* (watch) while drinking alcohol, like Josh Malihabadi did. Majaz, a man of acerbic wit, responded that he would rather have a *gharaa* (water pitcher) than a *gharee* in front of him. The alcohol consumption continued. He died in his thirties. Josh, who rarely acknowledged a better poet, once admitted that, at the time of death, Majaz had achieved only 25 percent of his poetic potential. Imagine the loss to Urdu poetry!

When it came to alcoholism, the undisputed champion was Akhtar Shirani. Many would find it hard to believe, but Akhtar Shirani was more popular in the 30's and 40's than any other poet in India, including Iqbal, Josh, and all the rest. The prince of romantic poetry used to galvanize the youth by his heart-wrenching renditions. Who can forget the following verse?

Hey zulm magar faryad na kar
Ae ishk hamen barbad na kar

Son of a highly respected scholar, Akhtar died at forty-three, estranged from his family, a destitute who had descended into opium addiction too.

Agha Hashr was a huge name in India. He was multitalented—a successful playwright and a decent poet. Having made his name all over India, he returned to Lahore in his last years. He had many plans—more plays to be staged, movies to be produced. But those who saw him were alarmed at the decline in his health. The Indian Shakespeare had been indiscreet with alcohol too, and it had taken its toll. He looked like a dead man walking and did not last long. Ashiq Batalvi, a friend of his, noted that Hashr once reprimanded Akhtar Shirani for a verse that was mediocre by Shirani's standard. Hashr then improved on it there and then. Such was the talent that was consumed by alcohol.

There was hardly a bigger name in Urdu journalism than Charag Hasan Hasrat. Those who had the privilege of working with Hasrat rated him very highly. He was a decent poet too. Just look at this verse of his:

Ghairon say kaha tum nein, ghairon say suna tum nein
Khuch ham say kaha hota, kuch ham say suna hota

Like Faiz Ahmad Faiz, Hasrat joined the British Indian Army during WWII. There were decent salary, plenty of free time, and access to inexpensive alcohol; he became an alcoholic and died at fifty.

Abdul Hamid Adam, a popular poet who used to work in military accounts, was one of the few who overcame his alcoholism. Before he accomplished that, however, he had many funny stories about this; the funniest was when, while drunk, he jumped from the second floor of a hotel in Anarkali and sustained a severe facial injury. When discovered, he refused first aid and instead asked for more alcohol.

Josh Malihabadi's alcohol use had become a legend; a more disciplined user of alcohol is hard to imagine. He drank four pegs and always began precisely at sunset. He was never seen drunk but "suffered like a dog with intractable itch" (his own words from a letter to Z. A. Bhutto) when 1977's prohibition affected his alcohol supply. His influential friends helped restore the alcohol supply, and the revolutionary poet's itch presumably went away. In a verse of his, he described his alcoholism as "I begin to rise when the sun sets in."

Another casualty of alcoholism was K. L. Saigal, arguably the greatest male singer of his generation. In his last days, he needed alcohol to steady himself, not the other way around. It was a tribute to Naushad that *Shahjehan*'s immortal songs were recorded. Saigal was forty-two at the time of death.

While alcoholism was more common in writers and poets, other professions were not immune from it. George Best, consistently rated among the top ten footballers of the twentieth century, wrecked his career by alcoholism. Having received a liver transplant, he resumed drinking and died at fifty-five. Unlike Pelé and Maradona, he is remembered more for alcoholism than for his football skills. Pal Gascoigne may have been the best football player of his generation in England. He never achieved his full potential and has been in and out of alcohol rehab.

Politicians in Pakistan often try to conceal their alcohol use. Z. A. Bhutto was often accused of using alcohol. Fed up, he once blurted out in a public meeting, "I do drink a little but do not suck the blood of the poor." That was more than enough for his diehard followers to exonerate *Quaid-e-Awam*. Atatürk, the founder of modern Turkey, died at fifty-three of alcoholic liver cirrhosis.

In the late 60's, Sen. Edward Kennedy was involved in a single-car accident late at night. He escaped unharmed, but the other passenger in his car, a young woman, died. Kennedy, who was the driver, failed to report the accident for hours. There was a suspicion that a drunk Kennedy had deliberately delayed reporting to police. He managed to evade the legal trouble, but political damage was done. Many felt that Edward Kennedy would have walked into the White House with his political talent and the enormous sympathy that existed in the USA for his family at the time. But the lingering questions about the accident followed him everywhere. He did make a late run for the White House in 1980 but failed to get his own party's nomination. He spent the rest of his life ruing his decision to drink and drive.

The list of alcohol users included two maulanas as well: one was Kausar Niazi, a minister in Z. A. Bhutto's cabinet. Bearded Niazi had started his political career in *Jamat-e-Islami*. Insiders used to ridicule him as Maulana whiskey. Ironically, he was the one to recommend banning alcohol as a political ploy to Z. A. Bhutto to deflate PNA's 1977's political agitation. The other name few would have guessed was Abul Kalam Azad. Late Indian writer Khushwant Singh had accompanied Azad to a conference in Paris. Khushwant reports that, as he made an unannounced entry to Azad's hotel room, *Imam-ul-Hind* was enjoying his scotch all by himself.

The menace of alcoholism is not new. One only has to look at the Mughal Dynasty to get an idea. All three of Akbar the Great's sons were alcoholics. Murad's alcoholism was so bad that "his friends had to spoon-feed him two cups of arak every morning before he was able to do anything, because he was shaking so badly." Daniyal, a gentle character and of many talents, was nevertheless a hopeless drunkard who died at thirty-one. Muhammad Hakim, Akbar's half brother who governed Kabul, also drank himself to death at thirty-one. Jahangir (his son

Parvez had managed to drink himself to death) was "a complete physical wreck, plagued by the devastating effects of forty years of alcohol and opium addiction," noted Dirk Collier in *The Great Mughals*.

Need one say more about the devastation caused by alcohol? Back to my friend in Pakistan—to my dismay, I later discovered that he had resumed procuring local liquor using his non-Muslim house sweeper's alcohol permit.

References: *The Great Mughals* by Dirk Collier; *Chand Yadein* by Ashiq Hussain Batalwi

In Search of Bhagat Singh

Just over eight decades ago this week, fearless Bhagat Singh walked up to the gallows, accompanied by his comrades Rajguru and Sukhdev. We are told he refused to wear the mask over his head, was allowed a parting embrace with his fellow prisoners, and proclaimed, "Now the world will see how the revolutionary sons of India embrace death." On the way to the gallows, the three of them kept chanting, "Long live the revolution." Their fellow prisoners reciprocated from inside their cells. A local congressman, Pindi Dass Sodhi, who lived nearby reported hearing their slogans clearly in his house. Soon afterward, a deathly silence fell over the infamous jail as the hangman performed his job, which was to silence this brave son of Punjab forever. He was only twenty-three at the time, and the fateful day was March 23, 1931.

As often happens, the reality gets mixed up with legend over time; this has also happened in the case of Bhagat Singh. On a recent trip to Pakistan, this scribe visited the roundabout in Shadman, Lahore; this roundabout was reportedly the exact spot where the gallows stood before the infamous Lahore Central Jail was demolished. A picture taken by legendary press photographer Chacha Chaudhary of *Pakistan Times* exists that shows the gallows. As I stood there, I realized not many passersby really knew the significance of this historic spot. Almost four decades later, the same roundabout was to witness the assassination of Nawab Ahmad Khan Kasuri in 1973. Legend had it that Mr. Kasuri had been the only magistrate willing to sign the death warrant for Bhagat Singh. If true, this would have been a remarkable coincidence. However, an article by R. K. Kaushik—an Indian Administrative Service officer who had reviewed the official record of the execution reports that Sh. Abdul Hamid and Lala Nathuram as the duty magistrates present.

Bhagat Singh was born in Banga, a small village in Jaranwala, near Faisalabad. At the time of my visit recently, Bhagat Singh's ancestral house still stands. The current resident is a refugee from eastern Punjab and reports frequent visitors from abroad, particularly India. We were told that, a few years ago, an old and ailing brother of the late freedom fighter visited and has since died in India, where the family migrated at the time of partition. The primary school where Bhagat Singh studied still stands but just barely. Incidentally, the final resting place of the legendary lovers Mirza and Sahiban is also located in the same area; that is a story for another time.

BS's family were politically well informed and very active. Both his father and paternal uncle were members of the Ghadar Party. His uncle had to flee abroad to avoid arrest and eventually ended up in Brazil. His father had also spent time in prison.

It seemed that the young lad from rural Punjab was really moved by the Jalianwala Bagh Massacre and visited the place later, bringing back a sample of the soil as a memory. There is some disputed evidence that Bhagat Singh was present and may have witnessed firsthand the brutal beating of Lala Lajpat Rai in Lahore by police. Lala Lajpat Rai was a respected political activist and philanthropist. The Gulab Devi Hospital in Lahore, which stands to this day, was founded by him in memory of his late mother. Lala succumbed to his injuries a few days later. At the time, BS was a student in National College Lahore, which was founded by Lala Lajpat Rai too. Interestingly, the Bradlaugh Hall still stands—though in a dilapidated state—behind Data Darbar in Lahore.

BS and his companions swore revenge but, in a tragic case of mistaken identity, gunned down the wrong British police officer. The bullets were fired from the DMV College Lahore. After shooting, as the assailants ran away, they were given chase by Chanan Singh, a police constable who was also shot by BS before fleeing.

Sometime later, BS and Dutt exploded homemade bombs inside the legislative assembly in Delhi and courted arrest. Of note, Motilal Nehru and Quaid-e-Azam were in the building at the time. The trial that followed in Lahore was used by the accused not to defend themselves but to publicize their political goal. Death sentences were passed onto BS, Sukhdev, and Rajguru and carried out a day in advance to prevent disturbance since emotions were running high, and the authorities feared riots. The three dead bodies were whisked away to a spot outside Ganda Singh Wala Village and burned in a hurry and remains thrown in Sutlaj River.

So what kind of man was BS? D. N. Gupta, who had authored two books, had this to say of him: "Today Bhagat Singh is widely known to be a nationalist who sacrificed his life in the struggle for freedom. What is not well known is the fact that he was a Marxist and revolutionary who despite his young age, had already established himself as an intellectual. He was well read and was heavily influenced by the writings of Karl Marx, Engels and Lenin."

Ajay Ghosh, who was a codefendant in the same Lahore conspiracy case and was later to become the general secretary of CPI, wrote of BS's remarkable intelligence and the powerful impression he made when talking. Though not a brilliant speaker, BS spoke with such force, passion, and earnestness that one could not help being impressed. Ghosh noted that, although BS could be impetuous and lacked the coolness of Azad, he was of affectionate nature, frank, and open hearted with no trace of pettiness in his makeup; he was a man who claimed the love of all who were acquainted with him.

Many of BS's speeches and letters have survived. In a statement that he delivered to the court, he said, "The bomb explosions were absolutely necessary to get British government's attention; nonviolence as a strategy is a failure; there is justification for violence to achieve our goal and the new movement is influenced by the teachings of Guru Gobind Singh, Shivaji, Raza Khan, Kamal Pasha, Washington and Lennon."

Shiv Verma, another of BS's comrades, noted, "As a thinker, BS was far ahead of his contemporaries." BS wrote often from 1923 to 1930 on God, religion, language, culture, and political leaders; but more than anything else, he wrote on the political organization and revolution. However, one of his best writings came out in the very last days of his life, titled "Why Am I an Atheist?" It was published posthumously by his father in the weekly newspaper the *People*. This was an extremely well-written piece of about 12–13 pages. Take this statement for example: "The only consolation for me is that I am sacrificing my life for a noble cause. A Hindu believer can expect to be rewarded in next life while Muslims and Christians can expect the reward in heaven but what is in there for me? All I expect is a last moment when the nose will tighten around my neck and the board will move from under my feet. For me that will be the very end of a life of struggle; that by itself is a reward enough for me. I have spent my entire life fighting for independence without any personal gain or motive in mind. That is all I could have done." This is a very moving document that gives an in-depth look in his soul; one may disagree with his reasoning, but his commitment and conviction to his cause are hard to question.

Today the man who made the ultimate sacrifice and surely ranks right up there with Che Guevara, Castro, Hassan Nasir, Rosa Luxemburg, and the like has no memorial in Pakistan. There is a statue of him in the Indian Parliament building alongside that of Gandhi and Nehru. It would be befitting if at least the roundabout in Shadman, Lahore, is named after him. This scribe has recently seen a medical school as well as a road both named after a politician's father in Sialkot. Our claustrophobic politicians are too preoccupied with recognizing their families and cronies. We have come to a stage where the corrupt politicians and murder convicts are given the titles of shaheeds and have airports named after them while the real heroes like BS remain unappreciated. Will it ever change?

Reference: *Bhagat Singh* by D.N. Gupta

Bhutto Legend: Myth and Reality

"I feel that your services to Pakistan are indispensable. When the history of our country is written by objective historians, your name will be placed even before that of Mr. Jinnah." The writer of this infamous piece of consummate flattery was a young Z. A. Bhutto and the recipient Iskander Mirza, who should be in the political hall of shame, if one were ever to be erected in Pakistan.

Bilawal Zardari has recently made a lot of noise about Z. A. Bhutto's trial and demanded apology for the unjust verdict handed out to his grandfather. It has become very fashionable lately to call it a "judicial murder." This writer is not a lawyer. Nor am I a politician. I do, however, belong to the unfortunate generation that has witnessed the events of his grandfather's time in power and fall from it. It is said that legends ossify over time; in Bhutto's case, certainly, that appears to be so. Bhutto worship has become a relentless train that shows no signs of slowing down; instead, it keeps gathering speed. In the process, the established historical facts are being denied or distorted, and myths are being created. K. K. Aziz may easily write another volume of *Murder of History* with what we have heard recently.

Z. A. Bhutto was widely admired for his genius. Henry Kissinger may not have been way off the mark when he remarked, "Elegant, eloquent, subtle. . . . I found him brilliant, charming, of global stature in his perceptions. . . . He did not suffer fools gladly." It was, however, the other side of ZAB—the dark one—that needed to be revisited. In the process, perhaps we—as a nation—may learn some lessons and see things in the right perspective. Khalid Hasan, a lifelong admirer who knew ZAB firsthand and worked as his press secretary, may have written the most balanced and insightful short biography of ZAB. He has summed it up eloquently: "ZAB had all the makings of a classical hero, carrying the seeds of self destruction in him—he was a flawed genius, a god who turned out to have feet of clay. . . . ZAB had many personal failings, including an inability to trust others, a congenital suspicion of friends and high sensitivity to personal criticism."

With rare insight and objectivity, KH writes, "There is no evidence that US government or any of his agencies played a role in the overthrow of Bhutto. The time has come for us to accept that much of what has happened to our country and our leaders has been the result of our own mistakes. . . . ZAB believed that a country should have only one central figure as leader and all power should flow from him. It is a tragedy that a man of Bhutto's intelligence, education and sense of history did not appreciate that Pakistan could only survive as a federal state with the provinces enjoying the maximum autonomy. Bhutto could not abide rival claimants to power even if they were elected to their office. He could not work with the opposition run provincial governments in Quetta and Peshawar and squeezed them out; that was his undoing. Bhutto forgot that power in order to be kept, must be dispersed." KH also notes that it was Bhutto who revised ISI's charter to include domestic political intelligence.

It was widely believed that Bhutto was hanged for a crime that he did not commit. It is rarely, if ever, asked, who then was the real perpetrator? Mohammad Ahmad Kasuri was murdered in Lahore; the crime scene was found to have shells used by FSF—Bhutto's elite security force. Yet the investigation was not extended to FSF. I recall a statement by Hanif Ramay of Pakistan People's Party (PPP), then the chief minister of Punjab, that Kasuri family had many enemies. This was despite Ahmed Raza Kasuri's contention that there was no suspect but one—ZAB. This was not the first attempt on Kasuri's life; he had escaped one ambush in Islamabad earlier. These episodes had followed an angry exchange between ZAB and Kasuri in the National Assembly when ZAB called Kasuri a poison.

Chaudhary Sardar, former inspector general of police in Punjab, has provided the firsthand account of this case in his book, *The Ultimate Crime*: "FSF was created by a notorious dismissed police officer, Haq Nawaz Tiwana, and was headed ultimately by another infamous police officer, Masood Mahmood. The FSF did not bother about any law, assuming the role of Bhutto's private army. Soon after the imposition of martial law, an elaborate enquiry in to the affairs of FSF was initiated. The FSF had gained a reputation of being, Bhutto's gang of goons, for dirty works. During the enquiry, ASI M. Arshad of FSF, appeared before Ch. Abdul Khaliq, Dep. Director, FIA, Lahore and promised to tell everything truthfully if he were not tortured. He disclosed that he was a member of a special cell in the FSF headquarters, which had the most trusted officers for secret and sensitive missions—then he threw a bombshell. He said he was one of the FSF men who had fired on the car in which MNA Ahmad Raza Kasuri was ambushed."

So this was the first solid lead into the infamous murder case that led Bhutto to the gallows; legal intricacies aside, one was hard pressed not to see a connection here. Chaudhary Sardar then discusses the dubious character of the infamous trio of Masood Mahmood (director general, FSF), Saeed Ahmad Khan (chief security officer to Bhutto), and Sardar Abdul Wakeel (DIG Lahore); they all had been among the most trusted police officers of Bhutto and would commit criminal and illegal acts to show him their "devotion and loyalty." After his overthrow, they all were among the star prosecution witnesses in the case that led to his conviction. Sardar also confirms the widely believed rumor of the time that a procession of opposition women in 1977 was mishandled near WAPDA House, Lahore, by the Nath Force—a large number of prostitutes, recruited temporarily as policewomen, specifically for this purpose.

Kasuri's murder may have been the most famous one but was by no means the only one; this was a list that included Dr. Nazir Ahmed of JI, member of National Assembly (MNA) from Dera Ghazi Khan, who was gunned down in his clinic weeks after the provincial chief of his party, Syed Asad Gilani, had been warned by Khar (*Us ka anjaam acha naheen ho ga*). Kh. Rafiq was gunned down behind the Punjab assembly while leading a procession; Abdus Samad Achakzai was killed in his house in a grenade attack while Maulvi Shamshuddin, member of the Provincial Assembly and deputy speaker of Balochistan Assembly, was shot in his car.

Those who escaped attempts at their lives included Wali Khan, who lost his driver and personal bodyguard in the ambush; this was the fourth attempt on his life. Years later, Wali Khan was to warn Zia of Bhutto's vengeance. ("There are two dead bodies and one grave. Make sure Bhutto goes in first. Otherwise, you may be the one.") Ch. Zahoor Elahi, whose political heirs sit happily with Zardari at present, suffered more than most. Amnesty International once reported that there were 117 cases against him; this included a case of buffalo stealing. He survived in jail in Balochistan, courtesy of Gov. Akbar Bugti, who refused to do him harm. Small wonder that, after Bhutto's hanging, Zahoor Elahi requested and received the pen that Zia had used to reject the mercy petitions for Bhutto.

Mian Tufail was scandalously manhandled in jail, writes Sherbaz Mazari in his autobiography, *A Journey to Disillusionment*; it was rumored at the time that a naked prostitute was sent into his cell to humiliate the emir of JI. At the height of crises that eventually toppled him, Bhutto rushed in to see Maulana Mawdudi in Ichra; one wonders whether the founder of JI reminded ZAB of the treatment given out to his successor. Barrister F. Ibrahim, who was later to become chief justice of the supreme court, used to share the legal chamber with Bhutto in Karachi in the '50s. "Bhutto was very generous, but I sensed a streak of violence in him, a certain mean or vindictive quality," he told Stanley Wolpert, the author of *Zulfi Bhutto of Pakistan*.

Mukhtar Rana, a PPP MNA from Faisalabad, had earned the wrath of his leader by his divergent views. He was deposed as MNA, arrested, and after being subjected to severe physical abuse—according to one report, he almost died under torture—convicted in a military court and sentenced to a five-year term of imprisonment, all in a matter of days. Ustad Daman, dervish Punjabi poet, made the cardinal error of writing an anti-Bhutto poem; he had a case registered against him—he was accused of being in possession of a hand grenade.

Kaswar Gardezi was one of many to suffer vicious brutality; here is Mazari's narrative: "In a voice breaking with emotion, Gardezi related his horrifying experience to me. The police presented him with an egg, a potato and an onion, he said, and then asked which of these will he prefer to be inserted in to his anus. After undergoing this humiliation and barbaric ordeal, he was then threatened with sodomy; to his good fortune, this threat was never carried out. Instead, he was badly beaten with a stout cane, after which he was forced to lie naked on a solid slab of ice." At the time, Gardezi was secretary general of the National Awami Party (NAP), one of the leading opposition parties. Some people have been accused of going to irrational lengths in their hatred of Bhutto; incidents like above were perhaps the explanation for this.

One has to remember that Bhutto's own associates were not spared his wrath; J. A. Rahim, a senior member of the cabinet, learned this lesson the hard way. He annoyed Bhutto once by leaving early from a dinner hosted by the PM. Rahim also made the mistake of showing his resentment by calling Bhutto "raja of Larkana." What would follow was how Rahim described this horrifying experience to Wolpert: "On reaching home, I went to bed. . . . About 1 A.M., I was woken up by my servant who said that there was a crowd of people before the house. . . . Some men of the FSF were climbing up the front balcony for the purpose of entering my bedroom. . . . I went to the front door downstairs. . . . Saeed Ahmad Khan, Chief of PM's Security, who was at the head of that mob of armed FSF thugs, answered that he had come to deliver a message from the PM. . . . As the door opened, they rushed in. . . . Besides being beaten by fists, I was hit by rifle butts. I was thrown to the ground and hit while prostrate. . . . I lost consciousness. . . . I was dragged by my legs, then thrown in to a jeep. . . . bleeding profusely." Intellectually brilliant, Rahim had retired as Pakistan's ambassador to France, had been one of the founding members of PPP, and had written its manifesto.

Khalid Hasan was once asked by Bhutto to check out a certain person in Lahore. "I found out that the man was saying bad things about Bhutto all over the place," Khalid writes. "I came back and told Bhutto. His brow furrowed. 'His credit in my book has not quite run out yet,' he said. I shuddered to think what would happen when the man's credit did run out."

The Doctor From The East

Malik Meraj Khalid, in his biography, *Miraj Nama*, describes the extent to which Bhutto and Khar could go to harass their political opponents. Meraj Khalid once received a phone call from Zahoor Elahi's daughter, whose admission to Lahore College of Home Economics had been blocked by Khar. By nature a decent man, Meraj had to call Bhutto personally to rectify this. On another occasion, Meraj had to call ZAB again to stop Khar's plans to set on fire the house on Davis Road, Lahore, where Asghar Khan was staying. Asghar Khan was not so lucky with his house in Abbottabad though; it did burn to the ground in very suspicious circumstances.

No account of Bhutto's Awami Raj would be complete without Dalai Camp. It would be fair to call it Bhutto's Guantanamo Bay. It was used to secretly detain three political dissidents (Iftikhar Tari, Chaudhary Irshad, and Mian Aslam). These people were former PPP members who had fallen out with Bhutto and left PPP along with Khar. Two of them had been former provincial ministers. Fearing arrest, some of them had been granted bail before arrest by the high court. They vanished without trace one day, having been picked up by FSF, and were only recovered when Bhutto was deposed. Iftikhar Tari, who had the reputation of a goon, appeared broken after release. He narrated his ordeal on TV and could not stop crying in a program called *Zulm ki dastanay*.

Bhutto could not forgive. Mazari recounted the following in his memoirs: "Back in the 50's, Sir Shah Nawaz (Bhutto's father) went to see Ayub Khuro, who was then CM of Sindh. Bhutto went along. Khuro slighted them by making them wait for half an hour in the verandah, and then drinking tea without offering them any. Swallowing his pride, elder Bhutto requested the Sindhi politician for a job for his son in the foreign service. Khuro listened to the request and asked the elder Bhutto to submit an application in writing to him. He then dismissed them cursorily with a wave of his hand. Later in 1972, as soon as Bhutto achieved power, one of his first acts was to humiliate Khuro by having the walls to his home in Larkana razed to the ground."

At times, Bhutto's sensitivity reached absurd levels. Mazari notes: "In the mid 50's, Ahmed Nawaz Bugti was hosting a table for some foreign ladies at Le Gourmet. Bhutto, who was present at the restaurant, spotted him and asked if he could join the group. Knowing his reputation with women, Bugti declined. Years later, Bhutto visited Quetta as president to attend a formal dinner held by Governor Bazinjo for Princess Ashraf of Iran. Seated at the high table, he sighted Bugti, who was then Balochistan's finance minister, dining at a less august table than his. Bhutto asked his ADC to bring Bugti to his table, looked at him and said, 'Do you remember the time when you would not let me sit at your table? Well this time, I won't let you sit at mine.'"

Here would be another eye-opener for Bhutto fans; this is again written in Mazari's autobiography: "Over dinner at the Governor's House, Arbab Sikander Khalil, related a rather strange and unsettling story to me. It seemed that Bhutto had recently visited Peshawar and while staying at the Government House, had requested Arbab Sikander for a supply of whisky. The Governor politely informed ZAB that as he did not imbibe alcohol, he was unable to provide the President with liquor. Bhutto then sent his airplane to Islamabad to fetch whisky. When the plane returned that evening, it not only brought alcohol but also, a Federal Minister's wife too, to keep Bhutto company."

Here is an excerpt from Stanley Wolpert's book, *Zulfi Bhutto of Pakistan*: "One of the women Zulfi met at a cocktail party that fall (1963) was Rita Dhar, daughter of V. Lakshmi Pandit, the first woman president of the General Assembly. Mrs. Dhar recalled how immediately after meeting her, Zulfi eyed her lasciviously, inviting her to his apartment." Nehru's niece apparently declined, to Bhutto's chagrin. Pakistan's young foreign minister was in NY to attend the annual session of the general assembly. Ardeshir Cowasjee told Wolpert that Nusrat Bhutto had once attempted suicide and was hospitalized in Parsi Hospital in Karachi with a drug overdose; on another occasion, she approached Ayub Khan, through Nancy Cowasjee, after "having been thrown out of her own house by her faithless husband." She was staying in Mrs. Davies Private Hotel in Rawalpindi. It is to her credit that she stuck to her husband as he continued his love affairs.

A myth that refuses to go away is that opposition and Bhutto had reached an agreement and the army sabotaged it; the facts speak quite otherwise. Here is Mazari's account: "At 10 P.M., on July 3rd, Mufti Mahmood, Prof. Ghafoor and Nawabzada Nasrullah, handed over the additional nine points to Bhutto. Having consulted Pirzada and

Niazi, Bhutto returned to the PNA team and told them that he needed time for further consultation. According to Prof. Ghafoor, Bhutto's attitude appeared accommodating; but only two hours later, his stance hardened dramatically. Addressing a press conference at midnight July 3rd, he lambasted the PNA negotiating team for 'repudiating their earlier agreement.' It was clear to all that the PPP-PNA talks had broken down once again."

Gen. K. M. Arif gives a very similar account of events in his book *Working with Zia*. Arif quotes General Gilani, ISI chief at the time, that both he and Rao Rashid, newly appointed director of intelligence, had warned Bhutto repeatedly that the army's patience had been exhausted and that it was planning to act very soon. KH has also devoted many pages of his book to the crises of 1977. Here is an excerpt: "Tikka Khan (Bhutto's adviser at the time) told the PM, in the presence of Zia and Corps commanders, 'Sir, I would say we wipe out five or six thousand of PNA's men. That will cool them off.' Tikka Khan's mindless remark convinced Zia and his Corps Commanders that Bhutto and his men were bent upon doing just some such thing."

Gen. Gul Hassan and Air Mshl. Rahim Khan had played a key role in bringing Bhutto to power. They were both dismissed in a most humiliating way, having been forced to sign their resignations, taken hostage, and then driven to Lahore in the company of pistol-packing Jatoi, Mumtaz Bhutto, and Khar. Years later, while awaiting his fate in jail, Bhutto accused Zia of "biting the hand that fed him." He had conveniently forgotten his own treatment of Ayub, Gul Hassan, and Rahim.

"Bhutto trusted nobody," KH notes. "He was troubled by what he considered unrealistic and idealistic liberal approach to press freedom, basic rights and government by law. Long before his overthrow, he had deprived himself of those who were capable of honest and wise advice. . . . and chose to exercise power through civilian and military bureaucracy that he had once denounced. After his overthrow, he told Inam Aziz—Bhutto's last interview—that he now understood where he might have gone wrong. He said he wanted to start all over again, back to the real fountainhead of power." "But history is merciless," Khalid laments, "and had moved on."

Mazari's assessment is similar to KH's: "The press had to bear ZAB's determined onslaught. As soon as he attained power, he dismissed the chairman of National Press Trust (that he had vowed to abolish) and the editor of *Pakistan Times*. His rival from the Ayub days, Altaf Gauhar, who was then the editor of *Dawn*, was placed under arrest. The printer, editor and publisher of *Urdu Digest*, *Zindagi* and *Punjab Punch* were arrested for protesting against ZAB's martial law, were convicted and sentenced even before the writ petitions challenging their arrests could be heard in the Lahore High Court. Shorish Kashmiri of *Chataan* was also sent to jail; *Hurreyet* and *Jasarat* were banned and their editors imprisoned. *Mehran* was banned while Iqbal Burni's weekly *Outlook* was forced in to shutting down its publication." This is by no means an all-inclusive list of the journals and newspapers that suffered.

KH has analyzed the issue of rigging in 1977 elections: "As far the rigging, it was so unnecessary because he was going to win big anyway. There is no evidence that he ordered the rigging, but he did not exercise the vigilance that it was his duty to do as PM and chairman of the ruling party. His own unopposed election from Larkana encouraged the lesser figures in the party to use the muscle of the state wherever possible to ensure their individual victory. The first angled brick that Bhutto built was laid by the unanimous and unopposed election of the PM himself. This less than laudable example was followed by his CMs and some other PPP leaders in the four provinces. His rival Jan M. Abbasi of JI had been kidnapped earlier, to keep him from filing his papers." Wolpert traces this back to the highly unexpected defeat of Bhutto's father, Sir Shah Nawaz, in 1937 at the hands of Sh. Majeed Sindhi. "Young Zulfi may have taken too much to heart, the lesson of his father's election defeat, resolving even at his tender age, never to risk losing an election, no matter how high a price need to be paid to insure victory."

ZAB's intolerance had no limits. On March 23, 1973, an opposition rally at Liaquat Bagh, Rawalpindi, was disrupted. Here is the eyewitness account by Chaudhary Sardar, who was superintendent of police at the time: "It was in the air that armed workers would be present in the public meeting. . . . Then came reports that that armed PPP workers were also coming to the same public meeting. . . . By midday, we received information that large conveys of PPP crowds were coming from Punjab and some of them were armed as well. . . . DSP City told me that he saw some FSF men in plain clothes and suspected their involvement—On the FSF involvement, I was really shocked." The violence at Liaquat Bagh led to eleven deaths and hundreds of serious injuries. Almost four decades later, Benazir was assassinated at the gate of the same Liaquat Bagh; was this divine retribution? One has to wonder.

Arthur Koestler once wrote: "Nothing is more sad than the death of an illusion." Many Bhutto admirers never knew him firsthand. One wonders what their reaction would have been had they seen their leader's behavior at close quarters.

Back to the apology demanded by Bilawal, I am not sure if the Bhutto family deserves an apology for his hanging. One should certainly ask whether the Oxford-educated Bilawal has the moral strength to offer one to the families of those who have suffered his esteemed grandfather's vengeance.

References: *Rearview Mirror* by Khalid Hasan; *Zulfi Bhutto of Pakistan* by Stanley Wolpert; *The Ultimate Crime* by Ch. Sardar; *Merajnama* by Meraj Khalid; *Working with Zia* by KM Arif; *A Journey to Disillusionment* by Sherbaz Mazari

Bhutto's Last Days

Much has been written about Z. A. Bhutto's time in office and imprisonment. His life in power has been like an open book, but the period of his captivity continues to be shrouded in mystery and has led to great speculation and many conjectural stories. This writer has only recently come across a book written by an eyewitness to most of ZAB's time in jail as well as his execution. I am referring to *Bhutto's Last 323 Days* by Colonel Rafiuddin, who had been in charge of security in the Central Jail Rawalpindi and saw the events firsthand. To those who are looking for an authentic and unbiased account of this most tragic, sensitive, and controversial period of our history, this book is a must read.

Colonel Rafi tells us of ZAB's personal habits that some of us already knew of. He had rare charisma and elegance; he ate and slept very little, had a phenomenal memory and uncanny intelligence, cared deeply about his looks, and was an avid reader. He had amazing self-control and once went on hunger strike for nine consecutive days. One gains an insight into his political thinking from the book. Bhutto felt strongly about the poor and thought that, had he had more time at his disposal, he might have accomplished a lot more for them and the country. He considered the political awakening of the poor as his greatest achievement. Ayub Khan, according to Bhutto, had many good qualities but was not a man of crises, while Asghar Khan was too rigid and was unlikely to be a success in politics. Yahya Khan is described as intelligent and graceful except when he was drunk, which was once too often.

The Doctor From The East

ZAB had an inherent dislike for mullahs and considered them the root cause of many ills facing Pakistan. Among his children, ZAB had high expectations from BB and predicted that she would leave her mark on history. He considered Gen. Akhtar Malik the most outstanding military commander of his time; his ill-timed dismissal by Field Marshal Ayub in the 1965 war let Kashmir slip away. Bhutto considered Zia's plan to Islamize Pakistan unwise. About the Ahmadis being declared non-Muslims, he felt it was a decision of the National Assembly and not his own. However, on another occasion, he made a remark to Colonel Rafi that perhaps all his sins could be forgiven for that decision. Bhutto greatly admired Turkish and German nations and once predicted Germany's reunification. Colonel Rafi recalled a remark by Bhutto one day: "Were I born a Turk, that nation would have valued me more than my own that has forsaken me while I rot in jail."

Perhaps the most fateful decision made by Bhutto in power was his choice of Zia as chief of army staff (COAS). Colonel Rafi remembers that Bhutto had blamed the outgoing army chief Tikka Khan for influencing his decision. But facts spoke otherwise. There is overwhelming evidence that the cunning and meek Zia had very tactfully convinced the prime minister of his total loyalty and servile nature. In their memoirs, Raja Anwar, Gen. Gul Hassan, and K. M. Arif have given details of how Zia created a benign image of himself and fooled ZAB. It appears even a political giant like ZAB found it hard to acknowledge this colossal mistake.

The author has written at length about the Bhutto family's visits to jail. Begum Bhutto and Benazir visited often and resented the jail protocol and procedures. The family was in emotional turmoil and understandably under great stress. On one occasion, Begum Bhutto exchanged harsh words with the jail staff and threatened them with reprisal. Colonel Rafi reported one such outburst by Begum Nusrat Bhutto when she said, "Are we not great?" and "God has given us brains," while pointing to her temple. Tragically, the ladies were not aware of the gravity of the danger to Bhutto's life and could have shared his belief that his imprisonment and trial was no more than a political stunt. It was much later—upon being informed of the date of execution—that Nusrat Bhutto panicked and desperately tried to see the chief martial law administrator (CMLA). Her letter offering to take the former PM abroad was delivered to the CMLA but ignored. By then, ZAB's fate had been sealed.

While imprisoned, ZAB seemed to have great faith in the loyalty of the members of his party. Colonel Rafi reports quite a few conversations with him when ZAB expressed his total confidence in the party members; he was expecting great street protests for his release. Only much later did it dawn on him that, though devoted, there were not many who were prepared to face the wrath of the martial law administrators. Colonel Rafi noted the obvious despair in ZAB. "My party prefers a dead Bhutto," he once lamented.

One day he screamed in obvious anguish, "Where are the bastards who were willing to lay down their lives for me?" There is also a reference to a very ill-advised statement from some PLO members that they could get Bhutto out of jail whenever they wanted. No such attempt was made; the tall claims only led to more stringent security arrangements.

The author denies having seen any physical abuse of Bhutto, although he regrets that the former PM was humiliated in the last few days. ZAB's bed was forcibly removed, and the former PM spent the last few nights of his life sleeping on a mat on the floor.

If these memoirs are to be believed, it is quite obvious that ZAB did not believe in the gravity of the danger that he was faced with. He was convinced that the murder case against him was fake and that the whole drama was being staged to unnerve him. The author blames Bhutto's legal team, his family, and other visitors for consistently misleading him. The reality dawned on him much too late when the clock marking his eventual doom had begun to tick.

Colonel Rafi has painstakingly recorded the last hours of Bhutto's life, the details of which are moving, painful, and some quite bizarre, almost embarrassing for the nation. After hanging, the former PM's genitals were photographed, presumably to satisfy the military authorities that he was indeed circumcised. His expensive wristwatch went missing and was later recovered from the pocket of Tara Masih, his hangman. One claimant for that wristwatch, Colonel Rafi wrote with obvious disgust, was Yaar Ahmad Daryana, the jail superintendent.

Incidentally, Colonel Rafi also met with the three coaccused in the murder case of Mr. Kasuri. One of them, Sufi Ghulam Mustafa, confided to the author that he had supplied the weapons used in the attack on Mr. Kasuri's life and that the orders for the murderous attempt had come from the "higher authorities." The intended target was Ahmad Raza, the son of the victim. Mustafa had been assured of release by the authorities if he stood firm on his statement that implicated ZAB. After ZAB's hanging, Mustafa's usefulness was over, and he met the same fate along with the three other coaccused. This was yet another of Zia's promises that was not kept.

Bhutto once said he wanted to be remembered as a poet and a revolutionary. "Resting in peace in the timeless land of Sindh," wrote his biographer, late Khalid Hasan, "he may take comfort that many in this land remember him as such while majority of those who were responsible for his humiliation in jail have become part of the garbage can of history."

Books cited: *Bhutto's Last 323 Days* by Col. Rafiuddin; *Rearview Mirror* by Khalid Hasan

The Story of the Brontë Sisters

Some time ago, this writer came on an article in *Pakistan Link* about Urdu fiction writer Hajra Masroor, who died recently. The article described Hajra and her two sisters as the Brontë sisters of Urdu literature. Hajra Masroor and her sister, Khadija Mastoor, were prolific and successful writers and may have their place secured in Urdu literature. But who were the Brontë sisters they were being compared to? Herein lay the answer.

Charlotte and her sisters Emily and Anne were born to a clergy of Irish descent who worked in a small village, Haworth, in West Yorkshire, England, in the first half of the nineteenth century. Their mother died when they were very young, and they were brought up by their widowed father and a maternal aunt who moved in with the family. They had two elder sisters too, who died at a very young age upon contracting TB at school. The family was not wealthy, and the girls had to work as governesses at times to support themselves. After finishing school, Charlotte and Anne spent some time in Brussels learning French and music. It was upon their return home that their life story became rather unusual.

Mr. Brontë, their father, despite his humble origins in Ireland, had studied at Cambridge University and had a literary taste. It seems that he passed on this trait to his children. He owned a small library and had once brought a gift of toy soldiers from Leeds for his son. Unbeknownst to him, his children had started using those toy soldiers as characters for their stories and plays.

Haworth was as rural a place as they came. It was surrounded by gentle rolling hills known as moors. The family had very little contact with the village folks, barring elder Mr. Brontë's work in the church.

There was plenty of time. So what did the sisters do? They would walk on the moors for hours during the day, and in the evening, instead of sitting idly by, they would write. Charlotte's friend and biographer, Elizabeth Gaskell, has left a detailed account of their routine. We are told they would get together after supper in the parlor and would walk around the table, pacing up and down, while discussing the plots of their stories with each other. It was during one of those sessions that Charlotte said to her sisters with earnest conviction, "My heroine in *Jane Eyre* is going to be unattractive, small, and plain." Before long, they had completed three novels, ready for publication. But then they ran into a predicament.

Odd as it sounded, it was all being done in complete secrecy. Nobody, other than the three sisters, had any idea of their work. In the Victorian era, women writers were almost unheard of. Thus, the sisters wanted to preserve their privacy. Years later, Charlotte was to say, "The most profound obscurity is infinitely preferable to vulgar notoriety that I neither seek nor will have." And so they sent their manuscripts to a London publisher with assumed masculine-sounding names: Currer, Ellis, and Acton Bell.

After many disappointments, *Jane Eyre*, *Wuthering Heights*, and *Tenant of Wildfell Hall* were eventually published. *Jane Eyre* and *Wuthering Heights* became massive hits. Almost overnight, the authors had become literary celebrities. There had been rave reviews of the books in newspapers, including the *Times of London*. Yet nobody seemed to know the real identity of the authors. There was intense speculation. Even the publisher had only a vague idea until, one day, two shy young women with Yorkshire accent turned up at his London office. Their identities revealed, they returned home in haste, having asked him to keep their secret.

Unfortunately, as the gods of good fortune were beginning to smile at them, a series of tragedies started to strike. To begin with, their only brother—Patrick Brontë, who may have been the most gifted in the family—fell in bad company. He could not hold a steady job and became an opium addict after a disastrous affair with a much older married woman. He incurred a lot of debt, went through severe depression, and died of alcoholism; he was thirty at the time of his death. Within weeks, Emily—whose *Wuthering Heights* remained popular to this day—came down with TB and perished soon afterward; she was only twenty-nine. The family had barely recovered from the twin tragedy when Anne, the author of *Tenant of Wildfell Hall* and *Agnes Grey*, also developed pleurisy. Charlotte took her to the seaside town of Scarborough, at her dying sister's request. Anne had visited and liked the place while working as governess as a teenager. Anne died within days of going to Scarborough. Heartbroken, Charlotte went through the ordeal of burying her last sibling away from home all by herself in an attempt to spare her aged father the pain of yet another offspring's burial.

Charlotte returned home and eventually got married to her father's assistant, Arthur Nichols, who had been wooing her for some time. After marriage, she looked happy at last, having endured so much pain, but this was not to last. She became pregnant and developed severe hyperemesis gravidarum, a pregnancy-related condition that led to intractable vomiting. As her life was ebbing fast, she whispered to her husband, "Oh! I am not going to die, am I? He will not separate us. We have been so happy." Charlotte Brontë died at the age of thirty-nine, leaving her aggrieved father and husband to mourn her. And so over a period of just seven years, the most celebrated literary family of its time had been wiped out. Ironically, the elder Mr. Brontë outlived all his talented children.

On a visit to Haworth a few years ago, this writer wondered how on earth the Brontë sisters, who had had so little exposure to the outside world, had come up with their stories. It seems that they nurtured their hereditary literary talent with keen observation of their environment. Cathy's character in *Wuthering Heights*—the heart-wrenching story of doomed love between Cathy and Heathcliff, a role played by the incomparable Laurence Olivier on screen—had, in fact, many similarities to the author, Emily Brontë, who created her heroine just like herself—stubborn, impulsive, and sensitive. Charlotte's less famous novel *Shirley* was also the story of her sister Emily. The infamous Lowood School mentioned in *Jane Eyre* was based on the Cowan Bridge School that the Brontë sisters had attended, while the character of Helen Burns in *Jane Eyre* was based on their sister Maria, who had died of TB while at school. And yes, the cruel schoolteacher in *Jane Eyre* was also based on one of the real teachers of that school.

One can't but admire the Brontë sisters' tenacity. They may have had God-given talent bestowed on them, but their manuscripts were rejected several times. However, repeated disappointments did not deter them. Charlotte's first novel, *Professor*, was rejected by no less than four publishers. But she persevered. Her magnum opus, *Jane Eyre*, was started in a dark hospital room in Manchester, where she had been nursing her father after cataract surgery. Amid the loneliness, depression, and a severe toothache, she started writing. It is hard to imagine bleaker circumstances for a writer. Little did she realize that she had embarked on a story that was going to make her a legend.

This writer recalls a time in the late '60s when *Jane Eyre* was part of the BA curriculum in Pakistan. Dilip Kumar reportedly was so fascinated with the Brontë sisters that he had acted in three movies based on their stories. Between the three sisters, Charlotte wrote the most; she also outlived her siblings. Her biographer noted that Charlotte had been an indefatigable student, fond of reading from a very young age. Her demeanor was of a shy and reserved person. Some of her letters have survived and give the impression that she was a pessimist and may have suffered from depression. Here would be some excerpts:

> My youth is gone like a dream. What have I done in the last thirty years? Precious little—Hope and fear fluctuate daily. I have endured such tortures of uncertainty that I could endure it no longer—I am free to walk on the moors; but when I go out there alone, everything reminds me of the times when others were with me and then the moors seem a wilderness, featureless, solitary saddening— We are vanishing.

Her pain and bitter sorrow is there for all to see.

Unlike Charles Dickens, Leo Tolstoy, and other writers of the Victorian age, the Brontë sisters did not have the advantage of living in cosmopolitan cities like London, Paris, or Moscow; they had hardly any exposure to the literary atmosphere so essential to a writer's grooming. Yet they have left behind what many consider to be the classics of English literature. Their life spans were relatively short, but their literary fame has endured for more than a century.

Back to Hajra Masroor and her sister—history is replete with writers who are popular in their life, but their fame dwindles over time until they are almost forgotten. M. Aslam, the novelist from Lahore, used to outsell most of his contemporaries, but now hardly anyone remembers him. Will the status of "Brontë sisters of Urdu" decline or soar—like that of Saadat Hasan Manto—over time? We will have to wait for the verdict of history.

<u>References</u>: *The Life of Charlotte Bronte* by Elizabeth Gaskell; *The Brontes of Haworth* (movie) by Christopher Fry

From Potwar to USSR: Dada Amir Haider's Odyssey

Z. A. Bhutto was once asked about how he would like to be remembered. "As a poet and a revolutionary," he said. Dada Amir Haider considered himself a communist only, but his credentials as a revolutionary were a lot stronger than Bhutto's and many others of the kind.

Now that I think about it, I cannot recall the first time I heard of DAH; it may have been a review of his autobiography, but I am not sure. It was probably two to three years ago that a nephew of mine sent me Dada's autobiography. I started reading it and found myself mesmerized. On the last trip to Pakistan, I asked this nephew to accompany me to Dada's desolate village—Dada once described it as a "remote Godforsaken place." Deep in the Potwar region of northern Punjab, about twenty miles north of Gujar Khan, is Kalian Sialian, the place of his birth as well as last abode.

DAH's life story is fascinating. What inspired a poor, orphan boy from such a remote area to endure lifelong struggle? The answer is not simple. It seems that, early on, he became a drifter. Having lost his father at a very young age, he never got along with his stepfather. Having spent some time in a *madrasa* and experienced mullah's cruelty, greed, and fanaticism, he ran off to Calcutta and then onto Bombay. He was too young but managed somehow to get himself enlisted as a fireman on a commercial ship. The year was 1917, and the First World War was raging. Thus began his long career in the shipping industry, which was to take him around the world more than once; in the process, he transformed himself from a naive teenager into a trailblazing communist revolutionary.

It is not easy to put a label on DAH's multifaceted personality. He was a communist, revolutionary, trained pilot, marine engineer, auto engineer, and businessman—he once owned a dry-cleaning shop in NYC. He was perhaps all these, but above all, he was a humanist; having seen the exploitation and suffering of the masses around him at a tender age—his own paternal uncle dispossessed him from his inheritance—he embarked on an epic journey that took him from the shores of Asia to Africa, Europe, and North and South America many times over. In the process, he came across momentous events and had had the good fortune to see gigantic personalities. DAH wanted to change the world around him for the better; he did not succeed in his aim. What he did experience in the process was a metamorphosis.

DAH's autobiography brings to life the first half of the twentieth century for the reader and is full of astonishing stories of the bygone era. Here are a few of them: He witnessed numerous cases of racial discrimination in his journeys; he reports merciless beating of a fellow Indian ship worker by a British officer for a minor mistake; the British crew were paid five times the salary of Indians for the same job; the crew of his ship that had just docked at a port was separated in two; the Indians were segregated for quarantine, while the British were just let through despite both having come from the same port; the fresh water was limited for the Indian crew, who were toiling in the boiler room of the ship in burning hot weather in the tropics, while no such restriction applied to the whites. In Trinidad, West Indies, he came across descendants of Indians who were lured to West Indies by British to work on the plantations a generation earlier; DAH notes with great sadness the plight of these wage slaves and their longing for their distant ancestral homeland of India. Over the years, DAH developed immense hatred for the British; instances like these were perhaps the reason for this.

The USA of 1920s that DAH experienced was in the throes of Great Depression and had its own discrimination. DAH once saw the Negro crew of an American Navy ship at the French port of Brest working overtime to unload the supplies during the WWI; to DAH' surprise, they were not welcomed at the white's restaurants despite being there to fight with the French and were not given time off at Christmas. There were plenty of surprises in store for him down the road. While recuperating in a rural Indiana hospital from a plane crash, DAH saw a KKK procession with their dreaded hoods; he left the hospital in a hurry, having been informed that the hospital admin were KKK sympathizers. DAH happened to be in Detroit when the infamous murder case of the Negro doctor came up for hearing; this case made headlines across the USA for months and created huge tension along racial lines.

DAH came across scores of people in his travels, but the one to have influenced him the most was Joe Mulkane, an Irish sailor whose father had fought in the Irish uprising of 1916. Joe had strong anti-British views that he passed on to DAH. For DAH, Joe became a sort of political mentor; their association was brief, but it had a lasting impact on DAH. The other luminaries whose paths crossed that of DAH included Lala Lajpat Rai (he was visiting NY before his tragic death in Lahore by police beating, later avenged by Bhagat Singh by the killing of a British police officer); Dr. Syed Hussain, who spoke in Detroit about India's freedom struggle; and Agnes Smedley, that firebrand political activist who sympathized with freedom movements all across the world. It was also in NY that DAH met a Sikh activist based in San Francisco who worked for Ghadar Party of India; it was at his instigation that DAH agreed to carry secret anti-British literature to be distributed at various seaports during his travels. DAH carried out this assignment at great personal risk. Years later, while traveling on a ship from Bombay to Europe, DAH saw an old and ailing Rabindranath Tagore; being in disguise and traveling on a fake passport, DAH did not try to talk to the Nobel laureate.

DAH's career as a sailor ended abruptly in Staten Island in 1922 after yet another incident with raciest undertones. Never one to tolerate discrimination lying down, he resigned and moved on to other adventures. After a brief stop at a Dupont factory in New Jersey, he ended up at Oleans, upstate New York, and it was there that he experienced what he calls real America. He made friends in the community, lived as a paying guest with an American family while working at the local railway yard. Being interested in aviation, he learned to fly and bought a small airplane that he flew over Oleans, to the great delight of inhabitants. DAH describes with great relish his solo flight over Manhattan's skyscrapers. Having spent some time in Detroit, where he worked at the GM plant, DAH's path crossed that of Comrade Owen and Charles Ruthenberg; this was to be a watershed moment. Henceforth, the young man from Potwar was to leave American shores for good and was to embark on a new journey that was to take him to USSR and make him a diehard communist.

In 1926, DAH bid a final farewell to the USA and boarded a ship from New York Harbor. He made it to Moscow, having traversed the Atlantic Ocean, Strait of Gibraltar, and Mediterranean and Black Seas in 2½ months, having been stranded at Istanbul for weeks. DAH was enrolled in University of the Peoples of the East in Moscow and became Comrade Sukharoff.

DAH has left some interesting details of life in communist Russia of the time. He took part in the May Day parades in the Red Square. There is a passing reference to John Reed's grave in the Kremlin wall. He reports seeing Liu Shao Chi—the future president of communist China—as well as Thomas Mann in Moscow. There was a naked dip in the Black Sea with some fellow students. Overall, he found Russians in general and females in particular well disposed toward the foreigners. His training completed, DAH was shipped to colonial India in disguise to begin his revolutionary work.

The British were wary of this new communist philosophy and were on the lookout. Dada spent most of his time underground in Bombay and Madras, having had numerous narrow escapes. His narrative have some heartbreaking details of the difficulties experienced by his fellow communist workers. "Dr. Adhikhari opened his tiffin carrier and I saw some dry, stale *chappaties* which he was going to consume. His father was a provincial Bombay gazette government officer; he could have lived a very comfortable life, had he decided to serve exploitative colonial system. . . . At Calcutta, three of them lived in one room in a congested area, slept on mats, and survived on cheap Bengali food. . . . His body was only a living skeleton covered with skin but no flesh. If anything was left over, his wife gave it to him, otherwise he used to go without food and mostly starved."

As for Dada himself, "Matthew, in the morning used to take some milk and bread. I had not much money to afford to pay to eat any thing in the morning. I did not want to be a burden on Matthew. I used to pay six rupees per month to him for my share of food. This food had very little nutrition and even my eyesight was getting affected. These were the hardships faced by the men who, in the beginning, sowed the seeds of communism in the sub-continent while being accused of working for the Moscow gold," he laments.

There were lighter moments in his sojourns too. He once had a one-night stand with a young Italian woman in Naples who "was at par with me in every respect," he wrote with youthful exuberance. There were brief friendships with Jenny and Helen in Oleans, New York, and with Lolia Matrsova in Moscow. DAH called it "my cherished memories." But he was on a mission and had no time for courtships or marriage, and apparently, his female friends understood that.

DAH's memoir stops abruptly in 1936, when his luck ran out; he was arrested and imprisoned for long periods. After the creation of Pakistan, he based himself in Rawalpindi while continuing to work for the communist party. The circumstances were bleak, and the party was soon banned. More periods of incarceration followed. His fellow prisoners, at various times, included Faiz Ahmed Faiz, Ahmed Nadeem Qasmi, Hyder Baksh Jatoi, Allama Mashriqi, Qaswer Gardezi, Chaudhary Afzal, and Zaheer Kashmiri. Eventually released, he was forced to stay in his village under mandatory surveillance. It is not clear from his memoirs what type of treatment he received from the government of Z. A. Bhutto. During his last illness in 1989, he was treated at Pakistan Institute of Medical Sciences at PPP government's expense. He was laid to rest in his ancestral village in one corner of his beloved school that he had founded and seen to completion in his lifetime. Ironically, his beloved USSR came crashing down a few months after his death.

"DAH lived and died virtually unsung. That did not diminish him. It makes the rest of us look more small" was the tribute paid to him in *Pakistan Times*. He was a committed communist revolutionary in the mold of Sajjad Zaheer, John Reed, and Che Guevara, people who devoted their lives to a cause that they believed in. Communism may have been thrown into the garbage can of history, but would their dream of freeing their ancestral homelands from mass misery be ever realized? One can only wonder.

Reference: *Chains to Lose* by Dada Amir Haider Khan

Dilip Kumar: The Star of a Bygone Era

Way back in the '40s, a producer approached DK—then a struggling actor—and offered the lead role in one of his stunt movies. DK was tempted; the money was very good, and he was hard pressed financially so much so that he had asked his studio for a loan. There was one problem, however; stunt movies were considered C-grade stuff. Having thought it over, DK declined the role.

Many years later, when he was making *Kohinoor*, he found out about a scene that required him to play sitar in a song sequence. Naushad suggested that Ustad Jafar Khan would play sitar in the scene while the camera would focus on his fingers, and the audience would not know. DK did not like that and instead spent months training himself on sitar. When the day came for shooting, he was ready to play sitar. "Jadugar qatil" was the song, which can be seen on YouTube by those who wish to confirm this. DK knew early on how to be selective and had an unmatched dedication to his work.

Yusuf Khan, who was born in a conservative family in Peshawar, was forced to move to Bombay because his elder brother fell from a horse and sustained a serious back injury. It so happened that the nearest back specialist available was in Bombay, so the whole family moved onto Bombay. As luck would have it, Ashok Kumar—the established star of Bombay Talkies—was about to leave the studio. Devika Rani, the owner, was desperately looking for his replacement. Unbeknownst to his conservative father, Yusuf interviewed. It is not known exactly what impressed Devika Rani about the shy lad, but he was hired. She chose his filmi name Dilip Kumar in preference to Jahangir and Vasudev. DK's journey had begun, and what a ride it has been! The horse in Peshawar as well as Devika Rani deserve our gratitude for their role in making DK out of Yusuf Khan.

DK did not become a sensation overnight; he passed through a painful phase of successive flops. *Film India*, the leading film journal of the time, almost gave up on him, calling him "an anemic addition to the actors whose acting effort was nil" in *Jwar Bhata*, his first movie. DK was not a born actor as he has admitted on occasions. But he had something even better—a burning desire to excel. Over the years, he was to hone his craft by painstakingly studying the leading Hollywood stars Paul Muni, Spencer Tracy, Henry Fonda, John Gielgud, James Stewart, and Marlon Brando. Brando was a proponent of the method school of acting, and DK seemed to have acquired it too.

DK became a colossus with his relentless pursuit for excellence. His attention to detail was legendary. For *Gunga Jumna*, his own production that was based on a dacoit story from UP, the dialogues were written in the local Purabi dialect at the suggestion of Naushad, who came from the area. It took almost a superhuman effort to get the cast, which included South Indian Vyjayanthimala, deliver the lines in the local accent. Those who had seen *Gunga Jumna* today best remember it for the dialogues.

DK was soon to become synonymous with tragic roles. Mehboob Khan's *Andaz* started this trend, which continued well into the early '60s. In that period, the tragedy king gave his admirers *Deedar*, *Sangdil*, *Devdas*, and *Gunga Jumna*, among others. As time wore on, he started to move away from the tragic roles at the advice of his psychiatrist and began to accept lighter roles, the examples being *Azaad*, *Kohinoor*, and *Leader*.

The staff at Bombay Talkies were encouraged to read. The studio had a well-stalked library. Over the years, DK became fond of English classics, particularly the writings of the Brontë sisters; he had done four movies based on their novels—*Sangdil*, *Arzoo*, *Hulchul*, and *Dil diya dard liya*. It was sad that none of these did well at the box office, but that may be a reflection of the taste of audience than of the movies.

Over his long and distinguished career, DK has worked with most of the leading ladies of his time. Guess who impressed him the most? It wasn't Nargis or Madhubala; it wasn't the tragedy queen Meena Kumari either. It was Nalini Jaywant. He did only two movies with her, *Shikast* and *Anokha pyar*; years later, he would remember her as "punctuality personified who would bring extra warmth to her performance and would be extraordinary even in her first rehearsal." When asked about whom he considered his mentor, DK did not name Mehboob, who had catapulted him to stardom with *Aan* and *Andaz*, or Bimal Roy, who directed him in *Devdas*—that heart-wrenching saga of the doomed love that many considered to be his finest role. Dilip instead named Nitin Bose, who had directed him in *Milan, Deedar*, and *Gunga Jumna*.

A question is often asked about his best role. Many would point to *Devdas* and *Gunga Jumna* as ones that defined him. DK himself has never answered this question. The consummate artist in him is perhaps too proud to choose one among many.

DK had the reputation of being choosy about his roles. He took his time before making a commitment. Whereas he generally made the right decision, there were roles that he turned down that—with the benefit of hindsight—he should have accepted. His biographer, Sanjit Narwekar, reported that back in the early '60s DK was approached by David Lean and offered the role of Sharif Ali in his epic *Lawrence of Arabia*; DK asked for the lead, for which the Irish actor Peter O'Toole was already signed up. Besides, the role required a Caucasian. David Lean politely refused but may have wondered about the audacity of this Indian actor. The same role was then offered to Omar Sharif, who accepted it. We are told that DK turned down *Baiju Bawra* (given to Bharat Bhushan), *Mother India* (given to Sunil Dutt), and *Pyaasa*—a cult classic that ranks the highest among all Indian movies on the Internet (done by Guru Dutt himself, a role tailor made for DK).

His admirers include Amitabh Bachchan, who has said that had DK been in Hollywood, he would surely have collected multiple Oscars. Shah Rukh Khan has called DK his ideal. But perhaps the best tribute to DK has come from Manoj Kumar. Manoj, who had often been accused of being an imitator of DK, said, "Tell me which actor in the last forty years has the guts to keep his hand on his heart and say that he has not imitated or tried to imitate DK."

Despite being a reserved and very private person, DK has not been spared the gossip and scandals, which are almost a job hazard in the movie industry. In the '50s, he had a well-publicized love affair with Madhubala; her inability to choose between her stubborn father and DK ended it on a sour note. Before that, Kamini Kaushal—one of his early heroines—was ready to leave her husband for him. Well-educated, Kamini Kaushal was a graduate of Kinnaird College Lahore and the daughter of the dean of Punjab University. She was only dissuaded by Ismat Chughtai, whose husband, Shahid Lateef, was making *Arzoo* with Dilip and Kamini Kaushal at the time.

Dilip remained single until forty-three and then suddenly married Saira Banu. People were aghast. SB was considered a B-class actress and almost twenty years younger and had an ongoing affair with the already married Rajendra Kumar. Besides, she had done some roles considered quite offensive for those times. She was the daughter of Naseem Banu, herself an actress from the early '40s. Naseem's mother had been a well-known courtesan. Manto had written a sketch of Naseem Banu in his masterpiece *Ganjay Farishtay*. DK's marriage with Saira Banu has survived, although there was that bizarre Asma Begum incident in the early '80s that did strain it. Asma was a divorced socialite from Hyderabad whom DK had married in secret. His repeated denials of second marriage were swept away when marriage certificate was published in newspapers. Asma was eventually divorced. DK moved on, and today this episode that tarnished his image has been almost forgotten.

DK naturally had his detractors too. Industry insiders had known, for years, that DK had a habit of changing the script to enhance his role at the cost of others. Sanjeev Kumar, who worked with DK in *Sunghursh*, was very vocal about this. Mehboob Khan refused to change *Mother India*'s script for DK's role; DK was not thrilled, but Mahboob refused to budge and gave the role to Sunil Dutt. A. R. Kardar, one of the senior and highly respected directors, has always blamed DK for changing the script of *Dil Diya Dard Liya* so much that the movie bombed. Kardar pointed fingers at DK for the disaster that effectively ruined him. "DK was my Waterloo. He has never given happiness to anyone. He has always made life difficult for filmmakers," Kardar said once.

DK has a fair share of tribulations in his career. His one attempt at production, *Gunga Jumna*, was stuck with the censor board for almost a year. There were whispers that this was done to allow Raj Kapoor's *Jis desh men Ganga behti hai* a free run in the market. DK had to go all the way to PM Nehru. Nehru saw the movie, liked it, and cleared it. The episode so embittered DK that he vowed never to produce a movie again. He has been accused of being a Pak spy too and had to endure the indignity of a police raid on his house that came to nothing. His visit to Pakistan in the '80s and acceptance of Nishan-e-Imtiaz created a furor in India. Undeterred through all that, DK has stood tall with poise and class of his own.

The death of Dev Anand leaves DK the sole survivor of the famous triumvirate—Raj Kapoor having died many years ago—that had ruled the box office from the midforties through the late sixties. Nowadays, he lives quietly at Pali Hill, Bombay, leading a retired life. Years ago, there had been a brief foray in politics as member of Rajya Sabah. The crowds of admirers are long gone as are the producers, who had been only too willing to pay him exorbitant amounts for roles he will usually decline. Like a lion in winter, he is quiet and slowly fading away. We are told he will celebrate his ninety-sixth birthday soon. From a fan of his who lives far away in North America, I say "happy birthday" to the ever-young hero of our rapidly diminishing generation.

The Duke of Wellington once said that he regretted not having thanked those who served him so well. On behalf of thousands of DK's admirers who are scattered across seven seas, this writer therefore says, "Thank you, Dilip Kumar, for the happiness, excitement, and tears that you brought to our eyes. Despite your flaws, you have been, and will always be, remembered as truly one of a kind. You are the king as late Khalid Hasan once described you."

Reference: *Dilip Kumar-Tha Last Emperror* by Sanjit Narwekar

A Doomed Love Affair

Dev Anand arrived in Bombay in 1943 from Lahore. He was almost penniless and traveled third class in the Frontier Mail. It took him many years and a lot of struggle before he managed to find a niche in the highly competitive and cutthroat film world. Suraiya was at the peak of her popularity at the time. Although both of them were Punjabis, their backgrounds were different. Suraiya had come from a humble blue-collar family from Gujranwala.

Gujranwala these days is known for its wrestlers and good food. But in the years gone by, it had produced some outstanding personalities in the field of music, literature, and journalism. Just look at the names to have come from this area: Ustad Jandhe Khan (Naushad was his assistant once), Roshan, Kidar Sharma, Noon Meem Rashid, Maulana Zafar Ali Khan, Raja Mehdi Ali Khan, among others. There must be something in the water. An esteemed writer of *Pakistan Link* whose late father, Colonel Amjad, participated in the later stages of Pakistan movement also is from Gujranwala.

Suraiya had accompanied her mother and grandmother in the early 1940s to Bombay, where her maternal uncle Zahoor was a struggling actor. One never heard about her father. He may have died young, or perhaps her parents were divorced. Suraiya had a melodious voice but, unlike Noor Jehan and later Lata, hardly any training in music. But what she also had was the biggest asset of all for a heroine—good looks. Singing actors were in demand, and before long, she became a huge star.

Dev Anand was born in Gurdaspur, eastern Punjab. His father was a lawyer. He spent four years at Government College Lahore and

The Doctor From The East

completed his bachelor's in arts with English literature before moving onto Bombay. Two of his brothers, Chetan and Goldie, were also well educated, and both of them made name in the film world as directors.

As fate would have it, Suraiya and Dev were cast together in *Vidya*. They were young and good looking, and before long, the lovebug had bitten them. Now it was no ordinary infatuation. This was the real deal. Here is how Dev Anand reports it in his autobiography:

> From good friends to close friends, and then to lovers.... And our love affair became the talk of the town ... she and I were secretly talking of getting engaged ... the granny who controlled the ethical, moral and religious code of the family, as also its purse strings, became the main opponent to our relationship, though I always felt that Suraiya's mother was sympathetic to our cause.... Suraiya had no say in her own life; its sole arbiter was her granny ... I read the note scribbled by Suraiya. It read, "I cried as I read your [DA's] letter. It is mutual. I love you. I, too, am dying to meet you."... We held each other in a long, hot embrace. She did not utter a word, nor did I. After a long silence that said everything, we looked at each other. As I stroked her hair, she held her lips to me, ready for a kiss. The kiss lingered till eternity.... I went to Zaveri Bazaar and bought one of the costliest rings that would adorn her finger ... Suraiya had wept and wept and finally yielded to the pressure mounting on her.... They prevailed upon her. She took a solemn oath to throw me completely out of her mind. Later, as an act of desperate frustration, she took the ring I had given her to the seaside, and looking at it for the last time, with all the love in her heart for me, threw it far in to the sea, to sing songs about our romance to the rising and falling tides ... My heart sank, and my whole world shattered. There was no meaning to existence without her ... I cried on the shoulder of my brother Chetan, who knew the extent of my involvement with Suraiya who consoled me, "Life teaches its own lessons at every step. This chapter is closed for you forever, and you must start a new one."

Dev Anand followed the advice of his brother and moved on. In 1954, he got married to Kalpana Kartik, his heroine in *Taxi Driver*. That his marriage survived speaks volumes to the resilience of his wife. Dev Anand was a flirt by nature. It is hard to know what the outcome of his marriage with Suraiya would have been. What was widely known—and he freely admitted in his autobiography—was that he had had numerous affairs over the years. Some were highly publicized, like the one with Zeenat Aman in the 1970s. She was almost thirty years his junior. She was happy to use him to get a foothold in the movies. Once established, she ditched him.

For Suraiya, it was different. Although she continued to act and sing for a while, she started to live with the memories of her doomed love affair. She took early retirement from films in the early 1960s and lived a quiet and relatively secluded life thereafter. She had numerous marriage proposals over the years, including one from M. Sadiq, a successful director originally from Lahore who had made a name with hits like *Chaudvin ka chand*. He later migrated to Pakistan and made *Baharon phool barsao*. Some readers may recall a comic episode when a die-hard young fan of Suraiya, who was desperately in love with her, turned up at her door. He was dressed up as groom and refused to leave until his beloved accompanied him. He had to be forcibly removed. Suraiya never married.

Dr. Omer Adil, a famous TV personality in Lahore, narrates a strange episode. He spent some time with Suraiya in her apartment on Marine Drive, Bombay. As the interview finished and he was about to leave, Suraiya suggested that her visitor better leave from the side entrance to avoid inconvenience since there were always too many of her admirers on the front door. A surprised Omer Adil found an absolutely deserted front entrance with no one in sight. It seems that the unfortunate Suraiya had been living in the past, totally oblivious to the fact that life had moved on and that she had been almost forgotten by the public. Her mother and infamous granny had died years earlier, and the rest of her family had immigrated to Pakistan. She died in 2004 a lonely and forgotten person. Dev Anand, the love of her life, was in Bombay, was informed of her death, and chose not to attend her funeral.

Another aspects of Suraiya's life is also worth mentioning. It was said that she had an infatuation with Gregory Peck, the American actor. Frank Capra, the famous Hollywood director, once visited Bombay, and Suraiya met him. A picture exists of her sitting with Capra along with her mother and granny. It is said that Suraiya told Capra of her fascination with Gregory Peck and also asked him to pass on a picture of hers to him. As fate would have it, Gregory Peck was once staying in a hotel in Bombay, on his way to the Far East. Al Nasir, another actor in Bombay (one reads his name in Manto's piece on *Sitara, the dancing tigress from Nepal*), apparently managed to persuade Mr. Peck to visit Suraiya's house. Gregory Peck may have also recalled that picture from years earlier and agreed. Suraiya was woken up from sleep and was thrilled to see her idol. The meeting was brief, barely an hour. Some believe that Suraiya's love for Dev Anand may have been due to his resemblance to Gregory Peck.

Suraiya's last movie was *Rustom Sohrab* in 1963, in which the music was scored by the great Sajjad Hussain. The music was superb, but the movie flopped, and this turned out to be the swan song for both Sajjad and Suraiya. In that movie, Suraiya sang one of her evergreen songs, *Yeh kaisi ajab dastan ho gayi hea*. She may not have realized that her own life had become the epitome of the same song.

Reference: *Romancing with Life* by Dev Anand.

Father: The Aligarh Man

As I look back at my father's life, a few things stand out. He worked with clocklike precision and was organized to a fault. I suspect he had developed this trait back in his student days at Aligarh. He was an early riser, would go to mosque for prayer, and would then proceed to his morning walk. He did office work for an hour or so before proceeding to court; he was a lawyer. In the afternoon, he took a nap and on most days played tennis, followed by office work. Evening prayer was also in the mosque. By ten, he was ready to sleep.

Father could be a hard taskmaster. I recall his dictations to clerks at breakneck speed; heavens only know how the poor guys managed it.

The Doctor From The East

Later in life, he behaved impatiently at times; this is a trait he shares with those who value time and covet efficiency. He was a man of few words and grew restless when forced to hear long-winded stories from his legal clients. One of his junior lawyers once told me that, in court, Father's legal arguments were concise and to the point. He was an avid reader but, in later years, limited his reading to law journals and religious texts.

Father was a well-dressed man but not fussy about it; his court dress was white shirt and trousers, black coat, and black tie. In Zia's time, when local dress was allowed in court, he switched to white *shalwar* and shirt. The only constant was the Jinnah cap, although when young he wore Turkish fez, which might have been a legacy of his Aligarh days. In social gatherings, he wore a sherwani; while at home, he wore the traditional Punjabi kurta with *tehmad*. He had a pleasant, easygoing personality, was medium in height, had fair color and blue eyes.

Father was old fashioned in some ways. He was punctual but did not wear a wristwatch. In his youth, he used a pocket watch but later depended on the wall clock that needed weekly tune-ups. He owned a car but did not learn driving. Only grudgingly did he accept having a telephone in the house. He valued education—I distinctly remember his desire to see at least one of his children go to Government College Lahore. But, he was also a man of contradictions—two of our sisters did not go to college and were married off after finishing high school.

Although he never entered politics, he had strong political views. I recall a heated discussion between two groups on a train before the 1970 elections. Father was asked for his opinion of Bhutto; he offered his in crisp English. I do not remember his arguments except one, that Bhutto, despite his talent, was power hungry and untrustworthy. The fact was Father liked Ayub. Once, he returned from a morning walk, visibly excited. "Ayub has passed through our town this morning in Chanab Express!" He was unhappy the way Ayub had been ousted in 1969; for a few years after Ayub's fall, he expected his comeback. When lawyers came on the streets in 1977 after the rigged elections, he was in the lead.

Father's immense dislike for Bhutto, by default, led to a good opinion of Zia. He did not live to see the later part of Zia's era—the lies, deceptions, and all—otherwise, he might have changed his opinion.

In 1973, when the anti-Ahmadiyyah movement began, he was one of its leaders in our town. Father was not a religious fanatic but, on that occasion, joined in a cause that he strongly believed in. Little did he realize that the menace of sectarianism was being unleashed with that movement.

Father usually stayed away from the petty village politics, except once—a vagabond tried to rape a woman from a poor peasant family. Father took up that case and used his legal skills—and personal plea—to the presiding magistrate to get the accused behind bars.

Father was born in a rural area in a traditional Jat family and was one of the largest land owners in the village. Yet he was loath to use *chaudhary* with his name; nor did he ever write his caste (Gondal) with his name. It was plain and simple—Mohammad Mirza Khan, advocate. He had graduated from Aligarh but did not write *Alig* with his name. In a society where people are desperate to publicize their qualifications and pedigrees, he was an aberration.

Father was a practicing Muslim and had great faith in Allah. Little did he realize that his faith was to undergo a supreme test. It came in 1981. Father was then in his midseventies, still in full-time legal practice. Our elder brother Brigadier Safdar, then posted at Peshawar, died suddenly. The news was conveyed to our elderly parents at midnight. Having heard that his favorite son, the flower of his eyes, was no more, he bore the indescribable pain with a fortitude that surprised many. On that fateful day, no one saw him cry or shed a tear. While awaiting his son's dead body, he did not forget his prayer. His unshakable faith in Allah served him well that day. A few weeks later, our bereaved mother asked him, "Why do you not show any emotion?"

"My heart bleeds for Safdar," he said. "But remember, Allah gave him to us, and He took him away."

In financial matters, Father was upright. In 1975, I joined medical college, having done well in FSc and having secured—at least I thought—a merit scholarship for five years. It turned out that Father's income, reported accurately, had made me ineligible. I was aghast. Aware that many of my fellow students from wealthier families had qualified for scholarship (having not declared the actual income), I approached a clerk in Punjab University. That was no problem, the clerk said. All I needed was a statement from tahsildar that Father's income was less than stated in the original form. I was relieved. Father was the senior lawyer in town, knew everybody, and could surely manage that. It was evening when I reached home from Lahore. He was working in the office. As I broached the subject, he looked irritated and asked, "How much money do you need in a month?" I was taken aback and said five hundred. "I will let you have up to one thousand but do not expect me to lie for this." That was it. It took me a long time to overcome the disappointment of having lost my scholarship. Forty years later, however, I look back and admire his honesty.

Father was a great bedtime storyteller. It had started with his first child, and the tradition continued through to me. Being the youngest, I received more than my fair share of the bedtime entertainment that also included a gentle stroking of the skin that I greatly enjoyed. Alas, as Shafiq-ur-Rahman once wrote, I outgrew my childhood, and it stopped.

He had many admirers and acquaintances but a limited number of close friends. His busy and disciplined lifestyle left little time for social gatherings. He traveled abroad only once, for hajj. Otherwise, he was happy to make a weekend visit to our village. In summer vacation, he visited his eldest son, an army officer, at Rawalpindi. In his younger days, he had been to Delhi and Agra. Father would sometimes visit Lahore and stayed in Delhi Muslim Hotel in Anarkali. A few years ago, I was disappointed to see this famous Lahore hotel—once frequented by the Muslim middle class—in a dilapidated state.

Father had the opportunity to meet Allama Iqbal once. Accompanied by his maternal uncle, he approached Iqbal and sought the great man's help for a school that they wanted to build in our village. Iqbal did not disappoint them and wrote a letter to the nawab of Bhopal in support of the project. The nawab gave a donation as did many others. A beautiful multistory high school was built on a piece of land donated exclusively by Father. The school continues to function to this day, having become a beacon of light in a backward and relatively remote area of Punjab. Father rarely spoke about his donation—and many other acts of generosity. He was not that kind of man; the curse of self-aggrandizement had not touched him.

There was a portrait of Quaid-e-Azam that hung on the wall in our drawing room. Quaid-e-Azam was his hero. In the 1945 elections, Father supported the Muslim League candidate against a Unionist whom he knew personally. I also recall a comment that he once made about Gandhi's "mumbled speech." Only rarely did he speak of Aligarh days. Once, however, he made a comment about Sir Ross Masood, Sir Syed's grandson, and presumably, Aligarh's vice-chancellor during Father's student days. I knew nothing of Ross Masood back then, did not pay much attention, and decades later regret having not asked him the details.

Back in the '70s, Father wrote a letter of congratulations to Ch. Ahsan Alig, an old classmate of his from Aligarh whose young son had been made a minister in the PPP government. The young politician—who was highly educated, eloquent, and intelligent, having topped Central Superior Services exam in Pakistan—had the makings of a man whose star was on the rise and who appeared destined to do great things for Pakistan. Now fast-forward to 2020. Father and Ahsan Alig were long gone. As for the politician, he has been part of the some of the most corrupt regimes in the history of our country.

He received an unusual respect from his children. He was not loud or harsh but had somehow mastered the art of leading by example, persuasion, and polite reminders. Our eldest brother used to smoke but avoided it in his presence. We had a radio and were fond of music and occasionally, in excitement, would increase the volume but never in his presence. We were allowed to go to movies periodically but needed his permission, which was mostly given. We had learned, however, not to ask him more than once a month. Once, as I returned from a movie, he asked, "So what movie did you see?"

"*Jawani ki hawa*," I said triumphantly.

"So you have been exposed to *Jawani ki hawa*," he said and then burst out laughing. Being too young, I completely missed his point.

He would read Koran often, and sometimes aloud, with a beautiful rhythm. At Aligarh, he had been chosen to call adhan and received a scholarship for that. I remember his reverence for Ghalib, whom he once described as a poet with the ability to contain a river in a bucket. Once, as he returned from a *mushaira*, he described Murtaza Barlas's recitation as dazzling. Barlas had spent some time in our town earlier as a civil servant and, like another bureaucrat, Mustafa Zaidi, was a poet of considerable merit. Having read Persian, Father would sometimes quote Saadi.

Father had not detached himself from the simple pleasures of life. One day as he entered the house, he stopped, listened attentively to the song on the radio for a few seconds, and surprised me by identifying K. L. Saigal's voice. There was an old gramophone in the house with flat disc records bought years earlier by him. I never saw him use it, but my elder siblings had. Among female singers, Farida Khanum and Iqbal Bano were his favorites. Himself a tennis player, he would sometimes watch tennis on TV. To this day, I recall his admiration for the great Bjorn Borg with the way he used to dispatch poor Jimmy Connors at Wimbledon.

Father was rarely sick. Aside from a minor cold once in a while, he remained in excellent health most of his life. He was hospitalized only once; it turned out to be his first and last one.

Father's generation had lived through historic times. They had seen the struggle for independence, the creation of Pakistan, its early struggles, followed by the era of rapid progress in the sixties; they had also witnessed the breakup of Quaid's Pakistan. They had witnessed both the glory and the heartbreak.

Thomas Jefferson once said that "the art of life is the art of living with pain." Like the great American statesman, Father too carried on in life despite many personal tragedies. He personified a life of discipline, hard work, and dedication to his family, community and profession. He played his part on the world stage as the bard from Stratford once wrote. And when the time for exit came, he gently slipped into the night without much fuss. That was my father.

Flight of the Falcon: A Fighter Pilot's Story

It was November 1979. Pakistan was in the iron grip of martial law; the country's twice-elected PM had been executed, and all opposition had been crushed by brute force. Zia-ul-Haq came to address the elite of Pakistan Military at War College in Rawalpindi. While he spoke to "his constituency," the audience listened in silence. The wily dictator alluded to the difficult times at home and abroad and then made his point. "The armed forces will have to continue managing the country indefinitely until a nucleus of God-fearing, good Muslims enter politics." His address over, having reneged yet again on his promise to hold elections, Zia was ready to leave when Air Cdre. Sajad Haider stood up and asked for permission to speak. When allowed, SH made a statement for the ages; his words visibly shook Zia and had the audience—which included senior members of the cabinet—spellbound.

In his statement, dashing and flamboyant SH—twice-decorated ace of PAF in 1965 as well as 1971—questioned Zia's intentions and sincerity, criticized the intelligence agencies for their role in the fall of civilian governments, and brought up the sensitive issue of people's contempt for the uniform. For this extraordinary act of defiance, this outstanding officer paid a heavy price: instead of a well-deserved promotion, he was prematurely retired. This may be one of the very few examples in the history of our nation that truth was spoken bluntly with complete disregard to the consequences. SH, therefore, can rightfully claim to have performed the supreme jihad.

The fighter pilot par excellence, who has been hailed as "one of the gallant few who saved Pakistan in 1965" (by no less an authority than Air Mshl. Asghar Khan) and "the real and forever hero of the 1965 air war" by an Indian aviation expert, has recently come out with his autobiography that looks at behind-the-scenes stories of the wars of 1965 and 1971. But this book also has plenty of information for those who were fed up with the "murder of history" in Pakistan. He is forthright and candid and has hardly spared anyone. One may disagree with his opinion here and there, but his credentials are strong, and his patriotism is beyond any doubt.

In his memoir, SH takes the reader along on the incredible journey of his life that feels like an Indiana Jones movie. SH, who traces his ancestry to rulers of the Khwarazmian Empire, was born in Quetta, where his father—a physician—was posted; he went through Forman Christian College Lahore, PAF Academy Risalpur, and postings in Karachi, Dhaka, Sargodha, Peshawar, and Washington, DC, as air attaché in the Pak Embassy. As fate would have it, having fought in two wars and having earned high praise for his daring and leadership, he found himself in solitary confinement in the infamous Attock conspiracy case in 1972. Exonerated of all charges eventually but scarred, he tried to move on with his life and career, only to find a vindictive Air Mshl. Zafar Chaudhary in his way. Zafar Chaudhary's dismissal brought only a temporary relief in his ordeal since the shah of Iran came calling soon, asking for his dismissal on some very flimsy ground. Z. A. Bhutto was sympathetic to SH, but after his overthrow came Zia and then the episode mentioned earlier that ended SH's once promising career.

While SH's air force career had its ups and downs, his family life reads like a real roller coaster. He went through three failed marriages and a passionate love affair with a Hispanic lady whom he calls "the eternal love of my life." Living in retirement in Islamabad now, he has done us a huge favor by bringing out many facts previously known to a select few only. In the process, he has set the record straight and laid to rest many a myth.

SH has painstakingly produced numbers and figures to prove that, contrary to the popular perception, PAF performed quite well in 1971 and clearly outdid its performance of 1965. He has also analyzed the missions flown and went over the heroic deeds of many of his colleagues, some of whom were martyred. Sarfraz Rafiqui was shot down over enemy territory. SH lamented that no attempt was made by authorities to get our hero's dead body back to Pakistan. M. M. Alam's claim of shooting down five Indian hunters is dismissed (the likely kill was probably two), yet the author is generous in his praise for Alam otherwise and calls him "the undisputed ace of PAF."

There are many villains in this story, but no one has received more criticism than Ayub Khan. SH has gone way back in to the military record of Ayub from the Second World War and produced evidence that Ayub was "insecure, intellectually mediocre, with limited military knowledge, a failure as CO in Burma in 2nd WW" when he was relieved of command by General Rees. Ayub chose Yahya as his successor despite being fully aware of Yahya's moral depravity. SH uses scathing remarks for Yahya too and concludes that "the war of 1971 was lost at the strategic level owing to the cowardice, incompetence and moral turpitude of Yahya and his cabal. Tikka Khan was overrated and mediocre and—having risen through the ranks—never forgot to humble himself in front of all his seniors. General Niazi's dirty jokes, orgy, and debauchery has found a place too as did Air Mshl. Zafar Chaudhary's witch hunting and Air Cdre. Khaqan Abbasi's corruption.

Among SH's heroes was the late AM Rahim Khan. The author calls his former boss "a superb leader, gallant, true son of the soil, upright and a thorough gentleman." He has discussed Rahim's role in bringing Z. A. Bhutto to power, his unfortunate dismissal, and his post retirement difficulties. Rahim's death abroad in poverty and oblivion wrenchs one's heart. Asghar Khan's role in laying a very solid foundation for PAF is acknowledged as is Nur Khan's.

As for Operations Gibraltar and Grand Slam, the author feels that the abrupt change of command (Yahya brought in place of Akhtar Malik) at a crucial moment when Akhtar Malik was ready to capture Akhnoor was a fatal mistake. He goes further and finds sinister motives by Ayub behind this most unfortunate military blunder.

SH has gone in to Yahya Khan's overthrow; the credit is given to two outstanding army officers, Brig. F. B. Ali and Col. Alim Afridi, who were serving at Mangla in 1971. They threatened to march onto the presidency with tanks unless Yahya abdicated. A shaken Yahya, having been made aware of the mutiny at hand, reluctantly agreed. Now how many of us ever knew and cared to remember these two heroes? Late Khalid Hasan, I recall, had interviewed Brig. Ali in Toronto a few years ago. Wherever he may be, he and his fellow officers deserve our gratitude.

The author had mixed feelings about Z. A. Bhutto; he admired Bhutto's intellect, charisma, and leadership qualities but calls him a poor judge of character, having replaced professionally competent and exceedingly sincere officers like AM Rahim Khan with the vindictive Zafar Chaundhary and Gen. Gul Hassan with mediocre Tikka and later meek Zia-ul-Haq. As for Benazir, "She fell prey to graft, kickbacks and plunder. I was tormented by her demeanor because she had a large inheritance. . . . I felt devastated by her greed and arrogance."

In the epilogue, SH deplores our culture: "It discourages the spirit of inquiry and brands reprobate villains as heroes. Our emotions far surpass rationale, logic and the hard truth; we only believe hearsay." George Orwell said that "in a time of universal deceit, telling the truth is a revolutionary act." By Orwell's criterion, SH may perhaps be considered one too.

Reference: *Flight of the Falcon* by Sajad Haider

From Jhang to Trieste: The Story of Dr. Abdus Salam

When Dr. Abdus Salam walked up to the stage in December 1979 to receive his Nobel Prize, he broke from tradition. Instead of the customary suit with white tie, he wore a traditional Punjabi dress with a "shamla turban" and "gold khussa shoes." This may have been a statement of his pride as well as humility for a scientist born in a two-room mud house without electricity in the peripheral town of Jhang. In the Nobel lecture that followed, he described in vivid detail the great heritage of Muslim scientists; men like Ibn-Rushd (Averröes), Ibn Sina, and many more. When the news of his Nobel win flashed on the TV screens across the world, he became known to the millions instantaneously. But for those in his profession, he had arrived decades earlier.

Some time ago, this writer asked a few physician colleagues—all from Pakistan—of what they knew about Dr. Abdus Salam. The answers went like this: he won the Nobel Prize, lived abroad, and was Ahmadi, and that pretty much summarized it. To my shame, I also knew only a little more. It was with this background that I recently read a biography—*Cosmic Anger* by Gordon Fraser—of this great son of Pakistan and would like to share some aspects of his life with the readers.

Dr. Salam's ancestors converted to Islam from Hindu Rajputs a few hundred years ago. His father, Mohammad Hussain, was a schoolteacher in Jhang. His paternal uncle Ghulam Hussain, later to become his father-in-law, was the first to convert to the Ahmadi sect. The other family members followed later. Salam, therefore, was born into this sect and did not convert himself. His academic journey took him from the backward waters of Jhang to Government College Lahore, Cambridge, Princeton, back to Lahore, and then back again to Cambridge, Imperial College London, and Trieste. The list of his academic accomplishments is very long. Suffice it to say that what started as first position in class one continued onto the Nobel win, KBE, and well beyond. *Cosmic Anger* is a well-written, balanced, and well-researched book that makes an interesting read.

Salam comes across as a very motivated, deeply religious, and hardworking individual. We learn that he had a "monk like devotion" to duty and worked up to sixteen hours a day. For him, time was a very precious commodity that could not be squandered. The most productive part of his day was early morning. The day began with prayer. He was an avid reader and did a lot of reading outside physics and math. He had been coached in poetry at Jhang by Sher Afzal Jafri. At Government College, he had been president of the college union, editor of the college magazine *Ravi*, and played chess. He stayed in the famous New Hostel, which he visited after his Nobel win to personally thank his servant, Saida, who had looked after him in his student days.

It was at Government College that he fell in love with Urmila, the beautiful daughter of the college principal, Sondhi. It is unknown if she ever responded to his charm or whether he ever approached her. It may have been like Meeraji's distant flirtation with the obscure Bengali beauty Meera Sen, but that is a story for another day. Unlike Meeraji, however, Salam moved on to better things in life; for that, we should all be very grateful to Salam, for he had too much work ahead of him.

Salam's family was in no position to afford his higher studies abroad. This was made possible by legislation proposed and passed by the efforts of Khizer Hayat Tiwana. It was Mr. Tiwana who suggested using leftover money—originally raised for the Second World War effort—to pay for the higher education of deserving students. Khizer Hayat Tiwana rarely gets a kind word in our history books. But by this action alone, he made it possible for Salam to move onto Cambridge, and the rest is history.

Salam's arrival at Liverpool docks in 1947 on a cold autumn day in a ship that had departed from Bombay weeks before was a very uncomfortable one. The young man on his way to Cambridge, with a trunk load of books, was ill prepared for the cold British weather and was struggling to move his luggage when he was spotted by Sir Zafrulla, who had come to receive a nephew. Having seen Salam's predicament, Zafrulla offered help. This included giving his overcoat to Salam. They traveled to London together by train and stayed overnight in an Ahmadi mosque in Southfields, London, before Salam continued onto Cambridge the following day.

This was not the first time Zafrulla had given help or advice to Salam. Years before, Salam's father had sought advice from Sir Zafrulla—the leading Muslim of the Indian subcontinent at the time—about Salam's career. Zafrulla offered three very valuable pieces of advice: First, the family should take good care of Salam's health; second, the lessons should be prepared beforehand and revised after school and last, the boy should be made to travel to broaden his outlook. Dr. Salam and Zafrulla were to develop a very personal friendship over the years. Reading this biography, Zafrulla comes across as one of the most influential people in Salam's life, the others being his father and Paul Dirac, a famous physicist whom Salam considered the greatest scientist of the twentieth century, even ahead of Einstein.

Salam's life had its fair share of failures and tragedies. An amusing one was his failure to pass the dreaded British driving test at first attempt. He failed to do the parallel parking to his examiner's satisfaction. To the genius from Jhang who had always stood first, this must have felt strange. Many more setbacks were to follow, however. Salam and his family were threatened during the 1953 anti-Ahmadi riots in Lahore. At the time, he and his family resided on campus at Government College, where he was professor of mathematics; he had to be smuggled out of his residence for safety. Ironically, there is a hall in Government College named after him now.

Salam's Nobel win came in 1979. However, what is not commonly known outside the scientific community is the fact that Salam came within a whisker of winning it in 1956 were it not for sheer bad luck. At the time, he had come up with the theory of "massless neutrino" and was ready to send it for publication. As an afterthought, Salam sought advice from Wolfgang Pauli—widely considered the biggest name in physics at the time—who advised against its publication. Heeding the heavyweight physicist's advice, Salam held on to his paper for some time. As it was, the same theory won the Nobel for Lee and Yang, while Salam had to wait another twenty-five years to finally get his.

Salam's biography makes it abundantly clear that he was after a lot more than just the Nobel Prize. He had multiple goals. First, he wanted to explore the mysteries of the universe to better understand Allah's creation. Second, he desperately wanted to promote scientific research in the Islamic world. And third, he wanted to create an institution that would enable the third world physicists to come together to exchange ideas, interact, and reverse the brain drain to the West. There was no question he succeeded in the first objective; his Nobel win proved that. Salam also managed to create the International Center for Theoretical Physics in Trieste, Italy, which met the third goal. The International Center for Theoretical Physics has been a spectacular success and has been named after him posthumously.

It was in the promotion of science in the Muslim world where Salam tragically failed. Salam traveled far and wide in the Islamic world and left no stone unturned to plead his case. He made multiple trips to the oil-rich Middle East but without success. There were not many Muslim heads of state with the vision to understand his point of view. Part of the problem was his Ahmadi faith. Salam continued to carry a Pakistani passport all his life that declared him a "non-Muslim." He could have easily become a British or Italian citizen but didn't. This made him go through the long immigration lines at London's Heathrow Airport, followed by interviews with the arrogant immigration officers. He endured all that humiliation in his single-minded devotion to his goals in which he only partially succeeded.

Salaam died of progressive supranuclear palsy (PSP), a degenerative disease of the brain, in 1996 at his second wife's home in Oxford. Though very debilitated, limited in his mobility and speech, his mind was sharp to the very end. His dead body was flown to Lahore, accompanied by multiple family members, where—true to tradition—no high-ranking member of the government or politician came anywhere near the funeral. Many in our nation had disowned him along with his Ahmadi community years ago, branding them heretics. At least he was in good company since a similar fate had befallen Galileo Galilei.

Today the man who brought the first Nobel Prize for our nation lies buried in a simple grave in Rabwah, where this writer had the opportunity to offer Fatiha a few years ago. His death anniversary comes on November 21 and passes without much notice every year. There are still calls from our enlightened religious leaders to prosecute the Ahmadi sect.

Late Khalid Hassan wrote a very moving tribute to Sir Zafrulla a few years ago. Let me quote from his lines: "This nation has not had the grace to acknowledge, much less thank, its real heroes. Will that ever come to pass? One can only wonder."

Reference: *Cosmic Anger* by Gordon Fraser

Hadji-Murad: The Tragic Hero of Dagestan

Napoléon Bonaparte called his marshal Ney bravest of the brave; Jackson, a general in the American Civil War, was affectionately called Stonewall, a reflection of his calmness while under attack. There are many other examples. There was Bhagat Singh, who walked to the gallows with hardly any sign of fear; there were the defenders of Alamo. This scribe was thinking of men like these when he came across *Hadji-Murad*, a novelette by Leo Tolstoy, some time ago.

As Imran Khan continues to struggle, I began to think of HM—his magnanimity, integrity, daring, almost reckless disregard of danger and personal safety. Imran also has another trait in common with HM—the nation has not supported him the way they should. While he continues his sagging campaign, Pakistanis—like the Caucasians of 150 years ago—remain divided; we have our own Imam Shamils and czars to contend with.

So who was this HM? The introduction to Tolstoy's HM calls him "an epic hero." To the invading Russians, he was the Red Devil; he wore a red cap and dyed his beard red. In the Caucasus, he remains a legend to this day. According to Lesley Blanch, the author of *Sabers of Paradise*, "HM was Shamyl's greatest Naib, his most valued Lieutenant, and Russia's most deadly foe after Shamyl."

HM's exploits are recalled to this day: he once surprised a Russian garrison town and escaped, having done considerable damage while a ball was underway next door; on another occasion, he assassinated

Imam Hamzad Beg to avenge his foster brother's death, accompanied by his brother, Osman, only. Hamzad was surrounded by thirty murids with drawn swords. While Osman perished during the struggle, HM escaped, having killed Hamzad. Legend has it that he made off with the widow of his archenemy, Ahmat Khan from Djengoutai, another garrison town, with streets full of soldiers.

As a prisoner, once he was being escorted by forty Russian soldiers in heavy snowfall. The path went over a high mountain, was dangerously narrow, and had a precipice on one side. Lesley Blanch wrote:

> HM walked like a prince although his hands were tied. He went sure-footed, stepping cat-like beside the precipices. This was his native terrain. As they reached the highest, most precipitous ledge, HM suddenly turned on his captors and hurled himself headlong in to the abyss, dragging one of the guards after him. . . . He was written off as dead.

HM survived the 120-yard fall—he had counted on the snow to break his fall—albeit with serious injuries, from which he recovered except for a residual limp.

Tolstoy has left a brief physical description of HM. "HM's smile struck Poltoratsky by its childlike kindliness, a sort of innocence, who had never expected to see the terrible mountain chief look like that; and here was a vivacious person. . . . He had but one peculiarity: his eyes, set wide apart, gazed from under their black brows attentively, penetratingly and calmly into the eyes of others." While making a serious statement, HM would put his right hand over his chest—as he did while talking to General Vorontsov—after defection to the Russians.

Impressed by HM's daring, he was made naib by Imam Shamil, who was then directing a heroic struggle of the Caucasians against the czar's army. Shamil fought against the Russians from 1834 through 1859 against heavy odds with hardly any outside support. Shamyl valued HM, who was hoping to succeed Shamil. But Shamil felt that HM had become too powerful and too arrogant. Shamil nominated his own son as heir. This started a rift, and an enraged HM defected to the Russians while his family was taken hostage by Shamil.

The Russians were thrilled to have HM on their side. HM was hoping to get their support to get his family released from Shamil in prisoner exchange. After that, he wanted to lead an assault on Shamil with Russian support. The Russian viceroy General Vorontsov promised help but then procrastinated for months while the fate of HM's family was hanging by a thread. There were rumors that Shamil was going to gouge his son's eyes and give away his mother and wife to his murids unless HM returned to Shamil.

HM was in a predicament. While Shamyl continued to make offers of pardon, HM knew that the foxlike Shamil could not be trusted. The Russians too never believed his sincerity and kept on making false promises. Time was running out for him. He was very attached to his son and worried about his fate. Though apparently free, he was really in a gilded cage in Tbilisi, Georgia.

HM planned a daring escape in broad daylight. As a desperate measure, he had decided to try to rescue his family from Shamil on his own. During one of his morning rides that Russians allowed him, HM and his henchmen suddenly galloped away after killing their Cossack guards. Having gone six miles, they stopped to rest for the night in a thicket. They were hoping to resume their flight, expecting to be in the mountains in a few hours, where they would be safe. As fate would have it, they were discovered and soon surrounded by Russian soldiers.

HM's last stand with five of his followers was beautifully written by Lesley Blanch in *Sabers of Paradise*:

> Within an hour, the troops had surrounded the coppice, and HM and his five men were trapped and outnumbered, a hundred to one. The game was up, and they knew it. But not one of them spoke of surrender. While the Russian officers were shouting to them to lay down their arms, they set about making their last stand. . . . As the five hundred attackers closed in, they could hear the Murids intoning their ritual death-chant, mournful and glorious. HM and his men unsheathed their shashkas; their ammunition was almost gone, but they still had their steel.

The rest of the narrative is by the master storyteller Tolstoy:

> HM and his men fired only when any of the militiamen came forward, and rarely missed their aim . . . So it continued for more than an hour. . . . Then HM was wounded, the bullet piercing his shoulder. . . . Another bullet hit HM in the left side. He lay down in the ditch, and again plugged the wound with cotton. This wound in the side was fatal, and he felt that he was dying. Memories and pictures succeeded one another with extraordinary rapidity in his imagination. . . . Yet his strong body continued the things that he had commenced. Gathering together his last strength, he rose from behind the bank, fired his pistol at a man who was running towards him, and hit him. Then HM got quite out of the ditch, and limping heavily, went dagger in hand straight at the foe. . . . Some shots cracked, and he reeled and fell. . . . But the body that seemed to be dead, suddenly moved. First the uncovered bleeding shaven head rose; then, with hands holding to the trunk of the tree, the body rose. He seemed so terrible that those who were running towards him stopped short. But suddenly a shudder passed through him; he staggered away from the tree and fell on his face, stretched out at full length, like a thistle that had been mown down, and he moved no more.

And so it came to pass that the most haunting and extraordinary character among the Caucasian heroes was no more, defiant to the very end. A young Winston Churchill, while working as a war correspondent in Sudan in 1898, had witnessed Khalifa Abdullah's fearless charge before being shot and with admiration called it "a dramatic dignity sometimes denied to more civilized warriors." HM certainly had this dramatic dignity in abundance, although Mr. Churchill may not have been aware of it.

The news of HM's death was conveyed to the czar by General Vorontsov with a tribute:

Thus on April 24, 1852, HM died, as he had lived, desperately brave. His ambition equaled his courage, and to that there was no bound.

The czar was later to receive HM's severed head as a battle trophy in Saint Petersburg. Little did the despot know that, just two generations later, his great-grandson, Czar Nicholas—along with his entire family—would be butchered by the Bolsheviks, bringing an end to the Romanov Dynasty. As for Shamil, the so-called imam was to surrender tamely to the Russians in 1859. Having lost HM, his most daring naib, for nothing else but nepotism, he was never the same force again. His designated successor and son, Khazi Mohammad, also surrendered with him, bringing to an end the Murid wars, a tragic chapter in the history of Caucasia. The memory of HM lives on, and he is widely believed to be the most haunting and extraordinary character among the Caucasian heroes.

A mountain song from Dagestan runs like this:

> The earth will dry on my grave,
> Mother, my Mother!
> And thou wilt forget me,
> And over me rank grasses wave,
> Father, my Father!
> Nor wilt thou regret me,
> When tears cease thy dark eye to lave,
> Sister, dear Sister!
> No more will grief fret thee!
> But thou my Brother, the Elder, wilt never forget,
> With vengeance denied me!
> And thou, my Brother, the Younger, wilt ever regret,
> Till thou liest beside me!
> Hotly thou camest, O death-bearing ball that I spurned,
> For thou wast my Slave!
> And thou, black earth, that battle-steed trampled and churned,
> Wilt cover my grave!
> Cold art thou, O Death, yet I was thy Lord and thy Master!
> My body sinks fast to earth; my Soul to Heaven flies faster.

It is said that HM was very fond of this song and would often ask one of his followers to sing for him. He would listen intently, and as the song would come to the end with its mournful tone, HM would close his eyes. Perhaps the valiant warrior had a premonition of things to come.

<u>References</u>: *The Sabers of Paradise* by Lesley Blanch; *Hadji Murad* by Leo Tolstoy

Ibn Battuta: A Traveler Par Excellence

I have indeed—praise be to God—attained my desire in this world, which was to travel through the earth, and I have attained in this respect what no other person has attained to my knowledge.

—Ibn Battuta

Ibn Battuta dictated the above lines to Ibn Juzayy after he had returned to his native Morocco, having put behind him seventy-three thousand miles in three continents, an area equivalent to forty modern countries. He began his globe-trotting at twenty-four and did not return until he was forty-seven. During this lengthy absence, both his parents died while he himself went through enormous hardships. But in doing so, he has left behind a remarkably detailed record of the places that he visited and the people he met. The reading of *Rihlah*—the book of his travels—reortedly is a fascinating experience.

Rihlah provides very few details of his personal life. All we know is that he was a Berber from a family of legal scholars in Tangier and had some training in jurisprudence. It appears that his original intention was to perform hajj. He set out from Tangier with this purpose in mind in 1325. It took him eight months to make it to Egypt, a distance of almost two thousand miles. Egypt and Syria at the time were ruled by Mamluks who enjoyed great prestige among the Muslims for having inflicted a crushing defeat on Mongols of Persia that had saved Egypt from the catastrophe that had befallen the Abbasid caliphate and many other countries.

The Cairo that Ibn Battuta visited had a population of five hundred thousand and thus was fifteen times bigger than London at the time. We also hear about the enormous size of caravansaries in Cairo, some of which could accommodate up to four thousand guests. Having spent some weeks in Cairo, he moved onto Hejaz through Syria upon joining the official Mamluk hajj caravan. About Meccans, he reported, "They are elegant and clean in their dress—use perfume freely—and the women are of rare and surpassing beauty, pious and chaste."

His religious obligation over, Ibn Battuta had a change of plans. Instead of returning to Morocco, he decided to move onto Persia. Indeed, he was to be a relentless traveler for almost thirty years, which took him to the very boundaries of the Islamic world and well beyond. Since he was no longer part of the hajj caravans, he ended up making his own travel arrangements. He spent weeks in the camel litters in the Middle East and Africa; horse was used in the Indian subcontinent while ships of various kinds were used at sea.

Reading *Rihlah*, one is amazed at the young Moroccan's ability to befriend and gain favors from private citizens as well as high officials. During his time on the road, he stayed in all kinds of places—including Sufi hospices, private residences, colleges, and madrassas—and survived on charity and gifts. Traveling in those days was far from safe, but he continued his single-minded quest to explore the world. In the process, he came close to losing his life a few times and lost all his possessions once when he found himself on the south coast of India. There were also sicknesses, including one that made him so weak that he was tied to the horse saddle to prevent a fall.

From Hejaz, he went to Persia through Iraq, both being part of the Il-Khanat Mongol Empire founded by Hülegü Khan. At the time of Ibn Battuta's visit, it was ruled by Abu Said, whose father had converted to Islam. Ibn Battuta liked Abu Said: "He is pious, tolerant, generous and a committed Sunni and is the most beautiful of God's creatures." Shiraz gets high praise too: "Its inhabitants are handsome in figure and clean in their dress. There is no city except Shiraz that approaches Damascus in the beauty of its bazaars, fruit-gardens and rivers." On the contrary, his description of Baghdad is quite depressing: "Her outward lineaments have departed and nothing remains of her but name. There is no beauty in her that arrests the eye, or summons the busy passer-by to forget his business and to gaze."

The next stop was Anatolia (Asian Turkey of today). There, he had the good fortune to meet and be a guest of Orhan, son of the legendary Osman, the founder of the Ottoman Empire. His kingdom was still in infancy. Here is what *Rihlah* says of Orhan: "This sultan is the greatest of the kings of Turkmens and the richest in wealth, lands and military forces. Of fortresses, he possesses nearly a hundred—he fights with the infidels continually and keeps them under siege." Ibn Battuta may not have realized he was witnessing the historic rise of an empire that was to see a nonstop expansion—in all directions—for almost seventy years and was to last more than five centuries.

From Anatolia, he went farther north into Crimea on a boat through the Black Sea. The next few months were spent in the Caucasus Region and Central Asia. Oz Beg Khan, the Mongol ruler of the Golden Horde, was a new convert to Islam. Ibn Battuta noted with obvious surprise that Mongol and Turkish women enjoyed freedom, respect, and near equality in that land. Ibn Battuta then turned west and traveled with Oz Beg Khan's wife, who was to visit her family in Constantinople. He thus traveled as part of the royal entourage, did meet the emperor Adronicus III of Byzantium, and toured the historic city, almost 130 years before it fell to Sultan Mehmed the Conqueror. Upon returning, Ibn Battuta turned south and passed through the kingdom of Chagatai. He paints a very depressing picture of the historic city of Bukhara, which had been plundered by Genghis Khan a few decades earlier. "Its mosques, colleges and bazaars are in ruin." The great center of learning was not to recover from the havoc caused by the Mongol hordes for a long time.

Ibn Battuta continued his southward journey toward India and crossed into Afghanistan through the Hindu Kush Mountains. This route went through the famous Panjshir Valley, where Ahmad Shah Masoud led a fierce resistance against the Soviets in the 1980s. His entourage went through the Khyber Pass and eventually was led to Multan, which was the westernmost military post of the sultanate of Muhammad ibn Tughluq.

Ibn Battuta's arrival in India was quite unlike his previous travels and needs some explanation. It was believed that he had heard about the prestige and glamour of the court of Muhammad ibn Tughluq way back in Egypt. He may have been aware of the attractive job opportunities there, particularly to scholars from the Middle East. Being a faqih fluent in Arabic and with a résumé that included extended stay in Hejaz, Damascus, and Cairo, he may have hoped to impress the sovereign; he was not to be disappointed. Soon after his arrival in Delhi, he managed to get an audience with Sultan Muhammad ibn Tughluq, who was sufficiently impressed and appointed the young scholar as the qadi of Delhi. His annual salary was to be twelve thousand silver dinars.

Ibn Battuta spent almost ten years in and around India and devoted a considerable part of his book to it. He describes the sultan as "a tall, robust, white-skinned man, his legs tucked beneath him on a gold plated throne" and Delhi as "a vast and magnificent city, the largest in India, nay rather the largest of all the cities of Islam in the East." He also reports on a severe famine when "thousands upon thousands of people perished of want."

Ibn Battuta's fall from grace in the court of Delhi was quite sudden and unexpected. It was brought about by his Indian wife's father, who rose in rebellion against Muhammad ibn Tughluq. Being related to the rebel, Ibn Battuta naturally came under suspicion. As a result, he lost his job, remained under house arrest for a while, and even feared for his life.

After some time, the sultan relented and asked him to go to China as the head of his delegation. Ibn Battuta, being a compulsive traveler, jumped at this opportunity. As the head of the delegation, he was to carry with him some very precious presents for the emperor of China. As fate would have it, there was a terrible storm in the Arabian Sea, and the ship that was bound for China sank off the coast of Calicut with all the presents on board. Ibn Battuta miraculously survived the disaster but decided not to return to Delhi, being fully aware of Muhammad ibn Tughluq's wrath and unpredictable nature.

Having spent some time on the south coast of India, he sailed to the Maldive Islands, where he secured another judicial post but soon left and ended up in southern China, having passed through Ceylon, Java, and Sumatra. The sea voyage lasted many weeks. China under the Mongol rule impressed him: "China is the safest and the most agreeable country in the world for the traveler. You can travel all alone across the land for nine months without fear, even if you are carrying much wealth."

Being away from home for years and probably having grown homesick, he started the long trip back from China in December 1346 and made it to Morocco in November 1349, having seen the horrors of Black Death (plague) ravaging around him. He reports up to two thousand deaths a day in Damascus. However, his traveling was not over yet. He was soon crossing the Strait of Gibraltar and spent some time in the Islamic kingdom of Granada. These were difficult times for Muslims in the Iberian Peninsula. The Islamic power in Spain had been in decline for some time, and the Christian Reconquista had already begun. It was during his short stay in Granada that he met Ibn Juzayy, who would collaborate with him for his memoirs later.

His last journey was to the south in his own backyard in West Africa, but this may have been the most disappointing of all. He went through enormous hardships to cross the vast and treacherous Sahara Desert, where there was only one source of water in a stretch of five hundred miles. This was undertaken to see the gold-rich Muslim kingdom of Mali. During the course of his travels, Ibn Battuta had pretty much come to expect a preferential treatment and expensive gifts from the kings. But Mansa Suleiman, the king of Mali, greatly disappointed him. His predecessor, Mansa Musa, had become a legend in that part of the world, having spent a fortune in Cairo on his way to hajj just a few years earlier.

It was said that Musa's entourage spent gold so freely in Cairo that its price depreciated. But this was how Ibn Battuta described the king of Mali in *Rihlah*: "Suleiman is a miserly king from whom no great donation is to be expected. Mansa Musa, by contrast had been generous and virtuous."

Having returned to Fès in Morocco, Ibn Battuta was asked by Abu 'Inan, the Marinid ruler in his homeland, to write his memoirs. Over the next two years, he dictated—from memory alone—while Ibn Juzayy took notes and did the editing. His work finished and presented to the king, he retired to a quiet life of a private citizen in a provincial town. Ibn Battuta died in 1368. Not much is known of his later years.

Ibn Battuta's life was, by any standards, an exciting one. He traveled far and wide, interacted with extraordinary people, and saw extraordinary events. (He reported seeing the self-decapitation of a subject to impress a Hindu prince in the Far East.) But during his extended time on the road, he did not forget his own private pleasures. Frequently, he traveled in great style and luxury in the company of his slaves and servants. (He reported buying a very beautiful slave girl from Sylhet.) At one stage, he became quite wealthy, having received the most expensive gifts from various kings. He married and divorced frequently and fathered quite a few children, some of whom may have survived. It is quite possible that his descendants have been living among us. In one sense, he was lucky too since most of his journeys took him through regions that were at peace, but that changed soon after his departure. Some of the kingdoms and dynasties he had visited vanished altogether (Granada, Mongol Persia, and Yuan China) while the rest experienced great turmoil.

What is Ibn Battuta's legacy? Traditionally, he has been placed well below Marco Polo, who died in Venice a year before Ibn Battuta started his epic journey to the east. His book *Rihlah* remained largely ignored and was almost forgotten until the last 150 years or so. In recent times, however, it is being given its well-deserved recognition. This is how his biographer, Ross Dunn, has summarized the famous traveler's place in history:

> For the history of certain regions, Sudanic West Africa, Asia Minor, or the Malabar Coast of India, the *Rihla* stands out as the only eye-witness report on political events, human geography, and social and economic conditions for a period of a century or more. Ibn Battuta has inevitably been compared with Marco Polo and usually taken second prize. Yet, Ibn Battuta travels to, and reports on, a great many more places than Marco did, and his narrative offers details, sometimes in incidental bits, sometimes in long disquisitions, on almost every conceivable aspect of human life in that age and his story is far more personal and humanly engaging than Marco's.

Book cited: *The Adventures of Ibn Battuta* by Ross Dunn

Josh Malihabadi: A Flawed Genius

"I am a poet, lover, seeker of knowledge and a friend of humanity," wrote Josh of himself in his autobiography, *Yaadoon ki baraat*. In his memoirs, he went to extraordinary lengths to bare it all. He fondly recalls his love affairs (eighteen to be exact), his upbringing in Lucknow, his education at home and Agra, an ill-fated short stay in Aligarh University, and his family with all their glamour and eccentricities. (His grandfather had 30 wives and concubines and fathered around 120 children, all except one of whom remained illiterate. He hardly ever spent a night without a female companion and died of syphilis at eighty-eight.) *Yaadoon ki baraat* is a remarkably candid account of the tumultuous but exciting life of a man who rubbed shoulders with literary giants and saw history being made around him.

Josh was born in great affluence in a conservative family of Afridi Pasthuns in Malihabad, near Lucknow, in 1903. His father was a poet, and it was with him that Josh started to go to literary gatherings. In his autobiography, Josh recalls his first recital in a *mushaira*, where his poem received more applause than his father's. Tongue in cheek, he writes of his father's admonishment for having surpassed him. There was no looking back for the young poet, who was to write awe-inspiring poetry and has been considered by some to be one of the finest of his generation.

Josh has made some interesting observations of his contemporaries: Faiz wrote good poetry but spoiled it by poor recital; Iqbal was a genius but borrowed his idea of shahin from Nietzsche; Majaz took

75 percent of his poetry to grave because of early death, otherwise may have surpassed everyone else; Firaq was a jewel in the crown of Urdu poetry but remained unappreciated in India; Mustafa Zaidi's poetry was modern, graceful, and unique. Others received scathing remarks: Hafeez Jalandhari was an intellectual dwarf and Faraz immature. Josh spent six months with Tagore at his school, Shantiniketan. He found Tagore larger than life, sensitive, frank, and fond of beauty but somewhat of an exhibitionist.

Nehru was Josh's ideal. Josh considered him a man who is born once in a century, a thorough gentleman, a shining star, and his benefactor who shared Josh's love of Urdu. Josh recalls a conversation when Nehru lamented the threat to Urdu in India. "I favor Urdu but my hands are tied since majority of my party favors Hindi," Nehru was reputed to have said. Josh's decision to immigrate to Pakistan was painful to Nehru; having failed to dissuade Josh, Nehru conceded that the "narrow-minded patriotism of Hindu was a real threat to Urdu in India." Sometime later, Nehru toured Pakistan clad in a sherwani and was amazed at having been received by Pakistani officials and dignitaries mostly in Western attire. Nehru was given the welcome address in English. Being fluent in Urdu, Nehru put his hosts to shame by giving his response in Urdu.

Josh was obsessed with language and spared no one for a mistake. Mirza Hadi Ruswa, famed author of *Umrao jan ada*, had been one of his teachers. Famous journalist and writer Hameed Akhtar reported Sahir Ludhianvi once being admonished by Josh in a literary gathering for having mispronounced one word in his poem "Taj Mahal." On another occasion, Josh went looking for magnifying glass in a Bombay market, kept asking for *mukabbar-ul-wujh*, and returned home without one. None of the shopkeepers understood this Urdu word, and Josh refused to compromise on his beloved Urdu. Hameed Akhtar also saw actor Prithviraj Kapoor, then in his prime, advising young actors to read Josh to improve their language skills. With some amusement, Josh narrates a visit to Nehru when Josh presented to him a book. Nehru thanked him by saying, "Main ap ka mushkoor hoon." Josh corrected him on the spot. "Should have said *Shakir hoon*."

Josh was a prolific writer. He had twenty-four books of poetry published in his lifetime, while another eleven or so never saw the light of the day. Josh wrote often against the British and was proclaimed *shaer-e-inqalab*. He befriended Jawaharlal Nehru, Maulana Azad, R. Tagore, and Sarojini Naidu and was greatly respected by the leadership of Congress for having written against the British when some of his contemporaries like Faiz and Hafeez Jalandhari—later to write Pakistan's national anthem—were serving in the British army.

Despite his reputation for bluntness, Josh was by nature a simple, almost naive kind of person. As the story goes, a distressed former raja of a princely state needed some of his property restored to him by the Indian government. He approached Josh and, as a thank-you, gave him the keys of a new car. Josh called on Prime Minister Nehru and broached the subject. Nehru directed Josh to the interior minister, Sardar Patel. Having thought over it, Josh said, "I have no desire to see that man [Patel] with criminal face, and by the way, what am I supposed to do with the car keys?" An exasperated Nehru, having understood his poet friend's dilemma, ended up calling Patel himself, and the issue was resolved.

Josh was sensitive as well as uncompromising and suffered as a result. After his immigration to Pakistan, his well-wishers—including government officials—made numerous attempts to produce a steady source of income for him; they all failed. Here is a hilarious example: Josh was once given the allotment papers for a residential plot by a government official but tore it to pieces, incensed that the official did not stand up as Josh departed. An ill-fated interview that was recorded to be broadcasted posthumously was hacked from Radio Pakistan and used by the hostile right-wing media to relentlessly hound him for the rest of his life. Financial worries, barrage of criticism, and prohibition of alcohol made life very difficult for Josh, whose drinking had become the stuff of legends—he once described it as "I begin to rise as the sun sets in," a reference to his drinking that would start precisely at sunset.

Those who visited Josh in his last days saw a sad, forlorn figure, slowly fading away, having been disowned by his adopted country. Josh once wrote:

Adab kar us kharabati ka, jis ko Josh kahtay hain
Ke wo apnee sadee ka Hafiz-o-Khayam hai saqee.

Little did he realize that he would be lowered to his grave by only a few and would be quickly forgotten. He lies buried in a simple grave in Islamabad with hardly any mention of him on his anniversaries. Strange indeed are the ways of our nation.

<u>References</u>: *Yadon Ki Baraat* by Josh Malihabadi; *Ashnayan Kya Kya* by Hamid Akhtar

K. L. Saigal

My earliest memory of Saigal is from the late '60s. There used to be a program of old filmi songs from Radio Ceylon. It always began with a song of Saigal, whom I did not like then. One day as I was listening to a song on radio, my father walked in. He was an old-fashioned, Aligarh-educated lawyer who did not pay much attention to music—or so I thought. But that day, as I tried to turn down the volume, he asked, "Isn't that Saigal?" Being told yes, he paused for a few seconds, listened attentively, and as the song finished slowly moved away, humming the tune. Looking back, I suspect he was nostalgic since Saigal had been the most popular singer in his youth. Those few minutes changed my perception of Saigal.

"I am just an ordinary person with no acting experience. I used to be a salesman, and singing is my hobby" was how K. L. Saigal described himself to a young Kidar Sharma (KS), who had knocked at his door, seeking his help to enter the Calcutta film world of the early '30s. "Unpretentious, humble, gracious, and a man of few words" was how Saigal came across to KS, who was to write the dialogues and songs for the all-time classic *Devdas*. The two Punjabis became lifelong friends.

Saigal's voice has been described as "nasal, deep, penetrating, free flowing, feeling-laden with astounding range" by experts. But how good was Saigal as a singer? I am no connoisseur of music, but just look at the names of those who were influenced by him: Mukesh, Rafi (early years), C. H. Atma, M. Kalim, and Kishore Kumar. Just listen to Mukesh sing his first hit in *Pehli Nazar* for Anil Biswas; he almost sounded like Saigal in "Dil jalta hai to jalne de." Kishore was so obsessed with Saigal that he traveled to Bombay from Calcutta to see him. Saigal's life was ebbing fast by then; the meeting never took place.

S. D. Burman once visited Ashok Kumar and overheard his younger brother Kishore, then an unknown, aspiring singer, imitating Saigal. His advice was "Saigal was great, but you need to create your own style." Kishore complied and, in his time, became the most sought-after singer in India. But Saigal remained his ideal. In 1987, HMV approached him and reached an agreement: Kishore was to sing some selected Saigal songs. Kishore was thrilled and agreed but then had second thoughts and backed out. His reason: "Saigal was the best of all times. I do not want to insult his memory, lest any of my admirers feels that I sing better than him."

Mauseeqar-e-Azam Naushad Ali, who worked with Saigal in *Shahjehan*—Saigal's last movie—once described him as "one of a kind, decent, simple, almost innocent being." In the cutthroat culture of filmdom, Saigal was indeed an anomaly.

Devdas was ready for release when it was decided to add one more song at the last minute. KS and Saigal sat together the whole night. While KS wrote down the lines, Saigal himself composed the tune; the result was "Dukh ke ab din bitat nahi." Such was Saigal's devotion to his craft.

For music fans, here was a quote from *Bollywood Melodies*, a book by Ganesh Anantharaman:

> Saigal's supreme effort at singing was, of course, R. C. Boral's, Bhairavi Thumri *"Babul mora naihar chooto hi jaaye"* in *Street Singer* (1938). In terms of authenticity and feeling, no other Bhairavi comes close to matching this Boral-Saigal masterpiece. Saigal, playing the protagonist, insisted that this song be recorded live as he is walking the street, though playback was well in vogue by then. Saigal knew that it was through his voice that he conveyed the truths of his character, and the truth of street singer needed a live recording. The director complied, and the song was recorded live with Saigal walking the streets, singing while a mike followed him in a truck just behind!

No other singer would have dared a live recording. No other singer, therefore, has sung as intense a Bhairavi.

Saigal was idolized by thousands across India, including women. Yet it is said that he was very lonely and longed for love. By nature, he was reserved and shy, and this became his handicap. How ironic that the superstar of his era could not muster up the courage to ask a woman out. Some felt that, like Sahir, he too considered himself ugly. Alcoholism may have been his escape from loneliness and loveless existence.

KS narrates another incident from Saigal's early days. Saigal used to sell typewriters in Calcutta. To supplement his income, he would also sell saris that an aide carried with him. Now there was a young girl, Najma, who lived in one of the slums. She would often stop him and look at a certain green sari that she liked but couldn't afford. One day she made Saigal promise to return the next day since she expected to have the required ten rupees. The next day when he came, there was a sound of wailing from that house. It turned out the young woman had died unexpectedly during the night. Saigal spoke to her sobbing brother, who was struggling to come up with the money needed for burial. A shaken Saigal donated the same green sari to be used as her shroud. A sensitive man by nature, Saigal was so moved by the tragedy that he stopped selling saris altogether.

Hameed Akhtar and Sahir Ludhianvi once went to Saigal's house in Bombay, hoping to see him sing. Saigal was averse to sing for visitors unless the request came from a child. Being informed of this by Saigal's servant, they managed to find a child from the neighborhood who asked Saigal to sing. The great one immediately picked up his harmonium and duly obliged.

"Saigal had two passions," writes KS in his autobiography, "music and alcohol; one made him and the other destroyed him." The menace of alcoholism has claimed many precious lives; among its famous young victims were gems like Manto, Akhtar Shirani, and Majaz. It is generally assumed that social drinking sometimes leads to alcoholism. In Saigal's case, however, there were some other theories too. KS notes that Saigal suffered from sciatica and drank to dull the pain. There is also a suggestion that Saigal had convinced himself that he sang better under the influence of alcohol. Just before recording, he would ask his driver to bring alcohol from the car, would consume some, and then would declare himself to be ready. Once a drunk, Saigal staggered into the recording room. Seeing his condition, the music director was ready to cancel the recording when Saigal said, "Please forgive my staggering, but I do not sing with my body but soul." He steadied himself by keeping a foot on a chair and gave a flawless performance—in just one take. At the end, there was a spontaneous applause from the musicians.

KS has also narrated an incident that shows Saigal as a humane, gracious giver. There was a drinking party in Juhu, where Saigal went along with KS. As the party was in full bloom, Saigal felt restless and asked KS to accompany him for some fresh air outside on the seashore. It turned out that his sensitive ears had picked up a faint sound of a blind beggar who was singing Ghalib's "Nukta cheen hai gham-e-dil." Saigal was moved to tears, sat at the feet of the beggar, put his hand in his pocket, and gave him whatever he had in it. When they returned, someone reminded him that he had five thousand rupees in his pocket, all given away without counting on an impulse. And Saigal's response was "You think the one who gives me ever counts?" Such was his generosity and nobleness.

In 1947, Saigal returned to his roots in Jalandhar. Years of heavy drinking had taken its toll; his liver was almost destroyed by then. He was hoping to recuperate and then give up acting altogether, concentrating on playback singing instead. But unbeknownst to him, the doctors had already given up on him and told his family to let him have alcohol if he so desired. One day he asked his brother for alcohol. The brother pretended to pour alcohol but instead gave water, hoping that he would not notice. Saigal took a sip and quoted, "Bajaye mein diya pani ka ik gilas mujhey, Samajh liya mere saqi ne badhawas mujhe." These were his last words. The man who had immortalized Mir, Ghalib, Zauq, Hasrat, Ameer Minai, and Seemab Akbarabadi with his golden voice, it seemed, remained a poet to the very end.

At the very end of Anton Chekhov's story *Uncle Vanya*, one of the characters said,

> My heart aches. There is nothing for it. We must go on living, through long, long chain of days and weary evenings. When our time comes, we shall die without a murmur. And there, beyond the grave, we shall say that we have suffered, that we have wept, and that life has been bitter to us. We had no joy in life. We shall rest; we shall rest.

And rest he did; with Naushad's eternal "Jab dil hi toot gaya" playing at his funeral pyre, Saigal bade his admirers a final farewell as he embarked on his journey to eternity.

References: *The One and Lonely* by Kidar Sharma; *Bollywood Melodies* by Ganesh Anantharaman; *Uncle Vanya* by Anton Chekhov

About Khwaja Khurshid Anwar

Years ago, I asked an uncle of mine about who the best composer in Pakistan was. "Khurshid Anwar," he said.

"And the best director?"

His answer was "Khurshid Anwar." While some may disagree with his second answer, hardly anyone would with the first. My uncle belonged to a generation that had been dazzled by KA's music. While India had Naushad, S. D. Burman, and Salil Choudhury, Pakistan had been very fortunate to have KA, who decided to leave a successful career in Bombay in the early fifties and returned to his beloved Lahore.

I never had the privilege of meeting KA; in fact, his most productive years were well behind him when I heard of him. But then the passage of time has rarely diminished the aura of truly great ones. A lot has been written of KA—his vast knowledge of classical music, attention to detail, skillful use of singers and instruments. It is said that an artist's greatness may be measured by the respect that he generats among his peers. Using this approach, this scribe has made an attempt to write about some aspects of KA's life that are not well known.

Habib Jalib, poet of the people, said this of KA in his autobiography: "I was very fond of him; he had been one of the great musicians of India even before partition, was highly educated, had superb knowledge of music and was a good poet too." Jalib regretts a misunderstanding that did not allow him to work with KA and blames himself for the lost opportunity. The two of them did eventually work together for a couple of songs written for a Hameed Akhtar movie.

Jalib had a very high opinion of KA as a person too: "He was a decent man and had a strange sadness about him that would translate in to his compositions. His work will not be easily forgotten; people like him are immortals." Jalib narrated an interesting episode when he was incarcerated in Camp Jail Lahore and in desperate need of cigarettes. He sent a note to KA, who lived nearby. Lo and behold, the bearer of the message returned with ten packs of Gold Leaf in an hour. Jalib calls KA *Sahib-e-dil*.

Another contemporary of KA, Qateel Shifai—who wrote songs for many of KA movies, including *Intezar*—has also praised him as a very talented composer who understood the fine points and intricacies of music. In his autobiography *Ghungroo toot gaye*, Qateel has analyzed the combination of Noor Jehan and KA in some detail and given more credit to KA for the duo's successful songs from the *Intezar* era. Qateel Shifai notes that KA used to create specific tones that suited Noor Jehan's voice. He worked very hard at rehearsals before going for the final take. It was his extraordinary talent that gave us the evergreen music of *Intezar, Chingari, Ghoonghat,* and *Koel*.

The KA and Noor Jehan combination did not last long, however. The split was due to the crush that she had developed on KA. She had somehow convinced herself—wrongly as it turned out—that the feelings were mutual. Qateel reports an amusing episode when NJ asked KA to take an oath on Koran that he was not in love with her. KA did so, saying that he only respected her and nothing more; *Malika-e-Tarannum* was not amused and almost passed out in exasperation. The die had been cast, and one of the most successful combinations in music broke up.

KA moved on and continued to create melodies with less talented singers like Kausar Perveen, Zubaida Khanum, and Naheed Niazi; but for NJ, it was never the same (except for a brief reunion in *Heer Ranjha* and a few other movies). She remained in great demand but was not able to sing quality songs the way she did for KA, for there was no one else of his caliber around. Qateel regretts that NJ never acknowledged KA's enormous contribution to her success. Qateel has made some other interesting observation about KA too. He was a man of contradictions: He used to pray and drink, both fairly regularly, and had very serious demeanor; and by the time Qateel started work with him, his days of flamboyance were well behind.

The most revealing piece on KA has come from that firebrand journalist and writer, late Ahmad Bashir. Being honest to the core, Bashir admitts that he was not part of KA's inner circle, but he knew enough of him. Here is his narrative:

> KA took film making seriously, worked hard at it but was an average director; it is as a composer that he excelled and surpassed everyone else. His unique style was stamped both in his direction as well as music. He based his tones on sadness that would make your heart bleed. Having spent time in Shimla in his youth, he had a touch of Shimla's folk music in his tunes. He was of romantic disposition and frequently chose romantic themes for his movies.

Bashir has also clarified KA's role in the famous Bhagat Singh conspiracy case. KA used to supply chemicals (stolen from his college lab) to the youth involved in bomb making. After the discovery, KA managed to extricate himself with the help of an influential relative. Despite his intense dislike of the British, KA moved away from politics since, "by nature, he was principled as well as uncompromising and therefore, ill-suited for politics." He turned toward music, and what a legacy he has left. Bashir continues:

> KA was *sur samrat* and used to play with the tunes. It is amazing that he hardly ever gave the impression of knowing the heights that he had scaled in music. Either he was totally unaware of his stature, or perhaps, took it for granted and considered it unnecessary to discuss it. His tunes were usually simple but unique and were meant for ordinary folks. He was a shy man and would rarely sing in public; he used to create his tune in isolation, using match box as a rhythm instrument, took his time and only after

considerable effort, would call upon the whole orchestra for recording. He was multi-talented, knew philosophy, poetry, script writing as well direction but above all was a composer par-excellence.

Bashir's portrait of KA's last days is not very pretty and should be an embarrassment to us all. This is what he recounted:

> His last years were sad. He had hardly any work. He would go to *Evernew Studio* daily, sit in his office and returned in the evening having received no offers. Those who once admired him were loath to recognize him and at times made painful remarks like, "He is finished."

KA endured this period of virtual unemployment with dignity and grace that had remained his trademark all his life. These were the '70s, when the Pakistani filmdom had been taken over by *gandassa culture* and the makers of *Maula Jatt* and their ilk were reigning supreme. Many films being made in Pakistan were copies of Indian movies. KA simply refused to work with this kind of crowd and, as a result, remained out of work for most of this period. The creative soul in him must have been very restless, for he approached EMI and persuaded them to produce thirty long-play records that had the classical ragas rendered by the representatives of all thirty families with an introduction by KA before each.

KA, with his rare insight, had been concerned about the fate of classical music in Pakistan since *ustads* of various g*haranas* were a rapidly diminishing breed. This was a huge undertaking that kept the composer in him going. KA successfully saw this phenomenal project through that has secured the classical music for the future generations. We are told it has since become part of the formal syllabus in Calcutta University's music program.

KA died on October 30, 1984, having been long forgotten by the glamorous but treacherous world of the film industry that he had once helped stand on its feet. He had been sick for some time and had passed into a coma. "His death was not totally unexpected, "laments Bashir. He had been dying slowly for many years and then one day, like a gentle note of his *Meend*, that fades away very slowly, KA quietly slipped in to the night."

KA has been gone for thirty-five years. And yet his legacy survives. This is due to the treasure of melodies that he has left behind and his service to the classical music. It is fair to say that he left music in a much better shape than he had found it, and for this, he will not be forgotten.

References: *Jalab Beeti* by Habib Jalib; *Jo Miley They Raste Mein* by Ahmad Bashir; *Ghungroo Toot Gaye* by Qatil Shifayi

The Englishman Who Loved Lahore

The Jungle Book movie was released just a few years ago and was a huge success. It is based on Kipling's famous story, written in India, about a boy who found himself in Seoni Jungle (in the Indian state of *Madhya Pradesh*) and survived, having befriended animals. Obviously more than a century after *The Jungle Book* was written, Kipling's work is still popular. His writings have passed one test of a writer's greatness—the test of time.

Born to English parents in India, Rudyard Kipling learned Hindustani—presumably Urdu—as a child. Although the city of his birth was Bombay, the one that he really came to admire was our own—Lahore. Having spent eleven years in a boarding school in England, at seventeen years old, RK returned to India and became the assistant editor of the *Civil and Military (C&M) Gazette* in Lahore. It did not take him long to fall in love with the former capital of Akbar the Great and Ranjit Singh. RK's fondness for Lahore is often obvious in his writings: He exercised at the *racecourse*, played tennis in the *Lawrence Gardens*, danced in *Montgomery Hall* (old Gymkhana), had dinner in the *Punjab Club*, and became a member of the *Freemason society*. There were moonlit picnics at *Shalimar Garden*, even visits to Lahore's infamous *red-light* district, where the future Nobel laureate contracted a venereal disease. RK used to wander in the bazaars and alleys of old Lahore, which he once described as "that prodigious brick honeycomb." The Grand Trunk Road is described as "that broad smiling river of life" and

Delhi Gate "a compound of all evil savors that a walled city can breed in a day and a night . . . combining the foul smell of badly-trimmed kerosene lamps, and the stench of native tobacco, baked brick, and dried earth." While at Lahore, he wrote articles on *Muharram Festival* and *festival of lights* in the Shalimar Garden.

In 1887, RK was transferred to *Pioneer* in Allahabad, a sister publication of *C&M Gazette*, but missed Lahore terribly. As fate would have it, he was recalled to Lahore for a few months in 1888. Mrs. Hill, a friend of RK, noted how he did "love those wild men of the north, whom he called his 'own folk'; after living among the frog-like Easterners of Allahabad, he was happy to be back among the 'savage, boastful, arrogant, hot-headed men' of the Punjab."

RK spent about five years at Lahore. Having left in 1887, he returned to his beloved city only once. But like Manto, who once quipped about Bombay, "I am carrying my Bombay with me," RK seemed to have done the same with Lahore; and for his second novel, he chose the title *The Naulakha*. These days, *Naulakha* is a low-middle-class locality in Lahore. But in RK's time, it may have been different. It is quite possible that RK, who was single at the time, lived with his parents in or near *Naulakha*. One of the pavilions in Lahore Fort is also known as *Naulakha*. While it is not clear whether RK had the former or latter in mind, his fondness for Lahore is obvious. The novel was not received well. But RK was not quite done with Lahore. Years later, after he had married an American and had come to live in the state of Vermont in the USA, RK built a house in Brattleboro, Vermont, that he also named *Naulakha*.

Edward Robinson, the editor of *C&M Gazette* and RK's boss, reported this of RK's interest in Lahore:

> Deeply interested in the queer and works of the people of the land. He liked to hunt and rummage among them, especially in Lahore, "that wonderful, dirty, mysterious ant hill," a city he knew "blind fold" and which he loved to wander through "like Haroon Al-Rashid in search of strange things." . . . He found "heat and smells of oil and spices, and puffs of temple incense, and sweat,

and darkness, and dirt and cruelty, and above all, things wonderful and fascinating innumerable."

Another thing that connected RK with Lahore was his famous story *The Man Who Would Be King*. Some believed that this story was based, at least partly, on real events. David Gilmour, RK's biographer, reports that RK had come across a mysterious character who asked him to convey a package to another stranger at a train station at some distance. Perhaps RK created the characters of Daniel Dravot and Peachy Carnehan based on that encounter. RK may also have heard of an American adventurer, Josiah Harlan, who had managed to create a kingdom on paper in northern Afghanistan, having signed a contract with Prince Mohammad Refee of Ghor on October 16, 1839. Harlan had spent years in India and Afghanistan, having worked for East India Company, Raja Ranjit Singh in Punjab, and Amir Dost Mohammad Khan in Kabul. Harlan and RK's paths did not cross since the American mercenary had left India in 1839. But his exploits have become the stuff of legends, and RK may have used his writer's imagination to create the story. The contract mentioned above still exists in Chester County Museum, Pennsylvania.

Fact or fiction, *The Man Who Would Be King* remains one of RK's most famous stories, having been immortalized by John Huston in his classic movie of 1975. In the movie, Sean Connery played the role of Dravot, who along with his companion Carnehan deserted the British Indian Army and carved out a kingdom for himself. Dravot was perceived as God by the simple Kafiristan folks, until the truth was revealed when Dravot was killed. Meanwhile, Carnehan managed to escape and, after a lot of hardships, met up with a journalist in a newspaper office. The story ends at *the Mall* in Lahore, where a disoriented Carnehan, suffering from a sunstroke, was recognized by the journalist from the night before and is sent to an asylum where he died. It is ironic that *Bhavani Junction*, which was filmed in Lahore in the 1950s (when Ava Gardner created a sensation), was not about Lahore, while *The Man Who Would Be King*, with Lahore background, was actually made in Morocco.

RK wrote his masterpiece *Kim*, widely considered his best Indian work in 1901 twelve years after leaving India. He spent eight years writing it. Those who have read it are convinced that the writer had to be in love with India. The novel opens with the main character sitting atop *Zamzama Gun*, which still sits on the Mall, opposite Lahore Museum. It was in *Kim* that RK used the famous phrase "the great game." It was a reference to the struggle for supremacy between Czarist Russia and the British in Central Asia. This phrase, in fact, was first used by a Captain Connolly back in 1842, but RK was the one who publicized it.

"And his nostalgia persisted," writes RK's biographer, David Gilmour, "so that he used to yearn to revisit *Pindi racecourse* or the elephant lines at *Mian Mir*. But although his plans to return to India never materialized, his imagination remained there, encouraging him to write some of his most serious stories about Anglo-India and the imperial mission."

RK did have a dark side. At a rail station in England, RK—considering himself a celebrity—jumped the queue. Asked to go back in line, RK said to the stationmaster, "Don't you know who I am?" The stationmaster's response must have startled him: "I know who you are, Mr. Rudyard bloody Kipling, and you can bloody well take your place in the queue like everybody else." Jumping the queue was a trait that RK might have subconsciously acquired in India. It is also on record that the infamous Gen. Dyer, who had been condemned by the House of Commons for his barbaric massacre at Jallianwala Bagh, received a monetary contribution by RK. He may have loved Lahore, but RK was an imperialist and English jingoist at heart.

RK left India in 1889. A few years later, a young Winston Churchill served in India as a soldier and a war correspondent. His book *The Story of the Malakand Field Force* was written in 1897. It was published in the *Pioneer*, where RK had worked earlier. Churchill passed through Lahore on his way to North-West Frontier Province and visited the *Civil and Military Gazette* office in Lahore since *Pioneer* and *Civil and Military Gazette* were sister publications. RK's and Churchill's paths did not cross in India. But one is intrigued by the coincidence that both the future Nobel laureates had a Lahore connection. Majid Sheikh, whose father was the last editor of *C&M Gazette* and who has written numerous superb articles about Lahore's glorious past, wrote of a chair that reportedly had been used both by RK and Churchill at the *C&M Gazette* office. This newspaper ceased publication in 1963. But what became of that chair? Does anyone really care? Perhaps the publicity-seeking Shehbaz Sharif, once he has finished his megaprojects, can be asked to have at least a plaque placed on the Mall on the former site of that newspaper. This would be a well-deserved tribute to RK.

RK, it is said, contributed more phrases to the English language than anyone except Shakespeare. He was known to, and admired by, men in high places. (His poem "If" was the favorite poem of Woodrow Wilson, while King George V was a personal friend.) He visited six continents and lived in four. But through all that, RK did not forget and remained in love with Lahore.

On his next visit to Lahore, this scribe intends to stand on the Mall on the former site of *C&M Gazette* and bow his head in gratitude to the memory of the Englishman who loved Lahore and carried his *Naulakha* with him to Vermont and beyond.

Reference: *The Long Recessional* by David Gilmour

Leo Tolstoy: From Writer to Pacifist Saint

There is a saying in Russia that people visit that country for three reasons: to see Moscow, Saint Petersburg, and Yasnaya Polyana—home of Leo Tolstoy. More than a century after his death, Tolstoy continues to be the most popular writer in Russia. Ninety volumes of his works adorn the libraries in his home country. It is hard to believe that he had not set out to be a writer; he wanted to be a diplomat.

Tolstoy was the scion of an aristocratic family of such standing that some considered them higher than the czars. His maternal grandfather had been ambassador in Berlin and a confidant of Catherine the Great. His paternal grandfather had been governor of Kazan while his cousin was the home minister in the cabinet of Czar Alexander III.

Having lost both his parents at a young age, Tolstoy was brought up by an aunt. By a strange twist of history, his life was sandwiched between two major events in the history of modern Russia: the Decembrist uprising of 1825 and the communist revolution of 1917. The early loss of his parents and the failed Decembrist uprising—a second cousin of Tolstoy, General Volkonsky, one of the conspirators, was dragged in chains in front of the czar and sent into exile in Siberia, having his title and lands confiscated—left a lasting imprint on the mind of young Tolstoy.

Tolstoy was sent to Kazan University but failed to graduate partly due to bad company, which included his elder brothers. There were visits to brothels, gambling, and all kind of boisterous fun so typical of spoiled children of aristocracy. Having failed his exam in geography—he was unable to name a single French port and flunked some simple questions of Russian history—he withdrew from the university. The decision was made easy for him since, at age ten, he had come into inheritance, which included Yasnaya Polyana—his ancestral home, a large piece of land, and 330 peasants. Had he graduated, he was well on his way to a career in the foreign service; what a loss would that have been for literature!

Upon his return home, he made a master plan of self-learning. He would learn math, law, languages, geography, history, medicine, agriculture, music, and painting. Oddly missing from this long list was writing—the literary giant of the future had no inclination in that direction yet. Having become bored at home, he went off to Moscow and then Saint Petersburg, where he resumed the customary life of a young aristocrat—visiting bathhouses, gambling, and drinking in the same spots that were to be frequented by the infamous Rasputin a few years later. Having incurred heavy losses at cards, Tolstoy enlisted as an NCO in the army and was posted in Crimea. He saw active combat in the Crimean War, which was to sow the seeds for *War and Peace* as well as *Hadji-Murad.*

As often happens, somewhere along the line, Tolstoy decided to become a writer. He sent his first manuscript, *Childhood*, to an editor in Saint Petersburg with the following cover letter: "My request will cost you so little labor that I am sure that you will not refuse to grant it. Look through this manuscript, and if it is not fit to publish, return it to me. Otherwise evaluate it and send me what you think it is worth, and publish it in your journal." There was palpable nervousness in the words of the young writer, who seemed uncertain of the merit of his novel. *Childhood* was accepted for publication, and the rest is history. *War and Peace* and *Anna Karenina* were to come years later, but *Childhood* had launched the literary journey of Tolstoy.

Tolstoy married Sofia Bers, the beautiful daughter of a Moscow physician. She was eighteen years younger than him, cultured, and intelligent. Their marriage produced a partnership rarely seen in the history of literature. Sofia not only was to inspire him but also did the editing and drafting for many of his writings, including *War and Peace*, many characters of which were based on their family members.

Pierre, the shy and awkward hero, was based on Tolstoy himself while Tatyana, his sister-in-law, became the model for the heroine, Natasha. Tolstoy went through enormous difficulties to write *War and Peace*, the compelling saga of Napoléon's invasion of Russia that has enthralled generations; this included a visit to the battleground of Borodino, the only large-scale battle fought between the Grand Army and Russia.

War and Peace was initially serialized in a magazine. Incidently, another masterpiece, *Crime and Punishment* by Dostoyevsky, was also being published in the same magazine at the same time. The two writers were probably wary of each other. It is mind boggling that they never met, although they might have moved in similar literary circles. One has to attribute this to the unfortunate trait of jealously so inherent in writers; surprisingly, the great ones are not immune from this either.

Tolstoy was a prolific writer and, over the years, was to bring out many more novels. *Anna Karenina,* the story of tragic love between a young Russian army officer and a married housewife, was also based on a real incident that took place not far from Yasnaya Polyana. Having finished *Anna Karenina*, Tolstoy went through a period of depression and stopped writing for a while. When he decided to resume, it refused to come. Sadly, somewhere along the line, Tolstoy had lost what his biographer, A. N. Wilson, calls 'his sustained brilliance'. For years, he had desperately wanted to write a novel on Peter the Great; he had the material—it just would not come. After seventeen attempts, he gave up. The same fate awaited his long-postponed desire to write of the Decembrist uprising; it came to nothing. But by then, Tolstoy's mind was beginning to move in a different direction.

Life in Russia had been intolerable for decades. Over the years, there had been many attempts to overthrow czars. In 1886, six students were caught by police with explosives, accused of plotting the czar's assassination, hurriedly tried, and hanged. The czar showed no mercy to the unfortunate hotbloods. The failed coup leader's brother vowed revenge; his name was Vladimir Ulyanov. Years later, when he returned to Russia from exile to lead the communist revolution, he was better known as Lenin. The czar's successor was to pay dearly for the cruelty of his father when Czar Nicholas and most of his family were butchered by the Bolsheviks in 1918.

Tolstoy was well aware of the miserable conditions of the poor. The famine of 1892 had claimed thousands of lives. Tolstoy moved tirelessly in the famine relief; he established hundreds of kitchens, feeding almost thirteen thousand people daily, and raised more than half a million dollars from the USA and England. At that stage, the master writer had been transformed into a dissident. There was widespread discontent about the slow response of the government to famine. Seizing the opportunity, Tolstoy launched a devastating assault on the czarist regime, aristocracy, and wickedness of land ownership. Years before the Bolshevik Revolution, this is what he prophetically wrote in *What Then Must We Do!*:

> The hatred and contempt of the masses are increasing and the physical and moral forces of the wealthy are weakening; the deception on which everything depends is wearing out . . . To return to the old ways is not possible; only one thing is left for those who do not wish to change their way of life and that is to hope that things will last my time . . . That is what the blind crowd of rich are doing but the danger is ever growing and the terrible catastrophe draws near.

His warning was brushed aside.

The czarist regime was in a quandary. Tolstoy had become a menace but had always been seen as part of aristocracy too. He still had powerful friends and relatives at court. What was to be done with him? The authorities tried to deal with him in a gentle fashion. Some of his works were censored, others banned. His disciple Chertkov, who oversaw the publication of his works, was sent into exile. His school at Yasnaya Polyana for peasant children was raided by police. Undeterred, Tolstoy continued his onslaught against political oppression and aristocracy. But by then, he also had another target—the Orthodox Church.

Tolstoy dared to attack the traditional church doctrines of Holy Trinity, Christ's ascension, the miracles of the gospels and saints, and the theology of grace; he called these teachings real blasphemy. The church reacted the way it always had—he was excommunicated. Tolstoy had, in the meantime, turned into a holy man. Gone were his aristocratic ways; he quit smoking and drinking, preached manual labor, started making his own shoes, and insisted on simple living. His later writings reflected a deep conviction that the real peace lay in the simple life.

Around that time, an Indian lawyer working in Transvaal, South Africa, was starting his own struggle against apartheid; he wrote to Tolstoy, asking for advice. Tolstoy suggested passive resistance. The young man took this lesson by heart and carried it with him to colonial India. Years later, he was to make his name as Gandhi.

A few years before death, Tolstoy visited Crimea with his family. While there, he was visited by Chekhov (the renowned author was then dying of TB) and Maxim Gorky. Much older, Tolstoy was held in awe by the two young writers. Gorky has left an amusing account of their conversation. Without any premeditation, Tolstoy suddenly asked Chekhov, "How many women have you f——d so far?" Unprepared, Chekhov mumbled something.

With a mischievous smile, the old master then confessed, "I was myself an indefatigable f——r in my youth."

Tolstoy did have a dark side to him. He had had numerous sexual liaisons; one of his illegitimate children worked as a coachman for his son. He could also be intensely jealous and carried the seeds of self-destruction; this unfortunate trait destroyed a genius like Pushkin (who tragically lost his life in a senseless duel at thirty-seven), Mozart (a reckless spender and always in debt), Manto, and Majaz (both alcoholics). Tolstoy could also be impulsive and eccentric. He insisted that Sofia deliver their children on the same sofa where he himself had opened his eyes. He recklessly signed away the copyrights to many of his publication. His wife, being a shrewd businesswoman, resented that. Sofia also disagreed with his anticzar work but was unable to rein him in. As a result, the domestic life for the prophet of peace became an ordeal.

Things came to a head when, in a fit of anger, Tolstoy slipped away from home at night. He wanted to move away from all the pain, hatred, and miserable life at Yasnaya Polyana. After a couple of days on the road and having traveled in an unheated train compartment, eighty-two-year-old Tolstoy developed pneumonia and died at Astapovo train station. His last words before slipping into delirium were "Always keep searching."

Ignoring the excommunication from the church, his admirers came in thousands as the beloved writer was lowered to the grave. Wilson, his biographer, has given us an idea of the respect that his people displayed for Tolstoy:

> The huge crowd was full of reverence. They defied their priests by singing the ancient Russian funeral hymns. When his coffin passed, many fell to their knees. It was one of the most extraordinary demonstrations of public sympathy in the history of the world. No novelist has ever been given such a funeral, but it was not for his novels that they honored him. It was for the deeds which now seem to us half mad and quixotic; it was for those volumes of his work which most readers now leave unread.

Tolstoy had once financed the immigration of some poor Russian peasants to Canada. Upon their arrival in Canada, they were greeted by a local delegate who said, "I do not know the name of your emperor, but the name of your patron and friend, Count Tolstoy, is as well known in Canada as in Russia, and I hope that one of the boys now listening to me, fifty years hence, will fill, like him, with honor to his country, the literary throne of the world."

Count Tolstoy's legacy has endured the test of time. Even today, multiple volumes of his work are available in this writer's hometown library and bookstore in rural Pennsylvania. Just eight years ago, a movie based on his last days was nominated for an Oscar. What more can a writer wish for?

<u>Reference</u>: *Tolstoy* by A.N. Wilson

Madhubala: Jawani Pe Roye

A film critic once said of Ingrid Bergman, "She had a combination of rare beauty, freshness, vitality and ability that is as uncommon as a century plant in bloom." This comment might as well have been made about Madhubala. She was blessed with rare beauty and talent, but her life was nothing but tragic. At the time of death on February 23 1969, at the age of thirty-six, she was alone in Arabian Villa, her house in Bombay. Her film career had ended years earlier due to ill health while she endured a painful and loveless marriage until her broken heart finally gave way.

Born on Valentine's Day in 1933 as Mumtaz Jahan in a very conservative Pathan family in Delhi, she had no formal education.

Her father was redoubtable Attaullah Khan and she was one of six sisters. When her recent biographer Khatija Akbar tried to interview her surviving siblings, she was politely rebuffed. The family was apparently living hand to mouth and had moved off to Bombay to explore an acting career for baby Mumtaz.

Her first role was in 1942 as a child star in *Basant*, but unlike most child actors who faded away, there was no looking back for her. The first real breakthrough was provided by Kidar Sharma in *Neel Kamal* opposite Raj Kapoor, himself a struggling actor at the time. Her filmi name Madhubala was chosen for her by Devika Rani, who seemed to have a special talent for names—she chose the filmi name Dilip Kumar for Yusuf Khan too. Years later, Kidar Sharma reflected on his impression of Madhubala: "As an actress, she was far superior to Raj, was intelligent, had a good diction and was very beautiful." Madhubala never forgot her appreciation for this and considered Kidar Sharma her mentor. The movie was a success, and arguably, the most beautiful actress of her generation had arrived.

Madhubala's film career, as a heroine, spanned from 1947 to 1962. She acted in sixty-six movies opposite most of the leading actors of the time, including Dilip Kumar. Dilip had a prestige in the movie industry unlike anyone else. It was only natural that they were smitten by the lovebug soon. Madhubala and Dilip acted together in four movies, *Tarana*, *Amar*, *Mughal-e-Azam*, and *Sangdil*—the last loosely based on Charlotte Brontë's novel *Jane Eyre*. It is said that their love affair started in 1951 while filming *Tarana* and continued well into the late fifties. Both were Muslims, both families had their roots in NWFP, were equally successful, and were deeply in love. What stopped their marriage? The short answer is her stern father, who can safely be described as the villain in her life. He was in no mood to let go of the sole breadwinner of the family. There may also have been some mutual dislike between him and Dilip.

It all came to a head when Madhubala was stopped by her father from going to the outdoor shooting of *Naya daur*. Dilip, who was the hero, was approached by the distressed director, Chopra. Despite Dilip's pleas, Attaullah Khan would not relent. A furious Dilip asked Madhubala to choose between him and her father. Madhubala, ever the obedient daughter, was unable to disobey her domineering father; for this, she paid the ultimate price. Dilip walked away and was never to come back in her life. As a fallout came the court case where Dilip famously admitted—on record—his everlasting love for Madhubala, but the damage was done.

Dilip carried on as before, but Madhubala never recovered from the heartbreak. Being sensitive by nature, on the rebound, and to escape her painful past, she made a reckless decision and married Kishore Kumar. Kishore was a struggling actor and a second-rate singer at the time. She had been working with Kishore in *Chalti ka naam gaadi* at the time of her breakup from Dilip and found Kishore's comic personality soothing. Only later did she realize her folly. As a couple, they could not have been more different. He was very eccentric, Hindu, was already divorced and had a son from a previous marriage. His parents never accepted her. This was a marriage of sheer incompatibility, notes her biographer Khatija Akbar. And then her health broke down.

Madhubala had a septal defect (a hole) in her heart since birth that began to show around the time of tension in her marriage. A discouraging trip to doctors in London brought no good news, just the prediction of limited life expectancy. Advised to rest, she retired. Her dysfunctional marriage a constant strain, they separated, and she moved back to her house. She died a lonely and tragic figure. Those who visited her in her last days reported her longing for Dilip. Although two of them did see each other occasionally after the breakup, he had moved on in life.

Madhubala's style of acting was so effortless and natural that it went underappreciated for a while. Ironically, her extraordinary good looks were also a distraction from her acting. Most of her movies have been forgotten, but there are some that have left their mark, movies like *Mahal, Mr. and Mrs. 55,* and *Tarana*. However, it was her superb performance in *Mughal-e-Azam* as Anarkali that has immortalized her. Looking back, many critics feel that she was not careful in the selection of her roles. Part of the problem was her ever-present father, who was her manager too. But then Madhubala had always allowed her heart to rule her head. After all, she had been born on Valentine's Day.

How beautiful was Madhubala? It is said that Frank Capra, multi-Oscar-winning director, was so captivated by her looks that he offered her a role in Hollywood. Ustad Bade Ghulam Ali Khan, who came on the set to sing for *Mughal-e-Azam*, was mesmerized by her looks. A journalist once wrote that none of her published photographs did full justice to her extraordinary beauty.

Madhubala never won an acting award, but for those who understood this art, it was different. Dilip Kumar, widely believed to be the finest actor of his generation, who costarred with her in four movies, said that had she lived longer and been more careful with selection of her roles, she would have been far superior to her contemporaries. Kidar Sharma, who directed *Neel Kamal*, called her performance far superior to Raj Kapoor's in that movie. This was no mean tribute coming from one of the pioneer directors of Bollywood. Baburao Patel of *Filmindia*, feared for his sharp pen and sarcasm, was even more generous: "She is easily our most talented, versatile and best looking artiste."

Today Mumtaz Jehan Dehlavi lies buried in a simple grave in the desolate Bombay cemetery of Santa Cruz, where her neighbors include the great lyricist Sahir Ludhianvi, Naushad, and the king of melody Muhammad Rafi, who joined her eleven years later. Since her untimely death forty-two years ago, many actresses have come and gone. But like Meena Kumari and Marilyn Monroe, she too has left behind a mystique that refuses to go away. Like Cinderella, her clock struck twelve too soon. But her infectious smile is still remembered by a generation that is slowly fading away.

<u>Reference</u>: *Madhubala* by Khatija Akbar

Mukesh: Geet Sunata Jaoon

Some time ago, an eminent writer of *Pakistan Link* had asked this scribe to write on Mukesh. Hoping to find some authentic details of his life, I tried to find a biography of Mukesh and found none. I then tried to google Tom Jones, an almost forgotten singer from Wales, and found half a dozen biographies. Disappointed but not surprised, I went ahead. What follows is the haphazard information about Mukesh gathered from here and there.

Mukesh—unlike some of his contemporaries Rafi, Lata, and Manna Dey—had no formal training in music. Motilal (who played Dilip's fellow train traveler in *Devdas*) was a relative and helped him be introduced in the film world. Early 40s was the time of singing stars like Saigal, Suraiya, and Noor Jehan. Mukesh acted in a couple of movies too and sang his own songs without being noticed. The breakthrough came when Anil Biswas made him sing "Dil jalta hai" in *Pehli Nazar* in typical Saigal style. The song was a hit, and Mukesh's career took off. To Anil Biswas, who was among the first generation of Bollywood composers (others being Pankaj Mullick, Naushad, and Khemchand Prakash), goes the credit of composing the first hit song for Mukesh as well as Talat. Saigal was every singer's idol back then, and not surprisingly, Mukesh tried to sing in his style.

Naushad then took Mukesh under his wings and made him the voice of Dilip in *Mela* and *Andaz*. How times change, but at that point, while Rafi—a huge talent—was struggling, Mukesh was the lead singer of Naushad's team. As fate would have it, Dilip and Naushad later chose Rafi while Mukesh was selected by Raj Kapoor to be his voice. For the next two decades, Mukesh found himself part of Raj Kapoor's team that included Khwaja Ahmad Abbas, Shankar Jaikishan, Hasrat Jaipuri, and Shailendra.

While Mukesh sang for many composers, he was a favorite of the Kalyanji-Anandji (KJ-AJ) duo. Kalyanji is on record that Mukesh had been their ladder to success and recognition in the 60s. Just look at the following list; most of these songs were composed by KJ-AJ back in the 60s: "Chandan sa badan," "Mere toote hue dil se," "Main to ek khwab hoon," "Jis dil mein basa tha pyar tera," "Waqt karta jo wafa," "Koi jab tumhara hriday tod de."

Other than Naushad, the two musicians who used Mukesh early on were Anil Biswas and Gujranwala-born Roshan. Unfortunately, Mukesh's best work with Biswas and Roshan from the early 1950s has been forgotten because the movies tanked. Roshan, a childhood friend of Mukesh, had composed evergreen "Teri duniya men dil lagta nahin" (*Bawre Nain*, 1950); his sudden death deprived Mukesh of the support of a talented composer. In his book *Bollywood Melodies*, Ganesh Anantharaman, argues that while many of Mukesh's popular songs were from Raj Kapoor movies, he grew more as a singer with his work with Kalyanji-Anandji, Roshan, Salil Chaudhry, and Anil Biswas.

After the golden period of Bollywood (50s and 60s) came the 70s. Anantharaman called it the "melody-devoid" world of the 70s. The reasons are many and beyond the scope of this article. Suffice it to say that, in that decade, while majority of senior and respected composers like Naushad, Khayyam, Madan Mohan, C. Ramchandra, and O. P. Nayyar were sidelined, the second-rate musicians, the likes of Bappi Lahiri, and mediocre lyricists like Anand Bakshi took over. As expected, the music output was pathetic. R. D. Burman did make some quality music, but he had a strange aversion to Mukesh and hardly ever used him. Even Rafi, arguably the finest male singer of his generation, became a distant second to Kishore Kumar.

Mukesh did, somehow, survive the 70s Kishore Kumar juggernaut. Salil Chaudhry, who had rescued him once before, composed for him what some call one of Mukesh's best songs, "Kahin door jab din dhal jaye." This song was picturized on Rajesh Khanna, the most popular actor of the early 70s, in *Anand*. Also, in 1976, *Kabhi kabhie* was released. It almost turned out to be the swan song of two greats—Sahir, the poet (died at fifty-nine in 1980), and Mukesh. In *Kabhi kabhie,* Khayyam—who had not composed for movies between 1967 and 1973—came out with "Kabhi kabhie mere dil mein khayal ata hai" and "Main pal do pal ka shair hoon."

Mukesh had a solid fan base but also his detractors. Late Khalid Hassan has written of an amusing comment made by a music connoisseur, Agha Mubarak Ali, from Sialkot. Agha was a violin player and used to own a restaurant, Amelia, which the music lovers like Khalid used to frequent. Agha once described Mukesh as the one with a cemented throat. The comment might sound harsh but had some truth to it. Mukesh's voice did have a limited range. But despite that limitation, he has given the music lovers numerous gems that have not been forgotten yet. Back in the early 2000s, this writer got the opportunity to see the once famous Amelia Hotel, where—according to Khalid—a generation of young hearts had once enjoyed the music of Mukesh and others. Amelia was being demolished then and has since vanished from the face of the earth. Amelia may be gone, but the music of Mukesh lived on.

Mukesh's career had its ups and downs. Back in the early 50s, he wasted a couple of years in acting. A picture exists of Mukesh and Suraiya, his costar, from the movie *Mashooka* from 1953. Naturally, his singing career took a back seat. While his singer competitors surged ahead, Mukesh eventually realized that he was getting nowhere as an actor and quit acting. What rescued him was Salil Chaudhry, who gave him a *Madhumati* song, "Suhana safar aur yeh mausam haseen." This song was originally meant for Talat, who—ever the gentleman, being aware of Mukesh's financial difficulties—asked Salil to give it to Mukesh. The song was a hit, and Mukesh's career was rescued by the brilliant Salil, whom Khwaja Khurshid Anwar had once described as the musician of musicians.

Mukesh was a gentleman, and unlike his eccentric contemporary Kishore Kumar, who married four times, Mukesh's personal life and professional career remained without any major controversy. His son Nitin followed him in music and, in his father's lifetime, joined him in overseas concert tours.

Mukesh was a heart patient. In August 1976, he was in the United States on a concert tour with Lata. A few hours before performance in Detroit, he experienced difficulty of breathing in his hotel room;

the ambulance was called. Precious time was lost going down the elevator from the twenty-first floor. Mukesh breathed his last in the ICU of a Detroit hospital a few minutes after arrival, having received unsuccessful resuscitation. He was fifty-three. Ironically, while most of the female singers of that era—Lata, Asha, Noor Jehan, Suraiya, and Shamshad Begum—were blessed with long lives, some of Mukesh's male contemporaries—Rafi and Kishore—succumbed to heart attack too at a relatively young age (Rafi at fifty-five, Kishore at fifty-eight). Talat died in the 90s but had suffered a stroke years before and lost his speech. As a side note, Nitin Mukesh—who had had modest success as a class B singer—appeared completely out of shape physically in a recent YouTube interview. He had witnessed Mukesh's struggle with heart disease firsthand. One would expect that he would have taken better care of his health; he hasn't.

At the time of his death, Mukesh was financially secure, still in demand, had a solid following. He also had the satisfaction of seeing his son doing well as a singer. His sudden death came as a shock to the music lovers. I recall a tearful Raj Kapoor on Doordarshan lamenting the loss of Mukesh. "Today I have lost my voice," he said. Just four years later, Rafi too died suddenly. With their passing and Talat already out of music, the golden era of Bollywood music came to an abrupt end.

What is Mukesh's legacy? Where does he stand among his peers? Ganesh Anantharaman has summarized it best:

> There hasn't been, at least after Saigal, another voice in Hindi cinema that could articulate melancholy better. . . . Each time you hear his sonorous, masculine, yet vulnerable voice express the anguish of the failed lover, the despondency of a purposeless life, the ache of the loss assails you afresh. It can't just be a coincidence that that the emotions he articulated—gloom, sorrow and despair—went out of fashion in Bollywood after his death. Perhaps there was a realization that in no other voice would these feelings would ring as true.

References: *Bollywood Melodies* by Ganesh Anantharaman; *Rearview Mirror* by Khalid Hasan

Nahid Iskander Mirza

Nahid Iskander Mirza turned up in Qudratullah Shahab's office one day and told him to get rid of Ruth Boral, the attractive private secretary, a leftover from Ghulam Muhammad's time. "Her presence here can only create more scandals," she told Shahab. The first lady did not want another pretty face in the Governor-General's House. Ms. Boral was asked to leave.

Shahab has written of Governor-General's House parties where the high and the mighty used to have fun. Alcohol was freely consumed. Some would get drunk, some would flirt with women, and Iskander Mirza (IM), the governor-general, would enjoy the sight of people making a fool of themselves. During one such gathering, when IM was seen getting too cozy with a female guest, Nahid burst on the scene and put a stop to it. The embarrassed female guest tried to explain that IM was only looking at her sari. "This is precisely the way he had approached me," Nahid retorted.

On a state visit to Iran with IM, Nahid appeared obsessed with Queen Soraya and would make every attempt to outshine the queen. Once she complained that the press had failed to notice that while she was seen smiling in the pictures, the queen was not. Later, she asked Shahab to consider upgrading her husband's ADC. Having seen the shah's ADC—a general—she wanted the same in Pakistan.

IM once asked Altaf Gauhar to allot a plot to the Iranian Embassy that lay next to it. Gauhar was aware that Nahid and the Iranian ambassador were friends. He tactfully turned down the request on the grounds that the vacant plot was meant to be a children's playground. IM accepted his plea, but Gauhar was alarmed at the influence that Nahid had on her husband.

Javed Iqbal was invited to lunch by IM in the Governor-General's House. Also present were Nahid and the U.S. ambassador. Allama Iqbal's son was surprised that the entire conversation was either in English or Persian; missing was the national language, Urdu.

Years later, while in London, Shahab saw the former first lady at a grocery store, approached her, and asked to visit. Ayub allowed the visit grudgingly, having made a sarcastic remark "So she has come down to earth; she wanted to be the Queen of Pakistan." Shahab found the Mirzas residing in a modest flat in Kensington. The former president appeared hard of hearing and in poor health. As for Nahid, years after the debacle of 1958, she still sounded bitter about the unexpected midnight visit and the hostile attitude of the army officers who had delivered the ultimatum from Ayub. Shahab might have considered it impolite to remind her of IM's dismissal of Noon, Bogra, Suhrawardy, and Ch. Mohammad Ali.

In 1960, Javed Iqbal was in NY, part of a Pak delegation to the UN that included Z. A. Bhutto. It so happened that Mirzas unexpectedly turned up in the UN lobby. Javed recognized the former first couple, greeted them, and offered coffee. Just then, Bhutto passed by and, having seen IM, tactfully avoided his onetime benefactor. While Javed felt embarrassed, Mirzas were slowly and painfully getting used to the new life.

Born Nahid Amir Teymour, Nahid had royal lineage, being a descendent of Tamerlane. She was born in a wealthy and influential family of Khorasan. Her father was the interior minister in the Mosaddegh cabinet and her brother a diplomat. Her obituary in *Kayhan* reports that she was in an unhappy marriage with an army officer. IM was descendant of the infamous Mir Jafar of the Battle of Plassey.

During a reception at the Russian Embassy in Karachi, the fifty-two-year-old and father of six IM walked up to Nahid and simply declared, "You shall be my wife." Humayun Mirza (HM), IM's son, on the other hand, is convinced that it was Nahid who pursued his father relentlessly and that IM fell for her, making an error of judgment. In his autobiography, *From Plassey to Pakistan*, HM recalls being with his father in a hotel suite in London in 1953:

> I was assigned the task of answering the phone to preserve father's privacy. Everyday a woman calling herself Nahid Afghamy would call, and each time, under instructions from my father, I told her that the Sec. of Defense was not available. IM explained that she was the wife of the Iranian Military Attaché in Karachi and that she was pursuing him. I later learnt that such trips were being financed by certain Pakistani businessmen to compromise the Sec. of Defense to serve their own interests.

IM had two sons. The younger, Enver Mirza, was a pilot in PAF, who died in a plane crash. IM received the tragic news in a London hotel. That was where HM saw Nahid:

> My father, pointing to a woman sobbing by the window, said: "Look, Mrs. Afghamy is crying for your brother." In his grief, IM was touched by her performance. No one at the time realized that Nahid was using this tragic occasion to ensnare the future Pres. of Pakistan . . . Nahid did not conceal her intentions and openly flirted with IM, much to the embarrassment of others.

IM married Nahid, who was twenty years younger, in London in secret. He may have expected her to stay abroad. But he was in for an unpleasant surprise, writes HM:

> IM was alone in the house (in Karachi) when he received a fateful phone call . . . His face turned white as he listened to the caller, put the phone down, and without saying a world, rushed out of the house . . . The caller had informed a shocked IM that Nahid had turned up in Pakistan without warning and was ready to start a scandal.

A while later, IM visited his family and broached the subject of his marriage to Nahid. His daughters were upset and refused to allow Nahid in the house. The newlyweds were forced to stay in the Punjab Guest House. Just a few days later, IM failed to turn up for his only surviving son's marriage—in the same city. HM remains convinced that Nahid stopped his father from attending.

A U.S. Embassy's confidential report dated April 2, 1958, described Nahid as

> An extremely ambitious woman . . . lifted by Mirza from the Iranian military attaché in Karachi . . . bitterly resentful of Begum Viqar-un-Nissa Noon, whom she suspects of having designs on the first-ladyship herself.

HM ran into President Ayub in Washington, DC, one day. Ayub had known HM as a child and spoke to him affectionately. Ayub asked about his father's well-being and then "Is that woman still with him?" Having been told that she was, Ayub made a derogatory remark about Nahid.

On a subsequent visit to Pakistan, HM visited Ayub. This is what HM remembers of that conversation:

> Ayub spent the better part of the discussion trying to justify his *coup* against my father . . . He put the blame squarely on Nahid's shoulders . . . "I used to visit your house and was always graciously received by your mother. But when this woman showed up, she treated me like a

lackey . . . was rude and offensive in her behavior and tried to impress on everyone the hold she had on your father . . . The appointment with the President, his Military Secretary told me [Ayub], had to be cleared by her."

HM's own assessment of Nahid is similar:

> Nahid was not willing to keep a low profile. She aggressively promoted her own image and interfered in the country's political affairs. As an Iranian and foreigner, her interference was highly resented in Pakistani official circles. She also took every opportunity, not only privately, but worse publically, to demonstrate her hold on my father.

Life in exile was not easy. IM had a part-time job. Some friends helped, but London was expensive. IM was once hospitalized. Ardeshir Zahedi came to visit once and overheard the Mirzas worried about the medical bills and IM saying to Nahid, "Just let me die."

On another occasion, IM was seen carrying a bag of dirty linen on the footpath when a friend recognized him and asked where he was going. "To the Laundromat. Can't afford a taxi," he said.

Col. Abid Hussain, a landlord from Jhang, was hospitalized in London. IM came to visit. This writer's late brother-in-law was present and noted that IM appeared short of breath; a heart patient, he had walked a considerable distance to the hospital.

IM had some remarkable firsts to his credit—the first Indian to graduate from Sandhurst and the first president of Pakistan. He was, by all accounts, an intelligent, hardworking man who may have done great things for Pakistan. But marrying this ambitious and scheming woman led him to a path of self-destruction and harmed democracy in Pakistan. One can only wonder why. The answer may lie in the couplet by the saint from Jhang:

> *Dil darya samundron doongay*
> *Kaun dilan diyan Jaaney Hoo*

As for Nahid, having gone through a whirlwind romance and a few years of power, she endured a decade of painful exile, followed by fifty years of widowhood. In later years, she became interested in the poetry of Hafiz and wrote some herself. The fading Hollywood star Ava Gardner came to live in the same London neighborhood, and they became friends. They had met during Ms. Gardner's visit to Pakistan to film *Bhowani Junction*. The movie turned out to be mediocre, but Lahorites were thrilled to see George Cukor, Ms. Gardner, and Stewart Granger at work. Old-timers still talk about those days.

Nahid had sunk into oblivion decades ago. The news of her death recently was hardly noticed. "I am just a speck of sand in the desert of time," wrote a wise man once. Just a reminder to those who seek false glories. *Rahe naam Allah ka.*

<u>References</u>: *From Plassey to Pakistan* by Humayun Mirza; *Apna Gariban Chaak* by Dr. Javed Iqbal; *Shahabnama* by Qudratullah Shahab; Nahid Mirza's obituary published in *Kayhan*.

Nawab of Kalabagh: The Man Who Knew Too Much

As one enters the famous *Borh Bungalow* in Kalabagh, one is struck by its beauty. *Borh Bungalow* once served as Nawab of Kalabagh's (NOK) guest house for his personal friends and visiting dignitaries, which included many heads of state. A young Shah Faisal stayed there once. Its location, right on the western bank of mighty Indus, is picture perfect. The pictures on the walls and the decorations tell a lot of stories of the bygone era. NOK was once the second most powerful man in Pakistan; this was also where he breathed his last. The present generation may not know much about him. But no history of Pakistan is complete without mentioning his six years of absolute rule over what was then West Pakistan.

Nawab Amir Mohammad Khan of Kalabagh was the scion of a feudal family. In his youth, he developed a reputation for brutality—an unfortunate prerequisite for survival in rural society in his day. Somehow he gained the upper hand over his adversaries, the Niazi Pathans of Isa Khel and Pir of Makhad. He participated in the historic gathering at Minto Park, Lahore, and made a substantial donation to the Muslim League in 1940, when the Pakistan Resolution was passed. His swift rise to power was helped by the fact that he owned some hunting grounds that he used to entice people in high places, men like Ayub and Iskander Mirza. Interestingly, Z. A. Bhutto also used the same tried-and-trusted formula to get close to the duo. Of heavy build, NOK wore the traditional Punjabi dress, had a huge mustache, and was old fashioned in many ways. He had been educated in Aitchison and London and spoke good English. Ayub was impressed and made him governor of West Pakistan, preceded by a short stint as chairman of PIDC. This unusual partnership between the military dictator and a feudal lord was to last six years.

NOK governed West Pakistan with an iron hand. He developed a reputation as a harsh administrator who was well informed. His system of intelligence was almost flawless, based primarily on direct reports from the district administration and personal contacts. He once surprised Jahandad Khan, his military secretary, by telling him that before approving his appointment, he had looked deep into Jahandad's family background and knew that Jahandad's grandfather was the first in his area to have performed hajj.

NOK was financially clean. Decades after his exit, no financial scandals have been associated with him or his family. There is no evidence that his assets increased while he was in power. He was very punctual and hardworking. Well aware of the dangers of nepotism, he kept his family at a distance; they were not allowed to stay at the Governor's House. Muzaffar, his eldest son and heir apparent, once was harshly reprimanded by the governor; Muzaffar tried to sit with his father in the back seat of the official car; the governor made him sit in front with the driver, reminding him that the back seat was meant for the military secretary. NOK drew no salary and did not avail himself of any benefits from his all-powerful post. Fiercely loyal to Ayub, he would insist on mentioning the president's name in his monthly radio broadcasts at least three times.

He was very outspoken and perhaps the only one who dared to warn Ayub about his family's corruption. On one such occasion, when he broached this subject, Ayub was overheard telling him, "Do my sons not have the right to live in this country?" NOK was taken aback and later remarked in frustration that Ayub's decline would be hastened by his son's bad reputation. *Shahabnama* has a reference to one of Ayub's infamous sons who led a procession in Karachi after the rigged 1965 elections that resulted in violent clashes with the supporters of Miss Fatima Jinnah. Scores died; the exact body count is unknown to this day. Decades later, the same son—while a member of Nawaz Sharif's cabinet—used administrative pressure to get his car registration from Gujranwala so that he could proudly display "GA 1." This most unfortunate tradition of protecting one's corrupt loved ones has persisted and flourished in Pakistan, the most recent example being the son of a retired chief justice of supreme court; while the publicity-seeking father was generating headlines with his *suo motu's*, the son had been enjoying his "right to live in Pakistan."

Back to NOK, when asked to join the Convention Muslim League, he declined and was overheard saying, "Keep me out of that dirt." He was also not in favor of *Operation Gibraltar*, which was Bhutto's brainchild. He once remarked in despair that Ayub's foolish advisers would bring his downfall.

NOK was against Yahya Khan's promotion to the chief of Pak Army and said so. Yahya's fondness for alcohol and reputation as an inveterate lecher had not escaped the ever-vigilant governor. Ayub ignored his advice. The self-proclaimed field marshal was by then surrounded by sycophants, for some of whom he had become Daddy. Many would argue that Yahya's promotion was a watershed moment in the history of Pakistan.

NOK submitted his resignation in 1966, having realized he no longer had the president's confidence. For some time, there had been a strain in their relationship. The last straw was an election at Karachi where Ghaus Bux Bizenjo won with NOK's support against the official candidate of the Convention Muslim League. The parting of ways was amicable, unlike Ayub's dismissal of Bhutto. NOK drove up to Rawalpindi, had lunch with the president, exchanged pleasantries, and went home to Kalabagh, having bid a final farewell, and that was it; they were never to meet again.

Within a year of NOK's departure, all had gone awry; West Pakistan was in turmoil. Yahya Khan easily pushed out an ailing Ayub. Sometime after Ayub's fall from power, his wife was overheard telling an acquaintance, "NOK's dismissal was a mistake by Khan Sahib [Ayub]"; one wonders whether her husband felt the same way, having replaced NOK with the meek and subservient Gen. Musa. Insecure Ayub had earlier replaced the widely popular Gen. Azam Khan in East Pakistan too with another sycophant, Monim Khan.

NOK's reputation for ruthlessness created many myths: One was allegedly a slap to the principal of King Edward Medical College, a highly respected surgeon of Lahore who had annoyed the almighty governor by not approving a student's migration to his institution; another widely believed allegation was the attempted murder of Maududi Sahib of JI. Jahandad Khan, who has devoted many pages in his memoirs to NOK, is convinced that both rumors were baseless, probably spread around by the governor's political opponents; there was no shortage of those. NOK was an admirer of Amir of JI and once told Dr. Toosi, a personal friend, of his frustration with Ayub, who used to urge him to do something about "this dangerous Maududi." Some time ago, this writer wrote to the physician son of the alleged slap victim to clarify that incident—I never received a reply.

NOK's sons were educated abroad, but none had the talent of their father. What they did inherit from him was his weakness—the feudal mindset. He had been a harsh father and husband; there had been discord within the family. His return to Kalabagh set in motion an unfortunate series of events that led to his tragic death.

NOK had two daughters; one was still single. For some time, he had been mulling over the proposal of Dr. Tahir Toosi, who was the son of a close friend of his. This young man was well educated and handsome. But he was a Kashmiri, and that was not acceptable to Nawab's family.

This started a friction between him and his sons, who were supported by their mother and maternal uncle.

The sons had another concern too. NOK had given some indications that he was fed up with his sons and was considering transferring his property directly to one of his grandsons. This was too much for his sons. They say, "Whom the gods wish to destroy, they throw a bone of property to them." And so, on a day when NOK was relaxing in his famous guest house—where over the years he had entertained many rich, powerful, and influential guests—he was murdered in cold blood by no other than one of his own sons. Malik Asad allegedly shot his father point blank. With much-feared NOK dead, the whole family stood united behind Asad. NOK's dead body was disposed of in a hurry; it was taken to the graveyard in a trawler and buried overnight—no funeral prayers were allowed.

Thus ended the life of NOK, whose word was once law in the land. There was a trial. M. Anwar, the renowned attorney from Lahore, pleaded for prosecution in a case that generated headlines for months. At the end, nothing came of it. Malik Asad went scot-free. In his memoirs, Jahandad hints at some collaboration between NOK's family and the Ayub government, which may have been relieved to see the end of someone who knew too much. But God has his own way of dispensing justice. Years later, Malik Muzaffar—NOK's eldest son, whom many believed to be the mastermind behind his father's murder—was gunned down, in broad daylight, in Kalabagh by his political opponents, *Baghochi Mahaz*.

As I think of NOK, my mind goes back to that famous TV play of the late 70's, *Waris*. The main character of that play was a Chaudhry Hashmat, an old-fashioned feudal lord who found it hard to accept change. At the end of the play, Chaudhry Hashmat preferred to drown in flood rather than leave his ancestral home. NOK was also a representative of old times and feudal culture who found it hard to change with time. His way of life was fading away, but he was clinging to the obsolete old values. Ayub had made good use of him to keep West Pakistan under control, but times had changed. In Ayub's government, NOK represented the pro-West faction; the other was the pro-China group, represented by the popular Bhutto and Altaf Gauhar. Ayub may have felt that NOK had become a liability and let him go.

NOK was a well-read person. A visiting delegation from Imperial Defense College (UK) once called on the governor. After the meeting, one of the delegates remarked that the most well-informed person whom they had come across in Pakistan on international affairs was NOK. That surprised many but not those who knew of NOK's love of reading; he kept himself well versed in international affairs. At a banquet given in her honor, Jacqueline Kennedy asked him a question about a fruit that she had not seen before. Now NOK was no absentee landlord; he was a well-informed, experienced farmer who had over the years taken a keen interest in his farms at Kalabagh. His discourse regarding *guava* so impressed the first lady of the USA that she said, "I am going to ask my husband to make you his agricultural adviser."

This scribe has seen a picture in which NOK, the governor of West Pakistan, is seen chatting with a young Z. A. Bhutto, then the favorite minister of Ayub, while the visiting president of China Leo Chao Chi is standing by. All three seemed to be having a jolly good time. Who would have thought that, within a few years, all three would fall from power and meet tragic, violent deaths. Such are the ways of this world! *Rahe naam Allah Ka.*

References: *Shhabnama* by Qudratullah Shahab; *Pakistan: Qiyadat Ka Bohran* by Gen. Jahandad Khan.

Of Death and Dying

"Praskovya Fedorovna Golovina, with profound sorrow, informs relatives and friends of the demise of her beloved husband Ivan Ilyich . . . The funeral will take place on Friday at 1 P.M." Thus begins *The Death of Ivan Ilyich* by Leo Tolstoy. Tolstoy then takes the reader through the way Ivan Ilyich's colleagues respond to the news. Having thanked God for having spared them, they begin to think of the implications of his death on their career, oblivious to the fact that death awaits them too. The story takes us through the life of a judge who has done well in his career, worked with a cold discipline, and been a social climber but lacked empathy. In short, he has lived his life just for himself.

The death and the process of dying, though inevitable, is terrifying to most. There is great variation in the way we respond to it. Approaching the end of life, you look back—the ups and downs, the triumphs and tragedies. With the wisdom gained over decades, one's outlook about life—and hereafter—often begins to change.

Meeraji, a pioneer of *azad nazm*, was hospitalized in Bombay in 1949. Ijaz Batalvi, later a famous lawyer, was on his way to London. He heard of Meeraji's sickness and visited him at the hospital. This was what he wrote:

> I found it difficult to recognize Meeraji due to cachexia. He was reading a book. I asked if he was surprised at my visit. "Nothing surprises me anymore," he responded . . . during my visit, the patient next to him died that made Meeraji visibly scared. In that gloomy atmosphere, Meeraji

asked for his rosary, closed his eyes and started moving the rosary beads between his fingers. . . . A priest with a cross in his hand turned up and offered to pray to Jesus Christ for Meeraji who reminded the priest that the week before, the priest had prayed for the patient who had since died. An embarrassed priest asked Meeraji, "How long since you have been here?"

"Since eternity," said the bohemian poet who once wrote:

Nagri nagri phira musafer
Ghar ka rasta bhool gaya.

The traveler from Lahore died in the charity hospital of Bombay a few days later.

Decades later, another meeting took place between Ijaz Batalvi and another giant of Urdu poetry, Noon Meem Rashid, in London. Rashid was leading a quiet life in a retirement community. The two friends met in an Italian café and reminisced about old friends. Rashid told Ijaz about a retired Englishman whom he had come across. This Englishman had served in India before partition and kept talking of the magnificence of Peshawar. Rashid felt that it was not really the splendor of Peshawar that the Englishman missed; it was his youth, his longing for the bygone era.

The conversation then turned toward aging. Rashid sounded apprehensive about his health; he was getting scared of traveling. He was about to publish what he called his last collection of poetry. When asked why last, he made two observations: He did not want to repeat himself like some other poets; also, he did not want to outlive his utility as a man. Rashid died a few weeks later. The above-mentioned collection of poems turned out to be his last. His Italian wife got his dead body cremated, which generated a lot of controversy.

Hakim Ahmad Shuja, a man of many talents, wrote short stories, plays, and poetry. His stories were in such demand that Sohrab Modi of *Pukar* fame bought four of them for one lakh of rupees in the early 40s. It was with his renowned father's help that his son, Anwar Kamal Pasha, made many successful movies in the 50s and early 60s. His best days behind him, Pasha was leading a quiet life. Ashiq Batalvi, an old friend, returned to Pakistan after twelve years in the UK and visited him. Here is Batalvi's narration of their last meeting:

> Hakim Sahib used to have a wide circle of friends. But over time, it had dwindled to just a few. Other than an occasional visit to Maulana Ghulam Rasool Mehr, he was spending most of his time at home. With passing years, he appeared to be very lonely. Both daughters had been married off and were happy in their lives. His only son was preoccupied with his work. Before my return to London, as I went to bid him farewell, he embraced me and broke down. I was so moved that I myself started crying.

The two friends were not to meet again. In a moving obituary of his friend, Batalvi called Hakim Ahmad Shuja's passing the end of an era. It was in their last meeting that Batalvi persuaded Hakim Ahmad Shuja to write the history of Lahore's historic Bhati Gate. The booklet that came out of Shuja's pen turned out to be the most authentic history of Lahore's Chelsea.

Ahmad Bashir was terminally sick. His family were keeping a vigil at bedside. The dying father noted the mutual affection of his children and said, "The reason you are so close is because I am not leaving any assets behind. If I did, you would have been already worried about your share."

One day he suddenly asked, "When will death come?" The veteran journalist, a die-hard communist, was not afraid to ask the obvious, though painful, question. His daughter Neelam, who later wrote his obituary, does not report the answer given; he died soon afterward.

Khushwant Singh, an Indian writer, once wrote that he was only worried about pain and suffering. Beyond that, he was ready for the inevitable. For him, "Death was a final full stop beyond which there is a void that no one has been able to penetrate." His wish was granted; the agnostic writer reportedly died without much suffering at ninety-nine.

Patras Bokhari, who had served as the principal of Government College Lahore and director general All India Radio (AIR) before partition, had moved to the UN. Educated at Cambridge, and fluent in English, he used to dazzle his fellow delegates with his oratory. Back in the 50s, he visited London in an official assignment from the UN. His old friend Ashiq Batalvi met him there. This is what Batalvi wrote:

> Pitras asked me where to start. In response, I quotes a verse of Iqbal. Having heard that, Pitras went in to a trance and then, in a moment of despair, with tears in his eyes, said: "Ashiq, we have wasted our lives and have nothing to show for it." I responded by saying that we had done our best within the limitations of our abilities and circumstances….I did remind him about his decision to leave academic pursuits for AIR. "Did you not waste ten best years of your life in AIR rather than staying and teaching at Govt. College?" Pitras agreed that he had made a terrible mistake… The two of us then stated to talk about Lahore, its people, the colleges, poets, dramas, politics and the rest. We laughed and shed tears in a cozy hotel room in Hyde Park, oblivious to the thick fog of London and the noise of Oxford St outside. As I bade farewell, Pitras made me promise to return the day after to take a stroll in London…we did meet and kept walking the whole day in Central London … we talked of old times, discussed the friends, living and those who were not. I was alarmed to notice that Pitras's laughter had lost its vigor. He did not appear in good health. Perhaps he was beginning to sense the inevitable…the next day he flew off to Geneva…having returned to New York, he wrote me a long and interesting letter."

Patras and Batalvi were not to meet again. Patras, who had the distinction of having a poem of Iqbal addressed to him in *Zarb-e-kaleem*, died in 1958 and was buried in New York.

Barrister Manzoor Qadir (MQ) was one of the best legal minds in Pakistan. Son of a celebrated father, Sir Abdul Qadir, he had served as Pakistan's foreign minister and had later been chief justice of Punjab High Court, from where he resigned to concentrate on his legal practice. Khushwant Singh once wrote that he never saw a more upright man than him. MQ was agnostic. In 1974, he was admitted in a London hospital. Ashiq Batalvi visited him. A visibly sick MQ was happy to see his old friend. After the usual pleasantries, MQ asked Batalvi something that surprised him. MQ wanted Batalvi to read a certain verse from *Musaddas-e Hali*:

> *Wo nabyon mein rahmat laqab pane wala*
> *Muradein gharebon kee bar lane wala.*

Batalvi read the desired lines aloud and noted that MQ's eyes were full of tears. After a few recitations, also from Hali's *Musaddas*, MQ's condition took a sudden turn for the worse; he died the same day. Altaf Gauhar had visited MQ in CMH Lahore a few weeks earlier and noted that, in his last days, MQ had discarded agnosticism, had been reciting Koran, and had developed a firm belief in God again.

The Duke of Wellington had developed a reputation of being reserved. Unlike his famous adversary, Napoléon, who was adored by his men, Wellington was aloof. The day before the Battle of Waterloo, he described the men under his command as "the scum of the earth." Years later, as he lay on his deathbed, he was asked of any regrets. The man who had defeated Napoléon and Tipu Sultan and had been prime minister of Great Britain named one: "I regret not having thanked the men who put their lives on the line for me." The Iron Duke's perception of life and people around him had started to change as he approached the abyss.

Back to Tolstoy's story—they say that a patient with a fatal disease passes through four stages: initial denial, followed by anger, then depression, and finally acceptance of his fate. It seems that Ivan Ilyich had done the same:

> Ivan Ilyich became bitter and refused to believe he was coming to the end of his life . . . Reflecting on his current situation and his past life, his world view began to change . . . he realized how meaningless his life had been . . . Slowly he came to terms with his imminent death . . . and died in a moment of exquisite happiness.

<u>References</u>: *The Death of Ivan Ilyich* by Tolstoy; *Ijaz-e-Bayan* by Ijaz batalwi; *Gauhar Guzasht* by Altaf Gauhar; *Khushwantnama* by Khushwant Singh; *Char Chand* by Neelam Bashir; *Chand Yadeen* by Ashiq Batalwi

Of Love and Infatuation

Back in the good old days when we were in medical college in Lahore, a class fellow followed a female classmate all the way to her home in Gujranwala. The following day, sitting in the hostel canteen, as he was lamenting his inability to express his feelings to her, someone made a suggestion. He was advised to do what one of the characters in Shafiq-ur-Rahman's book *Himaqatain* had done. This character had written a letter to his beloved that went like this:

> When you will grow old, and will have wrinkles on your face, and your beautiful hair will be all white, in those times, perhaps, you will remember that long ago, there was an unfortunate soul who really loved you.

The lovebird duly jotted it down and got his love letter somehow delivered to the girl's hostel. No response was ever received. There is a follow-up to this, but we will return to that later.

According to the dictionary, *love* is "a profoundly tender, passionate affection for another person," while *infatuation* is "an intense but short-lived passion or admiration for someone or something." What differentiates the two is, therefore, the time factor. You can't predict early on which way it will go.

Several years ago, when *Bridges of Madison County* was released, the audience was mostly elderly and middle-aged couples. A reviewer noted with surprise that several of them were visibly in tears; he should not have been. Many among us have stories in our past like the one portrayed by Meryl Streep and Clint Eastwood in that movie. Most of those stories are never told. We take them to our graves.

Guru Dutt was a successful actor and director. He had to his credit classics of Bollywood, including *Pyaasa*, *Kaagaz Ke Phool*, and *Sahib Bibi Aur Ghulam*. Married to popular singer Geeta Dutt, he fell under the spell of Waheeda Rehman. Rebuffed, Guru Dutt—a sensitive man—committed suicide.

Mustafa Zaidi, a bureaucrat and a respected poet, was found dead. A young woman, Shahnaz Gul, was found in his room. The poet who wrote *Ham us ke paas jaate they magar ahista ahista* had been lonely and depressed. These lines might have been written for Miss Gul. Mr. Zaidi was also married with children.

Suraiya and Dev Anand wanted to marry, but her grandmother wouldn't allow. Having thrown her engagement ring in the Arabian Sea, Suraiya called off the wedding. While Dev Anand moved on and got married, Suraiya died a spinster. A few years before her death, as a visitor was about to leave her flat, she told him to leave by the side door to avoid the crowd of her admirers at the front door. When outside, the curious visitor looked back; the front entrance was deserted.

Sahir Ludhianvi and a married Amrita Pritam were madly in love. Both moved to India from Lahore after partition. Amrita's marriage broke down. Sahir was single. But they never married. A legacy of their doomed love may be Sahir's verse:

Chalo ik baar phir say
Ajnabi bun jaen hum donoon.

Professor Siraj had a love marriage, a son, and a distinguished academic career, being professor of English at Government College Lahore. But the married professor fell in love again, this time with one of his students. His first wife made hardly any fuss and moved abroad. One of his former students reports that the professor had a miserable life after his second marriage.

Having directed two successful movies, Shaukat Rizvi had a brilliant career ahead of him in Bollywood when he fell madly in love with Noor

Jehan and married her. They moved to Pakistan. A bitter divorce was followed by a public feud that effectively destroyed Rizvi's career.

Musarrat Nazir took an early retirement from the movies after love marriage, moved to Canada, and vanished from news. Decades later, she reemerged and released a music album before going back to Canada. The last we heard, she was divorced.

Napoléon fell in love with Josephine, who was many years older and a widow with children. He wrote passionate love letters to her: "I awake full of you. Your image and the memory of last night's intoxicating pleasures has left no rest to my senses." The emperor, who had once said that "power is my mistress," married Josephine. Desperate for an heir that she was unable to produce, he reluctantly divorced her and remarried. His new wife gave him an heir. As fate would have it, there was no empire left to govern. Years later, upon hearing of Josephine's death, he stayed locked in in his room for two days, refusing to see anyone. His last words reportedly were "France, the army, Josephine."

King Edward VIII fell in love with Wallis Simpson, a twice-divorced American. He made the ultimate sacrifice for love and gave up the throne for her. By all accounts, they had a happy life together, mostly spent in exile.

Taj Mahal, built by Shah Jahan in memory of his beloved wife Mumtaz Mahal, has remained a legacy of his devotion to Mumtaz and continues to inspire lovers to this day. Less known is the fact that, after some time, Shah Jahan lost all interest in the magnificent monument and hardly visited it. It was in a pitiful "state of disrepair" as reported by Prince Aurangzeb in 1652. As an added insult to her memory, the aged emperor "two years after her death, began to lead an active and quite licentious sex life, involving several concubines, dancing girls and married women," wrote Dirk Collier in *The Great Mughals*.

Salim and Anarkali's love story is stuff of legends. Anarkali's mausoleum does exist in Lahore. The inscription on her grave reveals "majnoon" Salim's devotion to Anarkali. But there is no mention of Anarkali in either *Jahangirnama* or any other document of the Mogul period.

Dilip Kumar had professed his love for Madhubala in a court of law during the *Naya daur* controversy. But he refused to marry her unless she disowned her father. She was unable to do so, and that was the end of it. Years after his marriage to Saira Banu, the aging superstar had a secret marriage with Asma, a divorced socialite. The wedding pictures were leaked somehow. The tragedy king, who had been denying the rumors all along, finally confessed. As expected, Saira Banu raised hell, as did the rest of Dilip's family. Within a few weeks, he divorced Asma. Dilip and Saira have been living happily ever after.

Keats, the romantic poet who wrote the immortal line "a thing of beauty is a joy forever," had his muse, Fanny. He wrote passionate love letters to her. Diagnosed with advanced TB, he moved to Rome to be in a warmer climate. Fanny received the news of Keats's death (he was twenty-five) in London. She mourned him for six years. Eventually, she did marry and had children. Before death, she gave them the love letters from Keats. These were published, creating much interest as well as controversy.

The romantic poets do need a muse. While Akhtar Shirani's Azra and Salma were fictional characters, Iqbal's Emma was not. The young poet had been in Germany for his PhD. His letters to the German beauty reveal that he may have been in love. Atiya Fyzee, who visited Iqbal in Germany, had a chance to see Emma and noted how overwhelmed Iqbal was by her. They used to dance, and at least, once, Iqbal tried to join Emma while she was singing an opera. After returning to India, Iqbal continued to write to her. In one, he wrote, "I have completely forgotten the German language, except for one word—Emma." There was some indication that he wished to marry her and settle down in Europe. That did not happen. Emma's loss was our gain. But she deserves our gratitude for becoming his muse.

Syed Hussain had everything that a young man could wish for— scion of an aristocratic, respectable and wealthy family, good looks, and the brains to go with it. Ashiq Batalvi, who heard Syed Hussain speak in Lahore, noted that Hussain may have been the best orator in India. Hussain was close to the Nehru family. Proximity to the Nehru household allowed him and Vijaya Lakshmi, Nehru's sister, to fall in love. They were not allowed to marry. Syed Hussain was packed off to the UK and then to the USA. While Vijaya Lakshmi was forced into a marriage, Syed Hussain never married. He returned to India after twenty-five years abroad. Those who met him in his last years saw a lonely man with a broken spirit. A few months after being sent to Egypt as India's ambassador, he died, received a state funeral, and had a Cairo Street named after him. He may have died of "broken heart syndrome," a well-recognized medical condition now. It is said that Vijaya Lakshmi was once seen laying flowers on his grave. Shakeel Badayuni may have written the following verse for the likes of Syed Hussain and Vijaya Lakshmi:

> *Ae mohabbat tere anjaam pe rona aya*
> *Jaane kiyon aaj tere naam pe rona aya.*

Here is an unusual case of love. Back in the 1930s, a married professor fell in love with a famous and beautiful prostitute, Inayat Begum of Lahore. He would visit her once a month. Out of his salary of seven hundred rupees, he would give six hundred to her and the rest to his unsuspecting wife. Inayat Begum, a seasoned member of the oldest profession, but with a heart of gold, soon figured it out. She started to send six hundred rupees to her devotee's wife every month. This peculiar bidirectional movement of currency continued for several years. The professor never found this out.

Back to our class fellow—his attention soon turned somewhere else. The young lady, whom he had pursued right to her doorstep, did marry for love later. She has been divorced twice since. "Never say you know the last word about any human heart" (Henry James).

Prof. Nasrullah Malik: The Gordonian Guru

Prof. Nasrullah Malik (PNM) once asked if I had fully understood García Márquez's *One Hundred Years of Solitude*. I answered in the affirmative. That pleased him. The truth was I had found it difficult to comprehend the twisted plot of the Nobel laureate's masterpiece. But Professor Malik, whom I regarded as my guru, had high expectations of his students. Although I had never been to Gordon College Rawalpindi,

I had simply forced myself into a long list of his former students and admirers who remained close to him after leaving the college.

PNM had a habit of recommending books. Once, he saw me stressed out and asked me to read Bertrand Russell's *The Conquest of Happiness*. I read it and have since reread it a few times. He was the one to recommend Manto's *Ganjay Farishtay* and Nirad Chaudhuri's *The Autobiography of an Unknown Indian* to me. He was a scholar and encouraged pursuit of knowledge.

Raja Anwar, who has authored many books, including *The Tragedy of Afghanistan* and *The Terrorist Prince*, had been one of his favorite students. The two of them shared political philosophy and fondness for Z. A. Bhutto. Raja became adviser to Bhutto in the mid 70's. After Bhutto's fall, Raja escaped to Afghanistan, and PNM was suddenly transferred to Dera Ghazi Khan by the military regime. The allegation against him was the preface written by him to one of Raja's books, *Jhootay roop kay darshan;* this book had nothing to do with politics and was simply a collection of Raja's love letters to a former class fellow. Being away from home was hard on PNM. He had to leave his wife and young children behind in Islamabad. But somehow he endured the enforced exile to D. G. Khan, reading his books and having made new friends.

Once I asked him about a famous, high-profile Pakistani journalist who had once worked with Bhutto. "Yes, I know him." There was a long pause, and then he said, *"Yeh log dunya walay hein, dil waley naheen."* I had realized years ago that Guru was not an ordinary soul; he had his faults, but he had a heart of gold. He despised hypocrisy; during long association with him, not once did I hear him tell a lie. He did go through financial difficulties at times. There were scores who owed him a lot and were financially well off. Only once did he borrow money from someone. Within a few months, he paid it back—every penny of it.

Once as we were talking about corruption, he noted with sadness that way back in the 40s, a relative of ours had made illegal money. It turned out that this was a well-kept secret in the elders of the family. Although many knew it, only he had the moral courage to admit and condemn it. It took him years to build his house. He had to wait until he received his long-overdue share of inheritance from his siblings. He spent most of his time at Gordon College in a modest apartment that was attached to the college hostel; he was content with that.

PNM was not very handsome in the usual sense and physically not very imposing. His real talent showed up when you had a chance to listen to him. He was an avid reader and, when in the mood, had the ability to run an impressive conversation on diverse topics—literature, history, music, movies, and politics among others. He was not professor by title only; he was the real deal. Sometimes I would wonder whether he had been an underachiever and should have gone onto bigger things, perhaps a PhD or a teaching post abroad. But his yardstick of success in life might have been different. I never asked him this question, but if I did, I suspect he would have looked straight in my eyes and—with his characteristic loud laughter—would have reminded me that he was not a *dunyawala*.

He was an astute observer; once, he reprimanded me for drinking too little water. The physician in me protested, but Guru was right, so I increased my water intake. On another occasion, he spent a night with me in my college hostel in Lahore. As I woke up, I saw a strange sight—there were two feet pointing toward the ceiling. Confused, as I sat up in my bed, I found him upside down, standing on his head. "Yoga is good for you. Nehru used to do it," he remarked. This was one of his advice that I was unable to follow.

In his youth, he had spent two years teaching in our village school. Guru considered those years the best of his life and felt very nostalgic about it. To this day, his former students and friends in our area remember him with fondness. He had touched the lives of many. In the mid 90's, he was asked to be the chief guest at the annual school day and appeared thrilled at the opportunity to be with the simple village folks again. As is customary, he was asked to deliver a speech. He was not known to be an orator, but that short speech was very moving and almost brought tears to one's eyes. The theme was "some things always change, while others always stay the same."

Back in the 80s, I accompanied him to Pakistan Television (PTV) Lahore. PTV was big then. He had to see an old friend, Younas Mansoor, the script editor. As we entered, we bumped into a handsome man dressed in impeccable baggy trouser and long shirt. That was the renowned producer Yawar Hayat. It turned out that Yawar Hayat had worked with PNM at PTV Rawalpindi way back in the late 60s, in PTV's formative years. PNM had had experience of direction from his association with the drama club at Gordon College and did occasional work for PTV. While we were having tea in Yawar Hayat's office, Jamil Fakhri—then a famous comedian—walked in. "Meet my mentor" was how Yawar introduced PNM to Fakhri. I then realized that PNM had been Guru to many.

Rahat Kazmi and Shujaat Hashmi, who made name in the PTV drama, were both nurtured by him at Gordon College. I recall a PTV interview that he had done with G. Allana, a friend and biographer of Quaid-e-Azam. There were many other programs that I missed since I had gone abroad. Just a few days ago, I saw a short clip on YouTube of PNM playing the role of a professor in a PTV drama about Kashmir's struggle for freedom. It was a short role, but he came across as a natural. I also vaguely remember a family gathering when he was asked to sing '*Heer*'; he duly obliged and did fairly well. PNM was multitalented.

Among his friends—and mentors—was Dr. Fazal-ur-Rahman. Today not many remember him, but back in the 60s, Dr. Fazal-ur-Rahman had been asked to return to Pakistan by Ayub Khan to head the Institute of Islamic Research. He was a scholar par excellence. Unfortunately, he was hounded out of Pakistan by the radical religious elements. PNM had high regard for him and stayed in touch with him until the latter's death in 1988. PNM's daughter, who later joined the prestigious CSS, had been named by Dr. Fazal-ur-Rahman.

Guru was a socialist at heart and had had high hopes for Bhutto. Bhutto's execution hurt him deeply. I once saw him in a serious discussion with my late brother—an army officer—about the flaws in the supreme court's decision in Bhutto's case. He told me with sadness once that Raja Anwar had been wrong to criticize the Bhuttos in his book *The Terrorist Prince*. "The facts are reported correctly in this book," he accepted, "but Raja has bitten the hand that had fed him." Guru was emotional at times but still a rational man, although it took him years before finally becoming disillusioned with the Bhuttos.

Guru had an uncanny innocence about him. A nephew of mine, a police officer with a rather inquisitive mind, once asked him whether he had ever been in love. Guru answered in the affirmative. When asked if he liked beautiful women, he said, "I did, but I was not a flirt, just an admirer of all things beautiful, including women." He liked the forbidden nectar too but was discreet about its use. Somehow he had convinced himself that the holy book's prohibition of liquor applied to prayer times only. He was not overtly religious but had a solid understanding of the religion. I once saw him reading Koran with two different books opened side by side; he was comparing the commentary of two authors, one of those being the late Amin Ahsan Islahi, whom he greatly admired. Salman Rushdie's infamous *Satanic Verses* made him quite upset. Unlike many, he actually read it and only then concluded that this book had little literary merit and that Rushdie seemed intent on maligning the Holy Prophet.

In the early 90s when I was doing postgraduate training in the UK, he wrote to me. Here is an excerpt from that letter:

> You must keep reading relevant literature on your subject. You must bring good name to the family by some outstanding contribution to make men, women and children more beautiful and good to look at. . . . You should also, learn to relax and be happy. Those who do not enjoy life have to endure its sufferings more acutely. Read good books on human relations and become a good healer.

Except for a minor heart attack, he remained in excellent health most of his life until age finally caught up with him. The last few years were difficult: A stroke had left him physically weak; it made him stop his long-cherished walk; his recent memory was impaired too, but he could still recall the fine details of his childhood abode Bhera. During my last visit to Pakistan, I could see that he was fading away; he had become just a shell of the man he used to be.

PNM, the beloved guru to many, is no more. He passed away quietly a couple of weeks ago in Islamabad, surrounded by his family. To my utter shame, being abroad, I missed his funeral. I have heard—from two different sources—that he had an unusual glow on his face after death. I wonder whether the Gordonian Guru, who was a great admirer of beauty, had a premonition of all the beautiful things that awaited him on the other side of the great divide.

Profiles in Courage

Sir Thomas More walked up to the chopping block in the Tower of London, looked at his would-be executioner, and calmly said, "I forgive you, right readily . . . be not afraid of your office. You send me to God . . . I die loyal subject of His Majesty, but God's first." Minutes later, More was beheaded. Thus ended the life of a remarkable man—one who was patient in adversity and showed little fear of death.

Henry VIII, the king of England, had decided to split from the Catholic Church, having failed to get his divorce approved by the pope. Desperate for an heir, he wanted to remarry. But the Roman Catholic Church wouldn't allow divorce. Thomas More, Henry's lord chancellor, a devout Catholic, was right in the middle of it, torn between his conscience and his duty to the Crown. Henry expected More to support his divorce and breakup from the Catholic Church. Thomas More, a man of principle, refused to go along and resigned. Furious, Henry—an unscrupulous ruler—had him arrested.

The trial held in a kangaroo court, an intimidated jury found More guilty of high treason and condemned him to death on the basis of the false testimony of Richard (read Masood Mahmood)—a confirmed liar and opportunist who, for his perjury, was rewarded with a post in Wales. With death staring More in the face, the English statesman delivered a heart-wrenching statement:

> Death comes for us all, my lords. Yes, even for kings he comes. In good faith, Richard, I am sorrier for your perjury than my peril . . . Why Richard? It profits a

man nothing to give his soul for the whole world. But for Wales? . . . I am a dead man . . . I am the King's true subject. I do none harm. I say none harm. I think none harm. And if this be not enough to keep a man alive, then in good faith, I long not to live.

Before the trial, when asked to bend the rule to facilitate the king's remarriage, More said, "When the statesmen forsake their own private conscience for the sake of their public duties, they lead their country by a short route to chaos."

When reminded that most of English nobility were supporting the king, he said, "The nobility of England would have snored through the Sermon on the Mount."

Finding her beloved father's life in danger, More's daughter pleaded with him not to defy the king. In response, More told her,

> If we lived in a state where virtue was profitable, common sense would make us saintly. But since we see that avarice, anger, pride and stupidity commonly profit far beyond charity, modesty, justice, and thought, perhaps we must stand fast a little, even at the risk of being heroes.

In 1954, Thomas More was eulogized by Robert Bolt in a play, *A Man for All Seasons*. More was not the first, or the last person, to have made the ultimate sacrifice. There have been others. But not many who could have easily saved themselves. Thomas More—a scholar par excellence, the author of *Utopia*, a world classic, and twenty other books—chose not to and immortalized himself in the annals of humanity.

Back home, there was Bhagat Singh. Twenty-three at the time, he courageously walked up to the gallows and remained calm to the last second. A statement, published posthumously, revealed what was going through the mind of the firebrand revolutionary:

> The only consolation for me is that I am sacrificing my life for a noble cause. A Hindu believer can expect to be rewarded in next life; Muslims and Christians can

expect the reward in heaven. But what is in there for me? All I expect is a last moment when the noose will tighten around my neck and the board will move from under my feet. For me, that will be the very end of a life of struggle; that by itself is a reward enough for me.

Che Guevara, had been Fidel Castro's right-hand man in Cuba. He decided to move on and was trying to duplicate the success of the Cuban Revolution in Bolivia. Captured by the CIA-assisted local army, he was summarily executed. His last words to his would-be killer were "I know you have to kill me. Shoot, coward! You are only going to kill a man!" Che would have been pleased to know that the foremost statesman of the twentieth century, Nelson Mandela, languishing in prison at the time, called him "an inspiration" while Jean-Paul Sartre described Che to be the "the most complete human being of our age."

Marshal Ney of France was captured after defeat at Waterloo. He was court-martialed and sentenced to death. As he faced the firing squad, he asked to be allowed to order his own execution. His wish was granted. He ordered the firing squad to shoot at himself. In so doing, he proved Napoléon right who had called him the bravest of the brave.

Hadji-Murad, the folk hero of Dagestan, had fallen out with his mentor, Imam Shamil, and had defected to Russians. Having realized that he had almost become a prisoner of Russians, Hadji-Murad attempted a daring escape with two of his associates. Pursued and then cornered in a field, they refused to surrender and fought to the very end. Their uncanny bravery and battle cries were narrated by Leo Tolstoy in a novelette. Tolstoy had met the daredevil freedom fighter.

As Z. A. Bhutto's fate hung in the balance in the late 70s, his supporters started a campaign of self-immolation. Raja Anwar, a onetime adviser to Bhutto who had organized that gruesome spectacle on behalf of Nusrat Bhutto, has given some details:

> On Oct 1st 1978, Wahid Qureshi got ready in Lahore to set out for Rawalpindi. Qureshi's wife had died some time earlier, leaving four daughters behind. He alone was now responsible for their care. The youngest was no more than four; she was the one most attached to him.

Qureshi worried about her, and instructed Lala Fazil in Gujranwala: "Lala, please tell Apa [Qureshi's sister] that she must have the youngest sleep with her at night because she is not used to sleeping by herself. I don't want her to be crying all night." He must have repeated this message several times before leaving for Rawalpindi. . . . Before he was driven off, everyone said to him that self-immolation bid was to be symbolic rather than real . . . "Don't any of you worry," he replies laughing. We believed him. . . . The same evening, the two men set themselves on fire in Rawalpindi . . . when those gathered there saw them burning, they began to dance around them raising excited slogans. . . . Qureshi was lost in ecstasy, caught in a kind of transcendental state. He was so carried away by the slogans all around him that he went on dousing himself with petrol. He was terribly burnt, and died after fifteen days, never again to have his little, motherless daughter fall asleep with her head on his chest.

Raja Anwar recounts another incident of self-immolation at Lahore:

Parvez Masih left a young wife and a daughter just eighteen months old, plus his old parents. Before the fire brought him to the ground, he was heard intoning Christ's moving words on the cross: "Eloi, Eloi, lama sabach thani?" (My God, my God, why hast Thou forsaken me?)

Only twenty years old, Chaudhry Azam—another devotee of Bhutto—had joined Al-Zulfiqar. Murtaza Bhutto had assigned to him the perilous mission of firing a missile at Zia's aircraft. This is precisely what Azam did in broad daylight from the busy Murree Road, Rawalpindi. How he managed to escape from a city that was teeming with intelligence is another story. He was later to lose his life in Amsterdam. The fascist who shot him did not know that his victim had no fear of death.

There are two kinds of men, it seems. The first kind are personified by Thomas More; they are endowed with extraordinary courage perhaps because they have sincerity of purpose and a supreme conviction to their cause. And then there are the rest of us. It is for the former that Faiz wrote:

Jis dhaj say koee maktal mein geya, woh shaan salamat rehtee hay
Yeh jaan to aanee jaanee hay, is jaan kee koee baat naheen.

<u>References</u>: *The Terrorist Prince* by Raja Anwar, *A Man for All Seasons* by Robert Bolt, *The Sabers of Paradise* by Lesley Blanch, *Hadji-Murad* by Leo Tolstoy, *Street Fighting Years* by Tariq Ali.

Quaid and Ruttie

"Pakistanis sometimes enjoy the delights of gossip more than the science of history, and they are already weaving legends about Jinnah's name," wrote Hector Bolitho, Quaid-e-Azam's first biographer, back in 1954. Years later, K. K. Aziz was to deplore our tendency to "place Quaid on a pedestal and revere him." That Quaid's was an extraordinary life is beyond dispute. For those who need some convincing, just two examples may suffice.

"He is young, perfectly mannered, impressive-looking, armed to the teeth with dialectics, and insistent upon whole of his scheme . . . Lord Chelmsford (Viceroy) tried to argue with him, and was tied up into knots. He is a very clever man. It is an outrage that such a man should have no chance of running the affairs of his own country," wrote Montagu, the secretary of state for India. He was referring to Quaid. Stanley Wolpert, the American historian and a biographer of his, may have paid Quaid the ultimate tribute by crediting him with "changing the course of history, altering the map of the region, and creating a nation state—all three of them."

But there was more to Quaid than some of us like to know. He had been a young man once and had the same passions that other young people did. There were aspects of his personal life that are rarely written about. His biographies by Hector Bolitho (1953), Stanley Wolpert (1980), and Khalid Hasan's book, based on K. H. Khurshid's papers (2001) have some interesting revelations. As one reads them, a pattern begins to emerge—an extremely hardworking, disciplined, dedicated life completely focused on the goals that he had set for himself. You'd also notice his admiration by women.

"Mr. Jinnah was one of the handsomest men I have ever seen; he combined the clear-cut, almost Grecian, features of the West, with Oriental grace and movement." This comment was from Lady Wavell. Begum Raana Liaquat Ali Khan (BRLAK) was also smitten: "The first time I saw Jinnah, *he captured my heart.*"

One of his admirers was the Cambridge-educated poetess Sarojini Naidu. Qazi Essa narrated the following to K. H. Khurshid: Quaid was once asked if he had ever kissed a woman outside his marriage. He mentioned an incident from the UK, from his student days, when he had been expected to kiss a woman in a game but declined on the grounds that it was prohibited in his culture to do so outside of marriage. When Qazi Essa reported this to Ms. Naidu, she started laughing and blurted out, "Liar, liar." The talented and popular Sarojini Naidu once resided at Taj Mahal Hotel in Bombay. How she paid for that most expensive hotel was the subject of all kind of gossip. She was not wealthy but did have wealthy friends. The future president of Congress and governor of UP used to write love poems to Quaid. Rumor had it that she had a crush on him. But as far as he was concerned, the nightingale of India sang in vain.

After his return to India from the UK, a young Quaid settled down in Bombay and devoted himself to his law practice. It took him about three years before success came. Besides law, his only other passion was politics. Having worked with Dadabhai Naoroji and later Gokhale, he was being seen as the rising star of Indian politics, an ambassador of Hindu-Muslim unity. But "there was no pleasure in Jinnah's personal life. No interests beyond work. Never a whisper of gossip about his private habits," wrote Wolpert. At that point, Ruttie entered his life.

The story of Quaid and Ruttie's romance and marriage has been written about often and would not be repeated here. But the events after their marriage are discussed less often. Wolpert has given some details of their rocky marriage:

> A spoilt child who had once been the center of her
> father's universe, Ruttie had been effectively disowned

> by her family. Mercurial, dashing, impulsive, and lonely young Ruttie found herself daily with more time than she could possibly devise ways to spend . . . Ruttie was precociously bright, gifted in every art, beautiful in every way . . . she seemed a fairy princess . . . For Jinnah married life was a solemn duty: for his young wife, it was also an opportunity for pleasure . . . Jinnah had to adapt himself to a social life too merry for his nature . . . The differences in their ages, and their habits, made harmony impossible.

Chagla, one of Quaid's legal assistants, witnessed some of those moments:

> In temperament they were poles apart. Jinnah used to pore over his briefs every day. I remember her walking in to Jinnah's chambers while we were in the midst of a conference, dressed in a manner which would be called fast even by modern standards, perch herself upon Jinnah's table, dangling her feet, and waiting for Jinnah to finish . . . Jinnah never uttered a word of protest, and carried on with his work as if she were not there at all. No husband could have treated his wife more generously . . . Just imagine how the patience of a man of Jinnah's temper must have been taxed by so demanding, so lonely a wife.

On another occasion, Ruttie came to see Quaid unannounced at Bombay Town Hall with a tiffin basket and told him that she had brought lovely ham sandwiches for lunch. A startled Quaid had to remind his naive wife that he was contesting a Muslim-separate electorate seat and could not afford to ignore the religious sensitivity of his voters. A visibly upset Ruttie departed.

Quaid might have realized by then the gross error of his judgment in marriage. Ruttie and Quaid separated, and she traveled to Europe accompanied by her mother. There were failed attempts at reconciliation. Diwan Chaman Lall, a friend and a fellow barrister, was with Quaid in Paris and noted:

> Jinnah is in a despondent mood . . . he is the loneliest of men . . . I had always admired Ruttie so much: there is not a women in the world today to hold a candle to her for beauty and charm. She was a lovely, spoiled child, and Jinnah was inherently incapable of understanding her . . . In the evening, I said to him, where is Ruttie? He answered, "We quarreled: she has gone back to Bombay." He said it with such finality that I dared not ask any more.

Here is Quaid's reaction to Ruttie's death:

> When an old friend called, to describe his wife's last hours, he saw a cold, discouraging look in Jinnah's eye. . . . Jinnah had endured all he wished of emotional relationships, and he permitted no one to disturb his disciplined, celibate, recluse habits.

Bolitho narrates an incident from Bombay when two young men were guests of Quaid. One night as they were about to go to sleep, there was a knock at their door by Quaid, who surprised his guests by a conversation not about politics but about his life in England and his early years in Karachi. As he was leaving, he said, "I wish that I had a son." There, one found a lonely man who may have been missing the comfort and intimacy that only a spouse could provide. These were the times when his wife had died, and Dina, his daughter, had moved in with her late mother's family.

Fatima Jinnah spent most of her adult life looking after Quaid. There were hints that the ever-present Fatima became too possessive and might have contributed to the rift between Quaid and Ruttie. Begum Liaquat reported to Wolpert:

> She [Fatima] hated any women he ever liked. Oh, how she hated Ruttie! I think she must have been jealous of us all! We used to call her the wicked-Witch!

Wolpert wonders whether Fatima's intense dislike of Liaqat Ali Khan and his intelligent and beautiful wife might have resulted from their persuasion that had brought Quaid back to India from England. Begum Liaqat reported that once in her presence, when her husband dared to speak to Quaid of the latter's loneliness and asked him to consider remarrying, Quaid smiled at Begum Liaqat and said, "I will if I could find someone like your wife." So here was yet another hint that Quaid longed for marital happiness that had eluded him. Did the domineering sister become a hindrance to her brother's remarrying? One has to wonder.

After Ruttie's death, Dina lived with her father and aunt Fatima in London, where she attended a private school while Quaid practiced law at the Privy Council. He adored his daughter and pampered her. It turned out that Dina had inherited the strong will of her late mother. She eventually became estranged from her father and married a Christian. The result was the same—another failed marriage. Aside from a well-publicized visit to Pakistan a few years ago, Dina spent the last decades of her life in Greta Garbo like seclusion in New York City. While writing her esteemed father's biography, Wolpert did seek an interview with her; the appointment was cancelled by her at the last hour for unclear reasons. A BBC correspondent did manage a short visit but was not allowed to record anything or take pictures.

In the final analysis, it seems that the brilliant parliamentarian and one of the shrewdest lawyers in the whole British Empire (Wolpert's words) failed himself in his choice of a wife. Quaid—the master of cold-blooded logic, a man of iron discipline who as a young man of sixteen had ignored the temptations of London—made a terrible choice and paid a heavy price, as did his future generation. It seems mind boggling. Perhaps Henry James was right when he wrote, "Never say you know the last word about any human heart."

<u>References</u>: *Jinnah of Pakistan* by Stanley Wolpert; *Jinnah Creator of Pakistan* by Hector Bolitho; *Memories of Jinnah* by K.H. Khurshid

Rahmat Ali: The Condemned Hero

The other day, this scribe asked three Pakistani physicians about Rahmat Ali (RA). One thought that he had written the national anthem; another said that he had designed the national flag. One knew nothing; only one knew that he had coined the word *Pakistan*. Now this is what K. K. Aziz wrote of RA:

> His distinction lies in that he was the first to ague, in detail, in favor of the two-nation theory, to offer a concrete scheme, to give a name to the proposed state, and to establish a movement to achieve the ideal. Some others had made suggestions and then forgotten them or passed on to other things. He alone devoted his life to it and stood like a rock in its cause. He had no material resources to lighten his labors. No crowds applauded him. No public deification buoyed him up in dark hours. No party advanced his name or his plans, or fought for his principles. With none to cheer his lonely exile, not even a wife to share his solitary existence, he literally lived and died with the idea which he had made the sole justification of his life.

RA's was an extraordinary life. Born in a low-middle-class family in East Punjab, he came to Lahore in 1918. Having spent twelve years in Lahore, in which he graduated from Islamia College, taught at

Aitchison College, and worked as private secretary to Mazari chief Dost Mohammad, he proceeded to England in 1930. He was to remain in Cambridge for the rest of his life, barring a few short breaks.

Interestingly, those who helped RA in his life included Sir Umar Hayat Tiwana, a landlord from Sargodha, and father of Khizar Hayat Tiwana, later prime minister of Punjab. Mr. Tiwana kept a house in London that was open to visitors from back home. RA was not only allowed to stay there but also received a favorable letter of reference from his host that helped him get in to Emmanuel College in Cambridge, an institution where Patras Bokhari had once been a student. The Tiwanas were Unionists and opposed Muslim League. But Abdus Salam, who was to win the first Nobel Prize for Pakistan, and RA who coined the name *Pakistan* were both helped by them along the way.

RA's odyssey began on January 28, 1933, when he wrote the pamphlet *Now or Never* from 3 Humberstone Road, Cambridge. This was followed by the launch of Pakistan National Movement and a grandiose plan that envisioned ten independent Muslim states in India. He was to spend the rest of his life in the relentless pursuit of this ideal.

There is an interesting version of how RA came up with the word *Pakistan*. While he had been thinking of this for a while, RA claimed to have had a moment of inspiration while atop a double-decker bus in London when the word *Pakstan* (without I) flashed in his mind. It was later that *i*–taken from Indus—was added to make it *Pakistan*. Ironically, the original demand for Pakistan did not include Bengal.

RA traveled often to plead his case. There is evidence that he met Adolf Hitler; the German chancellor, it may be recalled, had also granted audience to Allama Mashriqi and gifted him a car that can still be seen in Ichra, Lahore. Halide Edib, the famous Turkish journalist, had been to India and was about to write a book on India. RA met her in Paris and persuaded her to include a chapter in her book on Pakistan. At her suggestion, he not only wrote the entire chapter himself but also ensured that five hundred copies of her book *Inside India* were purchased by his fellow students in England. "Those who have read Halide's book," wrote Aziz, "are impressed by richness of RA's argument. There is hardly any point in favor of partition of India which he does not make. The case for Pakistan is argued in such detail that all the *Muslim*

League statements of the years 1940–1947 did not go beyond repeating, elaborating and clarifying what he told Halide. In some cases, the very words and phrases have been borrowed from him."

RA visited London frequently and met Muslim dignitaries who used to come from India for various conferences. At various times, he met and tried to influence Quaid, Agha Khan, Iqbal, and Khaliq-uz-Zaman among others. Zaman has left this account of his meeting with RA:

> I took a sincere liking for this tall graceful and well cut figure. When we started talking about the scheme of Pakistan I found that not only had he thought deeply over the question but was earnest about its realization.

Many Muslim students were influenced by RA. Mahbub Murshed, who rose to become chief justice of East Pak High Court and incidentally was also the CEC for the 1970 elections, was among them. M. Anwar, later a brilliant lawyer, worked closely with RA. Anwarul Haq, the future chief justice of the supreme court, had also been an acquaintance of RA. Aslam Khattak was one of the four original signatories of *Now or Never*. Anwar and some other students would go to the famous Hyde Park Speakers' Corner to propagate their cause. This was years before Quaid and the Muslim League took up the case of Pakistan.

RA was not a statesman; he was an idealist, a perfectionist, who failed to see the weakness in his complicated plan. He felt let down when Quaid accepted a much smaller Pakistan than RA had proposed. A deeply hurt RA exercised poor judgment at that point and berated Quaid; his scathing and most unfortunate remarks included derogatory terms like *Quisling-e-Azam*, and *Judas*. This colossal mistake was to be his undoing and lost him the sympathies of many.

RA did come to Pakistan in April 1948, quite oblivious to the hostility that awaited him. He intended to enter politics, pursue law practice, and bring out a journal. In Lahore, his friends prevailed on him to apply for a house since he was a refugee and had left property in India. RA agreed, and a spacious house on Jail Road, Lahore, was allotted to him. RA found it full of expensive furniture and decorations that he promptly sent to the treasury.

The Muslim League government was wary of RA, and his life was made miserable. He was being followed by CID; his host, a respected medical professor, was threatened, and RA's application for a Pakistani passport was denied. It had finally dawned on RA that he had become a pariah in Pakistan. In October 1948, a disillusioned RA—physically exhausted and broken in spirit—left for Cambridge; he was never to return.

On a bitterly cold, rainy day in January 1951, RA walked to the house of his former landlady Miss Watson. He had forgotten his overcoat and umbrella at home, was soaked wet, and was visibly shivering. Having collected his letters, he left in a hurry. Within days, he came down with a chill, was admitted in a nursing home, and three days later died; he was fifty-three.

In personal life, RA was a bohemian. He attached great value to time, worked hard and long hours, often worked late into the night, was addicted to tea, and was a chain-smoker. His obsession with cleanliness and taboos in food often created difficulties with his landladies. His contemporaries described him as a sensitive and restless soul. He changed his residence often; in Cambridge, he moved through at least five addresses. He never married, never had a girlfriend, and never had a female visitor. It seemed that he had suppressed the need for female companionship by intense devotion to the one and only cause that was dear to his heart. Those who met him were impressed by his confidence and power of persuasion. Having moved in an educated circle in Lahore, to some, he came across as an aristocrat.

Financially, he was often in dire straits. While at Islamia College, he had to suspend his studies at times for lack of funds; he supported himself by part-time work in *Paisa Akhbar*. Only a generous payment from Mazari Sardar enabled him to proceed to the UK. He was in heavy debt at death.

Sixty-five years have passed since RA passed away in exile. Since then, we have tolerated Ahrars, Khaksars, Jama'at-i Islami, JUI, Red Shirts, and the like; they all had opposed Pakistan. We have made heroes of many corrupt, incompetent politicians and generals. Yet RA's role remains unacknowledged in the freedom struggle. There is no sign that the remains of one of our real heroes are coming back anytime soon. There have been demands over the years for reburial, the last one by

Ch. Shujaat Hussain. We condemned RA years ago for his criticism of Quaid, which—though harsh—was based on principle. Quaid was, and should remain, the undisputed leader and founding father of our nation. But that should not deter us from carefully studying history and giving credit where it is due. Quaid, wrote Aziz, "is to be put on a pedestal and revered; to examine his career is to utter a blasphemy. This line of thought has been given the name of national ideology."

We are a strange people. When Awami League was denied the right to form government in 1970, hardly anyone spoke. When RA was hounded out of Pakistan, there was virtually no public reaction. When he died, the only sympathetic obituary came from *Nawaiwaqt*. Today, Subhas Chandra Bose's role in the freedom struggle is accepted in India, despite his serious differences with Nehru and Gandhi. Nixon has been rehabilitated in the USA, but in Pakistan, RA's name remains in oblivion.

"He died in neglect, indifference and apathy," writes K. K. Aziz. "No Pakistani brought him to the hospital, or sat near his bedside, or called to inquire about him, or prayed for him, or mourned him, or took his dead body away." Aziz laments that the nursing home expenses were paid by RA's former tutor at Emmanuel College, only a few English friends were present at the burial, and the Pak High Commission in London, though informed, had not responded. Here is the description of RA's last resting place: "It is a mere piece of vacant land, the size of a grave. . . . a nameless, flowerless, cheerless six feet of earth covering a box that contains the bones of a body which suffered much during its mortal span."

Back to my friends—perhaps, I should have quoted to them Pir Ali Muhammad Rashdi, who wrote, "RA occupies the same place in the Pak ideology as does Karl Marx in Communism. If there is any difference in their positions, it is this that while the people who profited from Marx's intellectual labours remembered him, those who gained from RA's intellectual exertions have forgotten him."

This writer, for one, is willing to offer a sincere and humble apology to RA's memory. As for the rest of our nation, his soul demands and deserves an explanation for a glaring injustice. It is long overdue.

Reference: *Rahmat Ali* by K.K. Aziz

The Curious Case of Sahir Ludhianvi

Sahir's car was once intercepted by a notorious gang of dacoits near Gwalior; he was forced to spend the night at their abode, where he was treated like royalty, lavishly entertained overnight, and was asked by his hosts to read his poetry. It turned out a popular lullaby written by Sahir for a Sunil Dutt movie *Mujhay jeenay do* had so moved the desperadoes that they were on the lookout for the creator. Deathly afraid at the time, Sahir may have realized belatedly the extent of his popularity. Sahir himself narrated this incident to his friend Hameed Akhtar.

October 25, 2010, would mark the thirtieth death anniversary of Sahir Ludhianvi. The lyricist par excellence may not be known to the present generation, but for those whose youth was spent listening to his melodies from All India Radio, his memory lives on. A lot has been written of his poetry by people a lot more qualified than this scribe. It would suffice to say that he wrote for the poor and oppressed and had leftist tendencies. It was Sahir the person that this article is about.

Sahir did not come from an educated family; his father was illiterate as was his mother. He spent his youth with his mother in Ludhiana, went to college in Ludhiana from where he was expelled, and then was admitted in Islamia College, Lahore, where he hardly spent any time. His interest lay in poetry, and so he began to move in the literary circles of Lahore and gained fame early. His first collection of poetry, *Talkhian*, was published in 1944. This brought him early recognition. After partition, he shifted to Lahore along with his mother and lived at

The Doctor From The East

Abbott Road, Lahore. Hameed Akhtar, the famous writer who was his friend, lived with him. Within a few months, however, Sahir vanished from Pakistan and was never to return.

What made him leave Pakistan? It turns out he had been followed and harassed by the secret police since he was seen as a communist. A letter addressed to him by Sheikh Abdullah of Kashmir did not help. It was intercepted by the police, and they were after him. Sahir, despite his revolutionary ideas, was not known to be a man of strong nerve and was deathly afraid. To disguise himself, he was reported to have covered himself in an overcoat, a muffler, and a hat in the month of June and managed to board a flight of Orient Airways from Walton Airport for Dhaka, from where he went on to Bombay; he was never to return to the city of his beloved Amrita Pritam. And so one of the finest poets of his generation was lost to Pakistan.

Sahir found enormous success in Bollywood after a brief struggle, and the rest is history. Suffice to say that he almost revolutionized the way songs were written and the lyricists were treated. He demanded and received five thousand rupees per song when Lata was getting this amount for singing; he was the one to insist that the lyricist's name should be announced with the song rather than just the singer's and composer's; he also was the first to demand and receive the royalties for his songs. He got away with all this because he was in great demand, and his filmi poetry brought a freshness, literary excellence, and intensity that was lacking before. He teamed up with S. D. Burman, and the two of them gave the hit music for numerous movies in the 50s. The pair eventually fell out, but Sahir continued to write and remained successful with many other composers like N. Dutta, Roshan, and Khayyam. Two *Filmfare* and a *Padma Shri* awards followed. In later years, he worked sparingly and imposed a Greta Garbo like seclusion on himself. He died of a heart attack in 1980 in Bombay.

Sahir led a strange life. He remained a bachelor all his life despite numerous love affairs. Some of these were high profile and well publicized like his ongoing affair with talented and equally successful Amrita Pritam. This began in Lahore—she was already married—and continued on and off for years in India. There was an engagement with the writer Hajra Masroor that was broken off by Sahir. The other names linked to him were Lata, Sudha Malhotra, and Ashwar Kaur, a girl from his college who left home for Sahir. But when the time came to make the decision, he lost nerve and could not decide. She married a distant relative instead.

There have been numerous theories about Sahir's unwillingness to marry and lead a normal life. Qateel Shifai, who knew him well, reports in his autobiography that Sahir, contrary to some speculation, was not sexually impotent. He noted that Amrita Pritam's son had a close facial resemblance to Sahir. Many people took it as a proof that Sahir had fathered her child, though Amrita denied this.

The most intriguing aspect of Sahir's later life was his reclusiveness. He seemed to have broken off most of his social contacts and hardly ever left home. Sahir's admirers should be indebted to Hameed Akhtar again for some insight into the bizarre behavior of this eccentric genius. Hameed reported going to India in 1979 with the sole purpose of visiting Sahir, who had survived a major heart attack some time earlier. The two of them had been close friends before partition and would have been reuniting after thirty-two years. Mutual friends Kaifi Azmi and Ali Sardar Jafri had warned Hameed Akhtar about Sahir's erratic behavior and suggested not staying with him. Hameed Akhtar proceeded nevertheless. This was what he reported:

> Sahir that I saw had reached the zenith of popularity and success, had made millions but as a person, he had changed; he was ill tempered, become a recluse, had detached himself from his past and all social contacts. He was leading an un-natural life and began to drink heavily. His companions drifted away slowly until no one was left to share his evenings; he was a lonely man.

Hameed Akhtar's portrait of Sahir is of a man who had attained everything that he wished for—wealth, respect, power, and popularity—but who was at a dead end. The success that he longed for had not brought any happiness; his friends avoided him, and there were all kinds of funny stories about him. Sahir was a sensitive person, an idealist but not a practical man; he lacked self-confidence. He had a peculiar theory of women: he had convinced himself that while women loved poets, they preferred to marry for money only. In later life, this conviction may have prevented him from marrying.

He may have been lonely in life, but after death, he had the satisfaction of joining the greats of Indian cinema; his neighbors in the cemetery include names like Naushad, Rafi, Madhubala, and Kaifi Azmi. A recent article in *Times of India* reported that the remains of the above as well as scores of others had been disposed of and their tombs demolished to make space for new bodies. This may be painful for the fans of Sahir, but the sensitive poet who once wrote, *pal do pal mayree haste hay,* may have foreseen this and may have preferred it this way.

References: *Ashnayan Kya Kya* by Hamid Akhtar; *Ghungroo Toot Gaye* by Qatil Shifai

The Tragedy of Salim Raza

The other day, this writer came across a piece in *Pakistan Link* about the Lollywood tragedies. The article had some information about the famous actors Sultan Rahi, Waheed Murad, and Nanha, among others, who died relatively young. While reading that article, I started to reminisce about Salim Raza, who was one of the most popular playback singers in the 60s when I was growing up. Salim Raza, whose voice had an uncanny resemblance to that of Talat Mahmood, then suddenly vanished from Pakistan. My late brother had once heard Salim Raza in an interview on Radio Pakistan; Salim Raza said that he was fed up with the film industry and that he was considering going abroad. Despite my intense curiosity at the time, I was not able to figure out exactly what drove him away from Pakistan. And then I got busy with life and almost forgot about him; that is until the late Qateel Shifai's autobiography solved this mystery for me. For the music lovers who had been wondering about this over the years, herein lies the answer.

In the early fifties, while struggling to be noticed by music directors, Salim Raza sought help from Qateel Shifai, who was then the leading poet in the film industry. Qateel introduced Salim Raza to Madam Noor Jahan and also wrote favorable remarks about him in *Adakar*, a popular weekly film magazine of its day that Qateel Shifai used to edit. Salim Raza had a good voice, was trained in classical music, and became popular in a short time. And then sometime in the 70s, he left Pakistan for good. So what drove him away?

I tried to google Salim Raza the other day and saw the same old story written all over. Salim Raza could not compete with new singers;

The Doctor From The East

he could not adjust to the new recording techniques; his voice was not suited to the new trends in music and stuff like that. But the real reason was something else.

It turns out that Salim Raza, who hailed from Amritsar, was not a Muslim. He was of Christian faith. His real name was Noel Dias. He moved to Pakistan after partition. In Pakistan, his religion created no difficulty for him in his chosen profession of playback singing until he crossed the line.

Qateel reports that Salim Raza had developed a liking for Kausar Perveen, a female playback singer of the time. She might have reciprocated. Kausar Perveen was a Muslim. Salim Raza's Christian faith then suddenly became a liability for him. Most of the music directors were Muslims and took offense at the Christian singer who was trying to woo a Muslim woman. They started to boycott Salim Raza. "I have hardly any work," he told Qateel Shifai, who found him back at the radio station one day.

Almost overnight, one of the most popular singers became persona non grata in the film industry. In desperation, Salim Raza turned back toward Radio Pakistan. But the die was cast. Salim Raza knew full well that he was finished in the film industry. Kausar Perveen, in the meantime, was coaxed into marriage with a music director, Akhtar Hussain Akhian, and resurrected her career but not Salim Raza. It is likely during this lean patch that my brother, who was a fan of Salim Raza, heard the above-mentioned statement in that interview. Salim Raza was forced out of his profession and livelihood in Pakistan, a country founded by Mohammed Ali Jinnah, a nonpracticing Muslim who himself had married a Parsi's daughter.

Salim Raza moved to Vancouver in Canada. Sometime later, Qateel Shifai—while on a tour in Canada—met him. Salim Raza had not forgotten the favor that Qateel had done to him years earlier. He received his benefactor warmly and went out of the way to help Qateel and his fellow poets in Canada. Qateel was shocked to find Salim Raza in poor health; he had developed kidney failure by then and was already on dialysis. Despite his poor health, he was trying to run a music school to survive financially. Soon afterward, in 1983, Salim Raza died, thousands of miles away from Pakistan, almost forgotten and abandoned by the notoriously treacherous and cutthroat film industry. Understandably, he was a bitter man; his last years in this world were marred by ruined health and financial strain. He was only fifty-one at the time of death.

And so it came to pass that the singer of *"Shah-e-Madina, Yasrab kay walee,"* arguably the most popular filmi naats of my generation, was almost hounded out of Jinnah's Pakistan. The bigots who had forced him out of Jinnah's Pakistan had perhaps forgotten the commitment given to the religious minorities by the founding father. In 1947, Quaid had given them reassurance that they were free to practice their religion and go to their temples. Salim Raza was an unfortunate victim of the religious fanaticism that was always lurking under the surface that has since become a menace and a shame for our country.

Salim Raza's contemporary singer Talat Mahmood also had a sad and unexpected exit from Bollywood. The reasons were somewhat different. But that is a story for another time.

Shamim Ara: Lakhon Mein Aik

Image source: imdb.com/name/nm0032669/mediaviewer/rm4239275008

Shamim Ara (SA) died in obscurity a few weeks ago in the UK, thousands of miles away from Pakistan. She had been in coma for years, and this news was not unexpected. Still, her death has severed yet another cord with our past. A few years back, she was being interviewed. When asked to give a message for her countrymen, she broke down and asked them to remember the expatriates' love for Pakistan. Back in the 70s, Rajinder Singh Bedi was being interviewed on Amritsar TV. He started sobbing when asked about Lahore. The celebrated short story writer of Urdu had spent his youth in Lahore before 1947. Such is nostalgia for one's youth.

My first memory of SA is from the midsixties. Late Agha G. A. Gul, the owner of Evernew Studio, had produced *Naila*. The movie, the first in color in Pakistan, was based on Razia Butt's novel of the same name. The director was Sharif Nayyar. The story revolved around the heroine who was loved by two brothers simultaneously. The role was played to perfection by SA. Now unlike Madhubala and Zeba, SA was no raving beauty. But she was a talented actress, well suited to play the type of role that required a shy, delicate, eastern woman who sacrificed her life for a doomed love. *Naila* was a huge success. I distinctly remember my elder sisters hotly discussing the plot of *Naila* with their friends. *Naila* was a trendsetter too. It ushered in the era of movies based on novels.

Decades later, SA was asked to pick her favorite song; she chose "*Tarapna bhee hamain ata hey*," sung by Mala and immortalized by the music director Master Inayat Hussain, who was born in Lahore's Bhatti Gate. (Hakim Ahmad Shuja called Bhatti Lahore's Chelsea, but that is a story for another time.) SA followed *Naila*'s success by producing *Saiqa*, also based on another popular Razia Butt novel.

Times have changed. But in those days, going to the movies was fairly popular and a safe type of entertainment for middle-class families. Many cinema halls would reserve, and often partition off, a part of the gallery for families with women and children. The culture of vulgarity, crudeness, and violence had not permeated our films. Urdu movies typically had social, romantic themes. I remember seeing late justice Aslam Riaz Hussain, along with his family, in a cinema hall in Lahore.

The other day, I glanced through a book by the late Yasin Goreja, who can safely be described as the encyclopedia of Pakistani film industry. Goreja had created a list of top one hundred movies made in Pakistan between 1947 and 2000. SA was the heroine in ten of them: *Saheli, Farangi, Naila, Aag ka darya, Lakhon mein ek, Hamraz, Dil mera dharkan teri, Saiqa, Mera ghar meri janat,* and *Salgira*. If one considers the fact that her acting career lasted from the late 50s through the early 70s, it looks like a remarkably successful career.

In the early 70s, SA made a smooth transition from acting to direction. It was a well-timed decision. She was successful at that too, although I had left Pakistan by then and did not witness that phase of her career. As a side note, SA's retirement from movies brought an unexpected, premature, and tragic end to the singing career of Mala. Mala's voice was very suitable for SA. Many of *Naila*'s songs filmed on SA were sung by Mala. With SA's retirement from acting, Mala had hardly any work. Having gone through severe financial difficulties, a depressed and abandoned Mala died; she was only fifty.

Like most actresses of that era, SA too came from a blue-collar background. It is unclear if she had any formal education. Apparently, she had migrated to Pakistan from India, and the family had settled in Karachi. One never heard of her mother or father. But there was that ever-present maternal grandmother who may have played a role in SA's marital disasters. And then there were professional difficulties. Qateel Shifai, who was producing a movie, *Ek larkee mere gaoon ke*, noted in his autobiography that his movie's distributor would often make crude sexual remarks in SA's presence. When rebuffed, he would become visibly hostile toward her and would use derogatory remarks, like calling her a prostitute. SA must have dealt with this type of adversity many times in her career. After all, this was and, to a degree, still is a man's world. Roger Ailes (the recently fired Fox TV chief) was not the first, or the last man, accused of sexual harassment. His kind have always existed.

SA reigned supreme when there were quite a few decent actresses around—Sabiha, Zeba, Neelo, Deeba, Shabnam, Nayyar Sultana, and Rani among others. Despite her success in movies, her personal life remained a fiasco. There were rumors of impending marriage to Mohammad Ali until he got married to her competitor, Zeba. For years, there was a statement attributed to SA that she intended to marry the army officer who would capture Kashmir. Later, she denied having ever said that. And then came a sudden marriage to Sardar Rind, a landlord from the south who died in a car accident. Her marriage with the director Farid Ahmed, the talented son of W. Z. Ahmed, did not survive long either. After yet another failed marriage with Majeed Karim, she finally settled down with Dabeer-ul-Hasan, a writer who predeceased her by a few years. She has a son, who lived in London.

Another memory of SA etched in my mind is her very emotional speech from Radio Pakistan in December 1971. Many artists had been asked to do this to increase the morale of the armed forces. Unaware that East Pakistan was sinking fast and that the Romeo Gen. Yahya Khan and his coterie were enjoying their alcohol, SA presented herself at Lahore Radio station and, like a dutiful, patriotic citizen, did what was asked of her.

The last years were difficult. Everything had been drifting downhill. Her health had broken down. A stroke had left her visibly weak. In a TV program with Bushra Ansari, she appeared depressed and emotionally labile. Ironically, a successful actress, producer, and director of her time was also going through financial problems. Having been dispossessed of her house in Gulberg, facing litigation, and having no other place of her own, she was forced to stay with the actress Bahar, an old friend. The catastrophic brain hemorrhage came a few years ago. She was flown to London and spent the rest of her life probably in a nursing home.

Two days after her death, I found myself traveling on the London Underground train. The third station, going from London Heathrow Airport toward central London, is Hounslow. That is where the heroine of *Lakhon Mein Aik* and *Naila* had found her last abode. As my mind wandered back and forth, it suddenly dawned on me that my favorite heroine had finally come to rest a stone's throw from Heathrow from where Pakistan International Airlines, Pakistan's flag carrier, flies back to the homeland that SA sorely missed.

Shamshad Begum: First Superstar Female Playback Singer

As a fifteen-year-old girl clad in a burka, Shamshad Begum (SB) had gone to AIR Lahore in 1937. She used to sing devotional songs at the time. Master Ghulam Haider—the legendary musician who had an uncanny ability to spot talented singers—noticed her and asked her to sing a piece. Before *asthai* was over, he was impressed and offered her a contract.

SB's place of birth is somewhat uncertain. Various authors mentioned Amritsar, while some others thought it was Lahore. What is not in dispute is the fact that she came from a very conservative background. After some initial resistance, her father relented, and soon she had followed her mentor, Ghulam Haider, to Bombay. SB tasted success quickly and, within a few years, had overtaken the lead female singers of the time; this included formidable names like Zohrabai and Amirbai. This was despite the fact that SB had hardly any training in classical music. Years later, this deficiency was to haunt her. In the late '40s however, SB was the most expensive female singer in India, charging one thousand rupees per song.

In Bombay, SB became the lead singer for Ghulam Haider as well as Naushad, who quickly took her under his wings. Ghulam Haider immigrated to Pakistan in 1947, but Naushad continued to use SB, and it was under his brilliant composition that she sang most of her popular songs in movies like *Shahjahan*, *Dard*, *Dulari*, *Mela*, and *Babul*. But perhaps her best song was for an unknown musician, Ram Ganguly, for Raj Kapoor's *Aag*. "*Kahe koyal shor machaye re*" was a huge hit and can be seen on YouTube today. Ironically, what may have been her finest hour may also have started her decline.

Raj Kapoor had a fallout with Ram Ganguly and decided to use a new musician duo by the name of Shankar Jaikishan for his next movie, *Barsaat*. Shankar Jaikishan decided to use a new struggling singer from Maharashtra—Lata—and dumped SB. By then, Naushad also had been smitten by the Lata bug. He used Lata in *Andaz*, and started to use SB sparingly. It seems that lack of classical training became SB's main handicap. At someone's suggestion, she did try to train herself in classical singing but gave up when told that this was going to ruin the natural flow of her voice.

SB's decline was as rapid as her ascendency. The real humiliation came in *Mughal-e-Azam*. Both SB and Lata were to sing the famous course "*Teri mehfil mein kismat azma kar.*" SB was under the impression that she would be singing for Madhubala, the heroine. As it turned out, SB's voice was given to Nigar Sultana, the vamp, and Lata's to Madhubala. Cultured but ruthless, Naushad had given his verdict: Lata was now his lead singer. By the late '50s, SB was at the margin and by midsixties almost forgotten. O. P. Nayyar did use her voice in *Kismat* in 1968 once in "*Kajra mohabbat wala*," but for all intents and purposes, this turned out to be her swan song; SB had become history.

SB continued to live in Bombay with her daughter and son-in-law, her husband having died in 1955. She virtually became a recluse and rarely gave interviews. A few years ago, Javed Iqbal from Ivory Club, Faisalabad, wanted to interview her but was dissuaded by Naushad, who knew that she would not agree for one.

SB's voice has been described as transparent, nasal, hearty, full toned, Punjabi-style. Naushad once remarked that the microphone had an affinity for SB's voice, and as a result, he would keep her at a distance of nine to ten feet from the microphone for proper recording; the distance for Lata was one to two feet. The most interesting description of SB's singing style has come from Ganesh Anantharaman in his book *Bollywood Melodies*. According to him, "SB had a spirit of abandon before the microphone." Lata once said that SB had more sharpness to her voice than melody and could sing only some songs well. Some would disagree with Lata's assessment, but then "beauty is in the eye of the beholder," as they say.

The Arrogant Ones

Sūleyman the Magnificent, the tenth Ottoman sultan, had the reputation of being a wise ruler. Over a period of forty-six years, his army had a track record of never-ending victories. One day he found himself at the gates of Vienna in Central Europe. The Austrians were not willing to face Sūleyman's invincible Janissaries in the open. And so they locked themselves up behind the city walls. A siege followed.

Tired of the long wait, Sūleyman sent a threatening message to the besieged Viennese. "Surrender; Sultan intends to have his breakfast inside Vienna the following week." The Viennese held their nerve and refused to surrender. Because of lack of heavy artillery, the siege lasted many weeks and was eventually lifted. As the Ottoman forces were leaving the area, a messenger duly arrived from inside the city. "The breakfast for His Majesty is getting cold," it said. Sūleyman's response to this humiliation was not recorded. But once in his life, it seemed, he had allowed himself to be carried away. This unnecessary bragging of the military might by *the lawgiver*, as he was affectionately known to his subjects, whose empire spanned three continents, has allowed this scribe to include the name of arguably the greatest of all Ottomans to be included in this list of arrogant people.

Napoléon Bonaparte ranks high on the list of conquerors. In the morning of the Battle of Waterloo, as the great general surveyed the battlefield, one of his marshals asked of the strategy. An overconfident Napoléon looked at his ever-victorious and menacing *Old Guard* and then at the opposing, hodgepodge army of Wellington across the field and declared, "This will be like a piece of cake." By the end of the day, the French Army had been decimated and Napoléon, who spent the rest of his life in captivity at Saint Helena, kept on trying to come up with what might have been. The great ones were also not immune from bragging.

As for the not so great ones, one can think of our own infamous General Niazi. The Tiger had landed in East Pakistan in 1971 and having taken over from Tikka Khan, declared that the battle would be fought in the Indian territory. Sometime later, as the Indian tanks were approaching Dhaka, he proclaimed that they would enter Dhack over his dead body. The rest is history. Years after capitulation, he came up with a book with the bizarre title *I Did Not Surrender*.

Not far behind Niazi should be the Indian C in C General Chaudhry. Confident of occupying Lahore in 1965, he had spoken of his intention of having alcohol at Lahore Gymkhana. But an unexpected and heroic resistance by the Pak Army stopped the Indian advance. Decades after the war of 1965, General Chaudhry has stayed in the history books more for this empty boast rather than anything else. He therefore finds a well-deserved place on this list.

Z. A. Bhutto—a political genius, a student of history, and a great admirer of Napoléon—faced a serious political crisis in 1977. As the PNA-led opposition was getting stronger by the day, Bhutto delivered a speech in the National Assembly. Instead of accepting the PNA demand for fresh elections (that he would have won), an emotional Bhutto allowed himself to be carried away. Looking at the armchair beside him, he paused for a few seconds, and then delivered the infamous line "This chair [meaning his administration] is very strong." The events that followed proved this an unwise utterance.

During his last days of freedom, after being deposed, Bhutto went to Lahore and was staying at Nawab Sadiq Hussain Qureshi's house. Inam Aziz, a Pakistani journalist based in London, had been promised an interview. Aziz was, however, finding it difficult to get access to Bhutto. Aziz approached Qureshi and sought his help to remind Bhutto of the promised interview. An exasperated Qureshi surprised Aziz by saying, "Brother, what makes you think I can go in Bhutto's room?" Apparently, Bhutto's room had become a no-go area for his host, the former chief minister of Punjab.

More recently, Pervaiz Rashid of *Nawaz League*—an otherwise sober politician—had a YouTube clip being circulated where he taunted Imran Khan, "who will be unable to earn one button of the sherwani that PM wears." Now while Imran sits happily as PM, Rashid's former boss Nawaz Sharif is having a tough time in Adiala Jail, where he has the dubious distinction of the company of his daughter (of "stop us if you can" fame) and son-in-law.

The world of sport has too many contestants for inclusion here. The one of particular interest to Pakistani readers may be Richard Charlesworth, a talented Australian who was not only a physician but also a superb field hockey player and a fairly decent cricket player. The 1984 Olympic hockey semifinal was about to start between Pakistan and Australia. Australia was heavy a favorite. As Charlesworth and his opposing center forward, Hassan Sardar, stood in the middle before the start, Charlesworth taunted Hassan, "Who will win?"

"Pakistan, with the grace of God," replied Hassan.

"Your God is in my pocket," said the supremely confident Australian. But Pakistani team carried the day against heavy odds. Many hockey fans remember the Australian coach sitting on the sideline with a bowed head after the final whistle. He had a look of utter disbelief.

And then there was the case of Anwar Kamal Pasha, who once ruled the Pakistani film industry. He had produced and directed multiple hits back in the '50s and '60s. As was to be expected, a crowd of flatterers was usually around him. His arrogance had hurt many. One day he bumped into Saadat Hasan Manto. Manto spared no one and, sometime earlier, had written a scathing piece on Pasha with the title *Loud Speaker*, in which he had made fun of Pasha's megalomania. Pasha approached Manto and asked for advice on a movie story that had become stuck. Manto being Manto gave Pasha a serious look and said, "I am not in the business of giving free advice." A visibly embarrassed Pasha had to produce a check before Manto allowed him to proceed. To onlookers' amusement, Pasha had finally met his match, for Manto allowed no one to bully him.

On another occasion, Pasha was sitting in the studio, surrounded by his cronies, when Sibtain Fazli—a fellow director, an educated, cultured man—walked in. As Fazli came close, some of Pasha's people stood up to greet him. Pasha, in a moment of extreme arrogance, admonished them, "You people work for me, get paid by me, and stand up for others." This was spoken within earshot of Fazli. Ali Sufian Afaqi, a journalist and later a director, was present and reported that a stunned silence followed Pasha's remark. After a brief exchange, Fazli—who must have felt hurt—left.

Some years later, Pasha's decline began, and it was relentless. Movie after movie flopped, and the crowd of flatterers disappeared. One day, Afaqi saw Pasha enter the same studio. There was a crowd of filmi people at the entrance. Hardly anybody noticed a subdued Pasha, who quietly walked right through them. The times had changed. The successful filmmaker of the past had fallen on hard times. Pasha, and the others of his ilk, would have been well advised to remember the following verse from *Surah Al-Isra*:

> And walk not on earth with haughty self-conceit; for verily, thou canst never rend the earth asunder, nor canst thou ever grow as tall as the mountains!

Noor Jehan: The Dark Side

When I think of Noor Jehan (NJ), my mind often wanders to two other singers who were her contemporaries. Both came from blue-collar backgrounds and rose to great heights after enduring early struggles. I am referring to Mohammed Rafi and Umm Kulthum. Rafi, during his long and illustrious career, remained above controversies, except for a brief rift with Lata. He had developed a reputation as a thorough gentleman. There were many examples of his compassion. Umm Kulthum was adored by the masses and elite alike in the Middle East. NJ had a similar blue-collar background and was successful too. But the similarities ended there.

Back in the '70s, Nisar Bazmi was arguably the most sought-after musician in Pakistan. One day he abruptly called it quits and retired to Karachi. The poor soul had infuriated *Malika-e-Tarranum* by his statement that no singer in Pakistan had the voice to satisfy him. Bazmi had worked in Bollywood before immigrating to Pakistan. He was entitled to his opinion but was hounded out of Lahore by NJ's lobby. I vaguely recall that Hassan Nisar had written a scathing piece on NJ about this in *Dhanak*, a magazine that ceased publication years ago.

In 1971, Yahya Khan (YK) was at the helm, and the occasion Ali Yahya's wedding. A picture appeared of Madam NJ sitting next to YK. They were holding hands. YK, in his sleeping gown, appeared almost drunk. NJ (Noori, as he fondly called her) was holding a drink. I would leave it to the imagination of the readers about the type of drink being served. On the same occasion, as she sat close to her *Sarkar* (as she addressed him), NJ was overheard having snubbed Gen. Gul Hassan, soon-to-be COAS, and Z. A. Bhutto (*chup karo way, kee barr barr laee ooee jay*). Such was her influence over the man who should have been paying more attention to Manekshaw's plans. While YK allowed himself to be distracted by NJ and the others of her ilk, East Pakistan was in turmoil. She was not the only one but certainly one of the most destructive influences on the wretched man who presided over the division of Quaid's Pakistan.

Nobody suffered more from NJ's hands than Shaukat Rizvi, her husband. Rizvi, it is to be recalled, was one of the few successful filmmakers who chose to immigrate to Pakistan in 1947 despite being in demand in Bombay. He had to his credit multiple hits like *Khandaan* and *Jugnu* (the first hit for Dilip Kumar, who had three flops in a row before that). Manto, who had written a sketch of NJ, noted that "Rizvi had a good head for business, an excellent reputation as a director and editor and would have done well even if he had not married NJ. He was a man who knew his art and who worked hard." But unlike Mehboob, Kardar, Rafi, Naushad, Dilip Kumar, and many others who stayed on in Bombay, Rizvi chose to come to Pakistan. Given the chance, he might have been one of the pioneers of the Pak film industry. Instead, he was dragged into controversies by his wife.

Despite divorce, their feud continued for years. As a result, a talented filmmaker was lost to the fledgling film industry that desperately needed him. Having renovated Shahnoor Studio, poor Rizvi could do nothing else. One can only guess what might have been. A few years ago, as this writer stood at the gate of Shahnoor Studio, it looked a ghostly site.

NJ's vengeance had no limits. At the height of her feud with Rizvi, she threatened to make a prostitute of Zil-e-Huma, her own daughter, in the red-light district and to prominently display her name as 'Zil-e-Huma daughter of Rizwi'. In retaliation, Rizwi produced NJ's birth certificate in his book *Noor Jehan kee kahani*, in which her family profession was given as *tawaif*. When Ijaz, her second husband, the love of her life as she often called him, left her for a much younger Firdaus, NJ started to spread all kinds of rumors about him. Once she confided to Khalid Hasan that Ijaz had many brothers and that they all had different looks. The readers can imagine the implicit filth contained in this statement.

NJ's influence at times reached quarters beyond music and movies. The careers that had been derailed included a young man who, at one point, had the world of cricket in the palm of his hand. In the formative years of Pakistan, one source of pride for the young nation was the cricket team. A. H. Kardar led team had won a famous victory at the Oval in 1954. Two years earlier, when the Pakistan's cricket team toured India, a young and stylish opener from Lahore had faced the first ball in test cricket for Pakistan and created sensation by scoring a century and carrying his bat in the test match at Lucknow. His name was Nazar Mohammad.

Nazar's elder brother was the musician Feroz Nizami, who had given the evergreen music of Jugnu, which starred NJ and Dilip Kumar. Not many from that generation can forget the NJ and Rafi duet from that movie, "*Yahan badla wafa ka bewafai ke siwa kya hai.*" Nizami later also worked with Rizvi for *Dopatta*, another hit. Nazar might have accompanied his brother to the studio. NJ saw him and, throwing all caution aside, started an affair with the cricketer whose star was on the rise. At the time, NJ had been married for years and had three children.

As fate would have it, the lovers were found out at their rendezvous at Ravi Road, Lahore. As an infuriated Rizvi, with a pistol in hand and accompanied by his associates, approached the upper-story room, Nazar tried to escape and jumped from the window, fracturing his arm. The fracture never healed. While NJ lost just one of her admirers and moved on to other adventures (she once counted sixteen of them on her fingers), Nazar's promising cricket career was over. Years later, he may have obtained comfort by seeing his son Mudassar play test cricket. Ironically, fifty years later, Nazar's name would be known more for his liaison with NJ than for cricket.

In music, NJ was at the very top. She was famous, had plenty of money, had hardly any competition, and had all kinds of accolades thrown at her. One would have expected that she would act like a mentor to the new singers. But she did no such thing. Instead, she allowed herself to be involved in petty squabbles and scandals.

The Doctor From The East

An aspiring actress by the name of Nighat Sultana was working in a movie that Rizvi was directing. Suspicious that Rizvi liked Nighat, NJ got into a physical altercation with her. The ensuing court case brought bad publicity to NJ and finished off Nighat's career. Ali Sufyan Afaqi interviewed Nighat Sultana after that incident and observed with sadness that Nighat was the sole breadwinner of her family; her father was blind and the family literally living hand to mouth.

Mukhtar Begum (of Agha Hashar fame) once approached Rizvi and sought help for her younger sister who was an aspiring singer. Rizvi was unable to help, he writes, due to NJ's jealousy. That talented singer later created a name for herself on radio and TV but never made it to the film industry. Her name was Farida Khanum.

Back in the 80s, Musarrat Nazir tried to make a comeback as a singer. NJ sent her threatening messages. Musarrat felt so scared in Pakistan that she moved back to Canada. There was a spat with Malika Pukhraj too. Her offense: she had made the cardinal error of reminding NJ of her humble origin.

An infamous incident of NJ's misbehavior involved Runa Laila who, like the actress Shabnam, was from East Pakistan and had stayed on in Pakistan after 1971. She was a popular singer but hardly a threat to NJ. But NJ had developed a dislike for her. One day as NJ approached the recording room, Runa did not stand up as NJ expected of all. NJ took it as a slight, went up to Runa, and in her chaste Punjabi scolded her for not paying NJ the due respect. Naive Runa responded in English that she did not understand what the problem was. NJ slapped the young singer in full view of the recording crew and musicians. No one intervened; not a word was spoken by anyone in Runa's defense. Such was NJ's iron grip on the film industry. A shocked Runa left the recording room and Pakistan soon afterward; she never returned.

Manto, who saw NJ and Rizvi in Bombay, has left a description of NJ that is less than flattering. He called her arrogant, her smile and laughter commercial and insincere. Manto then gives his most damning assessment of NJ:

> She had every single characteristic associated with the background from which she came. Everything about her was a put on. She was flirtatious but not in a cultivated way.

Manto wrote this in the early '50s. His description of NJ was spot on. The prophet of short story writers had seen back in the 40s what the rest of us did decades later.

Of all her feuds, the most puzzling was one with Khurshid Anwar. He was widely regarded as the best music director in Pakistan, highly educated, universally respected, and a cultured person. Many of NJ's best songs were composed by him. Just listen to his compositions in *Intezar, Koel, Jhoomer, Ghunghat,* and *Heer Ranjha*. KA took pains to create the type of tunes suitable for NJ. Qateel Shifai went to the extent of saying that NJ owed a lot of debt to KA but rarely acknowledged his contribution to her career. Fed up with NJ at one point, he was forced to use Kausar Perveen and Nahid Niazi. Such was NJ's behavior toward her mentor.

Zahoor Chaudhry has this to say of NJ in his book *Jahan-e-Fun*:

> NJ was a controversial figure. She was admired for her generosity but was also despised for her jealousy and vindictiveness. She made it impossible for any female singer to sing without her approval. She would humiliate her fellow singers and musicians. The first musician to have been insulted by her was Mian Shehr Yar who was forced to use Naseem Begum. She would insist that her voice would only be used for the heroine and had numerous fights with singers, musicians and poets. Those who had access to recording studios witnessed the humiliation of many musicians by her. She made life difficult for Naheed Akhtar, Kauser Parveen and Roona Laila. Because of her monopoly and dictatorial behavior, the film industry was not able to bring up the new generation of female singers. The way NJ misbehaved with Master Abdullah, a proud, intelligent musician was widely known.

Naushad Ali was an admirer of NJ who once conceded that NJ had a better voice than Lata. He had used NJ in *Anmol Ghadi* before partition. He once remarked that, in the latter part of her career, she allowed herself to sing below-standard, cheap Punjabi songs that not only damaged her reputation but also hurt the quality of her voice. Maestro, who rarely compromised on quality and would typically do one movie in a year, appeared disappointed at the greed of his onetime prodigy. Yasin Goreja noted in *Lakshmi Chowk* that while NJ's periodic announcements of donation to hospitals came to nothing, Inayat Hussain Bhatti, a second-rate actor, actually did it.

NJ has been dead for more than a decade. She was revered for her music. She had become a legend in her life and remains so to this day. There were stories of her generosity and kindness. But there was a dark and sinister side to her character. Though she reigned supreme in her profession, at times, her inherent insecurities would show up. In those moments, NJ would act more like Allah Wasai from Kasur, a ruthless bully hidden behind a mask of polite but fake polite demeanor. Umm Kulthum was idolized by the entire Arab world; her funeral was attended by millions, and Cairo came to a standstill. But NJ, who envied Umm Kulthum and copied the Egyptian diva's style by holding a scarf while singing, had tarnished her legacy, and that was her tragedy.

Voltaire is credited with the saying that "we owe consideration to the living and truth to the dead." It is with this spirit that this piece has been written. The readers are requested to keep this in mind.

References: *Mulaqaton ke baad* by Javed Iqbal, *Rearview Mirror* by Khalid Hasan, *Ghungroo toot gaye* by Qateel Shifai, *Jahan-e-Fun* by Zahoor Chaudhry, *Filmi alf laila* by Ali Sufyan Afaqi; *Ganjay farishtay* by S. H. Manto, *Noor Jahan kee kahani* by S. H. Rizvi, *Aik dil hazaar dastaan* by Agha Ashraf, *Ab woh Lahore kahan* by F. E. Chaudhry, *Ehad e Shabab* by Agha Jamsheri, *Lakshmi Chowk* by Yasin Goreja.

The Lady in The Lodge

ALL INDIA DEBATING TROPHIES AND SENIOR COLLEGE DEBATERS 1943
A. STANDING: KAPOOR, ALTAF GAUHAR, ANWAR KHAN, KUTAB, IJAZ BATALVI, MASOOD MEHMOOD, TAJAMMUL HUSSAIN, ZAHOOR, ILYAS
B. SITTING: URMILA SOONDHI, VED PRAKASH, G.D. SOONDHI, PROF. SIRAJ UDDIN, GUR BACHAN SINGH

Way back in the 1940s, Urmila was a student of English literature at Government College Lahore. Her father Professor Sondhi was the highly respected principal of the college. One of her teachers was the Oxford-educated professor Sirajuddin, who was destined to be the principal of GC himself. Now Professor Sirajuddin was no ordinary teacher. He was not the first, or the last, Oxford-educated professor of English at GC; he was preceded and succeeded by many with that qualification. What he possessed was, however, a rare gift for teaching with a deep understanding and passion for his subject. Dr. Aftab Ahmad, an old Ravian, has written a beautiful sketch of Professor

The Doctor From The East

Siraj in his book *Bayade sohbate nazuk khayalan*. Dr. Aftab reports that Professor Dickinson, who was the head of English department and also Oxford educated, would often refer students to Professor Siraj when asked a difficult question; such was Siraj's aura and prestige.

Urmila was beautiful and intelligent. Naturally, she had many admirers. Among them was a young lad from a low-middle-class family by the name of Abdus Salam. Salam had come to GC from the provincial town of Jhang, the land of Heer and Ranjha. The fate had great things in store for Salam, but that was to be in the future. At the time of his infatuation, however, Salam had a lot of competition; one of his competitors was Professor Siraj, who was already married.

It so happened that one day, as Professor Siraj was in the middle of his lecture, he received a note from his wife; he had been asked to return home, for there had developed a crisis of rather strange nature. As Professor Siraj hurried home, he encountered an irate Professor Sondhi—Urmila's father and the college principal. An unpleasant verbal exchange between the two led to a physical altercation that produced a minor injury to the face of Siraj. Having vented his anger, Professor Sondhi left. Inside the house were two women; one was Professor Siraj's wife, Razia, and the other Urmila Sondhi. It turned out that Urmila had been thrown out of the house by her father, who had belatedly become aware of her flirtation with Siraj. Since she had nowhere else to go, she ended up in Professor Siraj's house. And that was where her father had followed her.

Before her marriage to Siraj, his wife, Razia, it was said, had been a painter of some merit. Theirs had been a love marriage, but that was some time earlier. Now some years had passed, and Siraj, father of a son, was in love again with one of his students. It may sound strange, but Razia apparently was willing to give her consent to her husband's second marriage. After she accompanied their son, Imdad, to Oxford, her husband tied the nuptial knot with Urmila. We are told that Urmila had converted to Islam; her new name was Umrao. Professor Siraj went on to become the principal of GC himself in the '50s. Later on, he became the vice-chancellor of Punjab University and after retirement, because of his extraordinary talent as a teacher of English, was rehired as professor of English at Punjab University.

Abdus Salam, in the meantime, had proceeded to UK. Having completed his master's at Cambridge and now married too, he returned to Pakistan in 1951 and was appointed professor of mathematics at his alma mater. Ironically, the principal of GC at that time was no one else but Professor Siraj. By a strange twist of fate, the paths of those two extraordinary men, and former adversaries, had crossed again.

Salam did not find it easy at GC. The man who was to bring the first Nobel Prize for his nation had a miserable time at Lahore. For one, anti-Ahmadiyyah riots had engulfed Punjab. But Siraj did not help either. Here is the account of Salam's biographer, Gordon Frazier:

> Sirajuddin told him [Salam] sternly to forget about the research work he had done in Cambridge and Princeton . . . In addition to teaching, he was expected to be a good "college person," taking on extracurricular responsibilities . . . Salam chose to manage the college soccer team . . . The aimless gesture matched his own disappointment . . . Salam was to have more run-ins with Siraj . . . His 1951 confidential report alleged "Salam is not fit for GC, Lahore. He may be excellent for research, but not a good college man." . . . As Salam's research work stalled in Lahore, he became increasingly frustrated . . . For Salam, Physics was sheer delight. But in Lahore, his light of delight temporarily went out.

And so it came to pass that a disillusioned Salam finally left Pakistan and went back to Cambridge. One has to wonder whether Siraj's harsh treatment of Salam was connected to their shared passion for Urmila Sondhi from earlier times. Ironically, years later, Salam—already married with children—was also to fall under the spell of another young woman, a British physicist by the name of Louise Johnson. "It was an emotional lightning strike," writes Frazier, "such as Salam had not experienced since seeing the inaccessible Urmila at GC, Lahore, some twenty years before. . . . Salam and Louise Johnson were married in a Muslim wedding in London in 1968."

As I came across the story of Urmila Sondhi and her talented admirers, I became curious and developed a strange fascination with her. I began to wonder what she was like. I then started to reminisce about my own time in GC from 1972 to 1974. I can still remember the principal's residence, *Lodge*, not far from the main teaching block of GC. It then dawned on me that Urmila Sondhi had resided in the famous house twice, first as a student when her father was the principal and later as the wife of Professor Siraj. I may add that Lodge has a long and distinguished history of its own, but that is a story for another time; suffice it to say that *Niazmandan-e-Lahore,*—a group that included literary heavyweights like Patras Bokhari, Sufi Tabassum, Hafeez Jalandhari, Faiz Ahmad Faiz, and Dr. Taseer among others—used to gather under its roof.

But let us return to Urmila; I did not expect to find the answer to my quest until I came across a 1943 group photo of GC Debating Society. And there she was, sitting with poise in the front row, not far from Professor Sondhi, her soon-to-be estranged father and the college principal, and a young professor Siraj, her teacher of English literature at the time, and her future husband. There are other important people in this photograph too, some of whom have played important roles in the history of our country. Among those, one can recognize Altaf Gauhar (Ayub's information minister and the ghost writer of *Friends, Not Masters*), Ijaz Batalvi (one of the prosecution lawyers in the Bhutto case), Masood Mahmood (the infamous onetime head of FSF who eventually testified against Bhutto), and Raja Tajammul (Altaf Gauhar's brother, bureaucrat, and onetime Pakistani ambassador to Malaysia).

Decades have passed since Urmila Sondhi created sensation in Lahore with her marriage to an already married Professor Siraj. It was a big scandal at the time. But the cruel sponge of oblivion has since removed its characters from the slate of history, and now hardly anyone remembers it.

Talat Mahmood: The Singer with the Quivering Voice

Once upon a time, a young singer received a message. The year was 1949. The sender was a respected and successful musician in Bollywood by the name of Anil Biswas. Anil Biswas was among the first generation of musicians in Bollywood. He was a contemporary of Naushad Ali, Khemchand Prakash, and Pankaj Mullick. Music lovers may recall that it was Anil Biswas who made Mukesh sing *Dil jalta hai* for *Pehli Nazar* in Saigal-style. The recipient of that message was Talat Mahmood, a shy, aspiring singer from Lucknow. Talat was not new to singing. He had been singing for Radio Lucknow for some time and had also spent time in Calcutta, where he had recorded ghazels. But it was success in movies that he craved, and so he decided to test the waters in the highly competitive Bollywood.

Anil Biswas had heard of the singer from UP with the silky voice and decided to give him a chance. Talat duly arrived, and Biswas asked him to sing. A nervous Talat, aware that the graveyards of Bombay were full of failed singers and actors, started cautiously. The experienced maestro that Biswas was noticed that and asked Talat why he was hesitating. Talat explained that he did so because of the quiver in his voice. Obviously, Talat considered the quiver a handicap. Biswas reassured him that the quiver was not a handicap but an asset (*Tumheen isee laye to bulaya hey*) and told him to relax. A relieved Talat sang to Anil Biswas's satisfaction and was signed up by Biswas, who was composing music for Ismat Chughtai and Shaheed Latif's *Arzoo. Ae dil mujhe aisi*

The Doctor From The East

jagah le chal was recorded. Both the singer and the composer may not have realized at the time, but Talat's journey to stardom had begun. For the next decade, he was the most sought-after male singer in India.

How good was Talat? Just try listening to two songs; the first is *Ae gham-e-dil kya karun*, sung by Talat and Asha in *Thokar*, and the other *Jayen to jayen kahan*, sung by Talat and Lata in *Taxi Driver*. Raza Ali Abidi, in his superb book *Naghma gar*, is convinced that the Talat versions were superior to the Bhosle sisters'.

Fast-forward to the 1990s. Talat had been in poor health for some time and out of Bollywood for decades. Because of a stroke, he had lost his speech. The unique, silky voice with quiver was no more. A visitor came to see Talat. He was ushered in. Talat was gracious and asked his son to play his famous nonfilmi ghazel *Tasweer teri dil mera* and then, unable to speak but with visible pride, pointed to himself to say to the visitor that he indeed was the singer. During the visit, the mail arrived that brought a royalty check for Talat from a far-off radio station. Talat's son reported that royalty checks were still coming. It seemed that Talat, out of Bollywood for years, had still not been forgotten by the music lovers.

Talat's fall from the lead singer to virtual obscurity had puzzled many. The most popular male singer of the '50s had almost vanished from the music scene by the midsixties. What happened to him? Well, life has strange twists in store for us. To begin with, he ran into a problem with Naushad. *Mausiqar-e-Azam*, who had used Talat exclusively for *Babul*, in preference to Rafi and Mukesh, moved away from him for reasons that were vague. Picky Naushad, it was rumored, had earlier removed Majrooh Sultanpuri—considered by many to be one of the finest lyricists in India—from his team because of the latter's communist tendencies. Whatever the reason, Talat and Naushad—both from UP—were never to work with each other again.

But what really damaged Talat's singing career was his unwise decision to try acting. He may have hoped to cash in his good looks. He worked in twelve movies; only two of those clicked. By the time he returned to singing full time, Rafi, Mukesh, Kishore Kumar, Manna Dey, and Mahendra Kapoor had left little room for him. The music in the '60s was also changing. The ghazel that was Talat's forte was less in demand. By nature reserved, he was not the type to beg musicians for work. A dejected Talat then turned toward overseas trips, concerts, and private singing.

And so it came to pass that the man with the silky voice was lost to the cruel and unforgiving film industry, and to his fans, forever. He lived well into the 1990s. Visitors reported that he consoled himself by the knowledge that he had been at the top once and that his fan base—while slowly diminishing—still remembered him. Deep inside, one wonders whether he might have regretted his unwise foray into acting. That decision made the producers and actors wary of him since he became a competitor to those who were giving him work. As it turned out, he had neither the movies nor the songs.

Talat was a representative of Lucknow's old traditions. A gentleman to the core, he once declined a song offered to him by Salil Chowdhury for Dilip Kumar's *Madhumati*. He asked Salil to give the song to Mukesh instead, who was struggling at the time. An ever-grateful Mukesh ended up singing *Suhana safar aur yeh mausam haseen*. Just listen to this popular song, and you can tell that it was really meant for Talat.

Let us return to Anil Biswas. His fate was only slightly better than Talat's. By the midsixties, changing music trends had sidelined him as well. The only composer from the senior lot who survived the changing times was S. D. Burman. The rest were mostly cast aside by the late '60s. These included stalwarts like Naushad, O. P. Nayyar, C. Ramchandra, and Shankar among others. Seeing the writing on the wall, Anil Biswas quietly moved to Delhi, where he took a job with All India Radio as the orchestra director. As expected, he was also soon forgotten by Bollywood.

Many years later, a group of music lovers turned up at his door and asked to see him. An ailing Biswas was getting on in years by then. They were led to his room. The exited visitors started to talk about his marvelous music. But it did not take long for them to realize that the maestro was having a mighty struggle with his memory. As they tried to reawaken his memory by naming his famous movies and songs, he just stared ahead, oblivious to his glorious past and legacy. The visitors left in tears. Anil Biswas passed away in 2003, having outlived his protégé by five years.

The American from Mozang

Among his peers and students, he had developed a somewhat undeserved reputation of being too Americanized. He did not deny it either. Once, while sipping the forbidden nectar in a Christmas party, he told me that he had boarded the plane to the USA from Lahore in 1969 and had vowed to return to Pakistan immediately after his training in medicine and not to marry an American; neither vow was kept. This was vintage Usman Ahmad. I write this in the Saadat Hasan Manto tradition, who once famously wrote in the epilogue of *Ganjay farishtay* that he was not in the business of cleaning up his subjects to make them more presentable to the readers.

Back to Usman Ahmad—I once asked him what had made him choose the USA rather than the UK for postgraduation. "It was a no-brainer," he said. "The British are more style than substance while the

Americans roll up their sleeves and simply get down to the business." Having come from the UK at the time, I did not like his comment; but looking back, I find it fairly accurate.

As I think of him, a few things stand out. He was one of a fairly large crowd of young Pakistani physicians who came to the USA in the sixties and seventies and made their millions. But he was among the select few who rose to professional heights in their specialty; he became the program director of a residency program and professor of medicine. This was not easy; in a hushed tone, he once told me how—early on in his academic career—he had been forced to "walk behind" a senior Italian American physician who had been sympathetic to foreign physicians. Getting foothold in academia in white-dominated organizations is not easy as many of us continue to discover.

Usman Ahmad spoke English with a rare fluency and poise for a foreign medical graduate. I recall a farewell party for a retiring office manager of his in Pittsburg, where he delivered a speech. The audience—mostly white Americans—sat spellbound by his eloquence.

His punctuality was almost legendary. Being late is endemic in our culture, a despicable trait that many of us brought here from back home and never get rid of—but not him. Over a period of four years, I remember only one morning when he did not turn up for the morning report at seven sharp. Somewhat surprised, I looked outside the meeting report room, only to discover him on the phone in the hallway, taking an outside phone call from a distressed patient.

Usman Ahmad disliked using any language other than English in public. If you spoke to him in Urdu or Punjabi, he would answer back in English, but you would also receive a cold stare as a polite reprimand. On one occasion, however, I managed to hear him talk to a fellow Pakistani physician in typical Lahori accented Punjabi, but that was it.

He was a practical man and would, from time to time, pass on a word or two of wisdom to his juniors. When my son was born, he asked me his name. "Taimoor Javed," I said triumphantly.

"Look, unlike you, your son is a born U.S. citizen and is likely to spend his entire life here, so choose a traditional Islamic name by all means, but make sure it is easy for Americans to spell and pronounce," he said with conviction. He then went on to suggest a few names—Ali,

The Doctor From The East

Karim, and Hakim among others. My wife and I chose Ali, instead of Taimoor, and remain grateful to him twenty years later for this advice.

Unlike many of us, Usman Ahmad did not publicize his Pakistani origin. In fact, at times, one got the distinct impression that he was positively hiding his roots. It took me some time to realize that he did open up to a select few in private gatherings, and then the real *Mozangwala* from Lahore hidden deep inside him would surface. I was amused once to notice his car number plate; it read *Mozang*. Once, having just returned from Pakistan, he told me about a music show in Gaddafi Stadium at Lahore that he had been taken to by a friend. "Fantastic show, and this Arif Lohar is something," he said with a chuckle.

He was in love with Pittsburg and spent his entire career in the USA—training and practice—in the steel city. He played golf and was very fond of Tiger Woods. In 1997, I asked him why Tiger was considered better than Daly, who could hit longer tee shots. "Because Tiger has a much better thinking head on his shoulders," he said with a smile.

He loved the Steelers and once took me along with his young son to a Steelers football game. I then realized that he was a die-hard Steelers fan. With a twinkle in his eye, he told me that he had been present at the Three Rivers Stadium—since demolished—the day Terry Bradshaw had thrown that famous pass to Franco Harris, now referred to as *the immaculate reception* that has since become part of the Steeler folklore.

But the American football fan in Usman Ahmad had not been able to completely suppress the cricket fan inside him. Having seen Sri Lanka's triumph over Australia in the Cricket World Cup final in 1996, he remarked, "Oh, this was no contest." His excitement was palpable the way he described the match. After all, I realized, he had spent his youth in the city of the great Fazal Mahmood and the legendary skipper Hafeez Kardar.

His ties with the family back home remained close despite the obvious handicap of an American spouse. Many years ago, he was talking of a brother of his who had come down with a debilitating neurologic disorder in Pakistan. The treatment was expensive. "Is he able to afford it?" I asked him.

"I am his only Blue Cross," he said with sadness.

Usman Ahmad was not particularly handsome in the traditional sense, nor was he a particularly well-dressed person; it was his elegance and the warmth of his personality that impressed you and sometimes overwhelmed you. He would rarely miss an opportunity to remind you that we were in the USA rather than in Pakistan. Once I protested that he had taken a complaint against me from a nurse seriously. "A complaint from a nurse?" I said.

He was furious and retorted, "You should have left this stupid colonial mentality back home." Years later, as I think of his remarks and my unwise statement, I remain grateful to him for the message conveyed.

He did have a temper and would occasionally unleash his fury at a resident. Once, when a young intern from the Philippines broke down in tears from his scolding, I felt as if he also had not left behind his colonial baggage.

It was sometime in the midnineties that he introduced me to *Pakistan Link*. Clearly, he had more ties and affection to the land of his birth than he would freely admit in public. I subscribed to *Pakistan Link* at his suggestion and, except for a brief interruption, have been a regular reader and an occasional writer. Little did I realize that, one day, I would write his obituary in his beloved newspaper.

As I write these lines, Usman Ahmad has been buried in a Catholic cemetery in Pittsburg. I am told he had a cardiac arrest, having just returned from Lahore having visited his family, which included an elderly mother. A mutual friend reported that there were scores of people at his funeral from all walks of life to pay their respects to the talented Pakistani American. It seems as if the hidden but die-hard Lahorite wanted to pay one last homage to his beloved *Mozang* before finally calling it a day in his adopted homeland.

Waterloo: Napoléon's Last Stand

On a hot and humid day two hundred years ago, two armies faced each other at Waterloo. There were 140,000 soldiers and 30,000 horses all crammed inside an area under three square miles; another 60,000 men were only a few miles away. Both armies were led by outstanding generals—the French by Napoleon Bonaparte, arguably one of the finest military minds of all time, while his opponent on that day was the formidable Duke of Wellington, who had fought against Tipu Sultan in India and had defeated some of the best French marshals in Spain. "Wellington had the measure of the French," writes John Man. It was at Waterloo that these two military giants had their long-anticipated showdown.

The battle began at eleven thirty in the morning with massive cannonade by the French. An infantry assault led by Napoléon's brother, which failed to capture a chateau, was followed by devastating cavalry charges. Wellington intended to fight a defensive battle; he had placed his front lines on the reverse slope of a three-mile-long ridge that separated two armies. In the center and at both ends of his line were three farmhouses that he used to great advantage.

The fighting was ferocious; at one point, one British soldier asked another whether the Battle of Waterloo would be an exception in the annals of humanity and if there would be no survivors. Marshal Ney of France—Napoléon once called him the bravest of the brave—"had three horses killed beneath him and was almost speechless with rage and exhaustion," writes David Chandler, head of war studies at the Royal Military Academy.

Napoléon had to attack and win quickly. Aware that Prussian reinforcements for the British were approaching, he unleashed his full fury against the British lines, which—though weakened—did not break. In desperation, the Emperor decided to use his elite and much-feared Imperial Guards, who had the well-deserved reputation of being invincible. Napoléon personally led them forward and handed them over to Marshal Ney.

The menacing sight of the Guards' advance seized the British line with terror. That was the critical moment of the battle. Such are the moments that create legends and destroy reputations. "The excitement was at fever pitch," writes Elizabeth Longford, Wellington's biographer. "'Vive l'Empereur!' the Guards roared again and again in an ecstasy of pride, joy and gratitude."

But then the unthinkable happened; the British line held and poured such sustained and devastating volleys that the guards initially hesitated and then began to withdraw. Sensing victory, Wellington ordered a general advance with the order "No cheering, my lads—but forward and complete your victory." The whole British line surged forward, and the French Army was put to flight. What had been the best army of its time in the morning was a horde of fugitives by the end of the day. The Imperial Guard made a heroic attempt to cover the French Army's retreat by forming a square. Asked to surrender, their general gave the immortal reply "The Guard dies but never surrenders." The British guns opened up at the square; only a few guards survived.

It was a complete victory for the British and their allies. Napoléon escaped but, finding his situation hopeless, surrendered a few days later; he was banished to Saint Helena in South Atlantic, where he died a few years later, still agonizing over what might have been. No major battle was to follow Waterloo until the First World War.

When it was all over, Wellington surveyed the battleground on his horse and said, "Next to a battle lost, the saddest thing is to gain one; it was the most desperate business I ever was in . . . I hope to God that I have fought my last battle." Wellington had realized the extent of the carnage. There were 65,000 casualties in a battle that had lasted barely ten hours. His wish was granted; Waterloo was to be his last battle.

Why did Napoléon lose at Waterloo? Many historians believe that he delayed the attack by many hours, thus enabling the Prussians to arrive and save the day for the British. Poor choice of commanders was a factor too. Berthier, Napoléon's renowned chief of staff, was missing; his replacement, Soult, sent confusing and contradictory messages to the field commanders. As a result, one-third of the French Army under Marshal Grouchy remained idle just a few miles away from Waterloo. Napoléon also refused reinforcements to Marshal Ney at a critical moment; the delay allowed Wellington to stabilize his disintegrating center. Napoléon also underestimated Wellington. He used to ridicule him as a "sepoy general." The French marshals who had fought Wellington in Spain were apprehensive. But Napoléon was confident and felt that the odds were in his favor by 90 to 10. "Wellington is a bad general, the English are bad troops, and this affair nothing more than eating breakfast," Napoléon said to his staff in the morning of the battle.

Wellington kept his nerve, even though the battle appeared almost lost at one point. In those desperate moments, he was seen looking at his watch and was overheard saying, "Give me night or give me Blucher [Prussian general]." Uxbridge, Wellington's second-in-command, asked him of his battle plan. "To defeat the French" was the calm reply from Wellington as he pretended to resume his nap before the action began.

In the heat of battle, an English gunner approached Wellington and asked for permission to take a direct shot at Napoléon, whom he had identified at some distance. "The generals have better things to do than keep firing at each other," Wellington replied.

Wellington had a knack for paying attention to detail. He had even looked at Waterloo as a possible battle site some time earlier; he was well versed with the Napoleonic warfare, having fought the French in Spain for six years. Unlike others, Wellington refused to be intimidated by his illustrious opponent.

After Waterloo, some French veterans found their way to India. At least three of them were in the employ of Raja Ranjit Singh in Punjab, where they molded his *Fauj-e-khas* into a formidable fighting force trained on European lines. One of them, Avitable, gained notoriety by his harsh treatment of restless Pathans at Peshawar; another, Allard, died at Lahore. His tomb is still present in old Anarkali.

The Battle of Waterloo was a watershed in the annals of warfare. It has left its mark on the world stage. Many cities around the world have been named after the sleepy village that lies south of Brussels. It has even found its way into literature; Victor Hugo was to devote one full chapter in his masterpiece *Les Misérables* to Waterloo.

Wellington and Napoléon are long gone. But if they were to return to the earth now, they may fail to recognize the geopolitical changes in their homelands. Britain and France are connected via Eurotunnel and Napoléon's dream of a united Europe has almost become a reality. As for the battleground, some overzealous politician has gotten a huge mound built there that has swallowed up the famous ridge used so effectively by Wellington on that fateful day of June 18, 1815.

References: *The Illustrated Napoléon* by David Chandler, *Wellington* by Elizabeth Longford, *Battlefields Then and Now* by John Man, *Waterloo*, 1970 movie by Sergei Bondarchuk.

What is Wrong with Us?

The other day, as I was with two Pakistani friends—both physicians—a question was asked: what is the language of Pakistan's national anthem? Neither knew the answer. During my last visit to Pakistan, as I spent a solid hour in perhaps the biggest bookshop in Lahore, there were hardly any customers. The culture of reading has almost vanished. Sadly, it has been replaced by the abuse of cellular phone, Internet, and cable TV. A young and bright physician, who visited us recently from Lahore, made a passing remark that there is not much to do in Lahore except to eat out. I pointed out that Lahore has many libraries. He appeared surprised as I pointed out a few names, Punjab Public Library among them.

As we left the bookshop mentioned earlier, my nephew reminded me that it was lunchtime. I asked him to find any restaurant in the area that he liked. We stopped at two; both were full of customers, with long lines stretching almost to the entrance. It then occurred to me that food has taken a high place in our priorities. A visibly overweight former prime minister once generated headlines; on a tour of Sindh, where scores had died of starvation, he complained of the lack of a certain dish.

Our favorite pastime is *loose talk syndrome*. I once heard a gentleman in a gathering making a blank statement that everyone of Pakistan's rulers had been corrupt; everyone agreed. Someone reminded them that the curse of corruption did not always exist in our rulers. He then mentioned a few names—Liaquat Ali Khan, Khwaja Nazimuddin, Ch. Mohammad Ali and Junejo. Even the despised Yahya Khan was not financially corrupt. The conversation ended on a sour note.

Loose talk has become endemic. Regrettably, we talk too much and often talk nonsense. Part of the problem is that we have moved away from serious reading. Internet and TV are poor substitutes for reading. Most well-to-do, educated, upper-middle-class families—in the United States and Pakistan—have flat-screen TV, good car, and expensive furniture; only a few have a decent collection of books.

Many years ago, I met a Pakistani physician at Lahore Airport. As we exchanged pleasantries, I asked him about his family. With no hesitation, he said that he was divorced. Mian Abbas was one of the coaccused in the Kasuri murder case along with Z. A. Bhutto. Just before being hanged, as his last will was read out to him, he pointed out a minor mistake he wanted corrected. I never met Mian Abbas, and I had not seen that physician since. But I continue to admire both for the same reason—they were precise and truthful; neither was a loose talker.

Insensitivity to others' feelings is common. People boast of their luxurious lifestyle, oblivious to the fact that some of us may be living hand to mouth.

Safar waseela e zafar is a famous proverb. Among us, those who can afford often do so but rarely deviate from a set pattern. The religious minded keep going for hajj, and Umra. A friend has been to Saudi Arabia so many times that I have lost count. Some travel for better weather, others for shopping or entertainment; only a few travel to learn and explore. Mark Twain is credited with the saying "Travel is fetal to bigotry, prejudice and narrow-mindedness and many of our people need it sorely on these accounts. Broad, wholesome, charitable views of men and things cannot be acquired by vegetating in one little corner of the earth all one's lifetime." The acclaimed American writer had traveled to most continents. In the 1890s, he had gone off to India and traveled all the way to Rawalpindi from Bombay and Delhi before writing his travelogue.

But the mother of all curses is time wasting. It is mind boggling that despite living in the West, where punctuality is the norm, we do not acquire it.

I used to work with an American physician whose work started at six. He was late just once—in eight years. The CEO of my hospital was expected at a meeting. As the time approached, he was nowhere to be

The Doctor From The East

seen, that is, until he made a frantic call from outside the hospital; he was getting delayed in traffic and asked that proceedings should start on time without him. Back home, a parliamentary delegation from Pakistan was recently unable to see the speaker of Lok Sabha at Delhi. The reason—they were late by fifteen minutes; the speaker refused to see them.

If accurate, this speaks volumes about our representatives. "India's new religion must be based on a work-ethic—We must not waste time," writes the recently deceased Indian writer Khushwant Singh. He, a Sikh, then goes on to quote a Hadith of Prophet Mohammed that says, *La tasabuddhara; Hoo wallahoo*—don't waste time; time is God.

Gen. K.M. Arif, who spent years working with Zia-ul-Haq, has made scathing remarks about his chief's work ethic. Zia had made it a habit to delay reading files. Arif writes that Zia needed repeated reminders to finish his office work. For those whose files were stuck on the CMLA's desk, it would have been little consolation that he rarely missed his *tahajjud*.

Bhutto once kept the whole cabinet waiting for hours while he was nowhere to be seen. A tired J. A. Rahim left. His remark (I can not wait for Raja of Larkana) made in frustration, was conveyed to Bhutto. The result was a real thumping for Rahim by FSF and the loss of one of the few intellectuals for Bhutto. This ugly episode started with time wasting.

Economy with the truth is another problem. The highly educated are not immune from it. A case in point: when I was a student at Government College Lahore (1972–74), our principal, who was an acclaimed writer and a poet, had lost control of the students. There were frequent strikes and student unrest. He just was not cut out to be a good administrator. After two years, he was replaced; almost overnight, the order was restored. I came across his autobiography recently; he claims to have done a great job at Government College.

Some of us just hate to work. The founder of Pakistan was a hardworking man; he did not slow down despite being old and sick. He is credited with the saying "Work, work, and work." As for us, a fellow Pakistani American was envious of someone recently who "rarely goes to work and still gets paid". I recall a scene from Lahore that has remained etched in my mind—men lined up outside Bhatti Gate. I was told that they came from outside the city every day, hoping to be hired by someone for the day so that there would be bread on the table for their children. I shuddered to think what happens otherwise.

Back in the '70s, an old man had come from a village to pursue his case in the court. Being told that the hearing had been adjourned yet again for the umpteenth time, the dejected Pakistani raised his hands toward the sky and was overheard saying, *waa Angraiz, tera raaj*—O British, I miss your times. The pain of that statement still haunts me. Two generations later, lawyers in Pakistan still find reasons to strike often while the judges are in no hurry to dispose of their cases. That old petitioner is presumably long dead, but his heir may still be waiting for justice.

Back in the '90s, I visited some friends in Pakistan. Over breakfast as we chatted, I realized that they—a police officer, a magistrate, and a district surgeon—were getting late for work. Since none of them appeared to be in a hurry, I tried to remind them. None of them moved. "The work can wait," said one with a smile; the others agreed. The chat continued.

An old classmate of mine came to the United States and called me from Washington, DC. I was delighted to hear from him and invited him to visit and stay with me. I was unable to leave my clinic, however. My inability to bring him from Washington offended him so much that he abruptly changed his plans. I did not think he understood the concept of job responsibility. That was the end of our friendship.

When I was a junior doctor at Mayo Hospital Lahore, our professor had the reputation of being a superb clinician. He had been the best graduate of his class and had a picture of his, receiving gold medal from Ayub Khan, proudly displayed in his clinic. Later, he retired as principal of King Edward Medical College. But he was famous for another reason too—he rarely made rounds. Most of the patients from his ward left the hospital without ever seeing him. He would turn up typically at around ten to eleven in the morning, would consume tea in his office, would ask the registrar if everything was okay, and then would see a couple of VIP patients before disappearing to his private clinic.

The Doctor From The East

Corruption is not new in Pakistan. What is shocking is its acceptance. While waiting to board a PIA flight to Pakistan at JFK, I met a lady, a distant relative, whose brother was a police officer in Pakistan. When asked how he was, she said, "He has just returned from Okara and is very happy, having made a lot of *maal*." As I looked, there was sheer joy on her face. An acquaintance of mine had his son engaged to the daughter of a police officer. Someone asked the soon-to-be-father-in-law, "What is your son's fiancée bringing?" Three crores was the happy answer. So there it is.

In the heart of London lies Trafalgar Square with the column of Lord Nelson, one of the great heroes of Great Britain. Nelson had won a famous naval victory against France that saved Britain from invasion. Nelson's final signal before the battle has since become part of the English folklore: "England expects that every man will do his duty." In the famous *Gettysburg Address* Lincoln had paid tribute to the fallen soldiers "who had given the last full measure of their devotion" to their country. Quaid-e-Azam's Pakistan expects and deserves the same from us.

Yahya Khan: The Romeo General

An issue of *Nawaiwaqt* from March 23, 1971, has remained etched in my mind. It had three pictures alongside one another. In the middle was Quaid-e-Azam, with the caption "founder of Pakistan." On one side of him was Mujib-ur-Rahman, with the caption "traitor of Pakistan"; on the other side was a gentleman in army uniform with all the medals and regalia, with the caption "defender of Pakistan." The last picture belonged to Gen. Yahya Khan.

In the late '60s, my mother used to visit her brother in Rawalpindi who was an army officer. After one of her visits, Mother narrated an interesting episode. One day there was some anxiety in Uncle's house. Mother was asked to make sure she stayed in her room for a few hours since a VIP visitor was expected. The visitor, a female, did turn up and spent a few minutes with my uncle, who was then involved with some civilian affairs while on martial law duty. After she left, my mother asked her visibly relieved brother about her. In a hushed tone, she was told that the visitor had come to ask for some favor and that she had enormous influence and could only be ignored at one's peril. The readers may be able to guess the visitor's identity as they read along.

There is yet another picture of Yahya Khan that I can't forget. He is sitting, a glass—presumably of alcohol—in hand, next to singer Noor Jehan, who is all smiles. There are some other people too; all seem to be having a good time. Years later, NJ was to admit to Khalid Hasan that YK was very fond of her company. He called her *Noori* while our

The Doctor From The East

Malika-e-Tarranum addressed him as *Sarkar*. There was one song he was particularly fond of, and she would sing for him; she told KH, *Saiyo ni mera mahi merey phag jagawan aa gya*. The Romeo General would have been well advised to read the following description of his *Noori* written by the incomparable Manto in *Ganjay farishtay*:

> She had every single characteristic associated with the background from which she came. Everything about her was a put-in. She was flirtatious but not in a cultivated way. I was surprised at how Shaukat [her husband] who came from the heart of UP, could get along with this diehard peasant Punjabi girl.

Twenty years after Manto wrote this, YK was getting along with his Noori, learning to "conquer the fort of *Chataur*" (Manto's words, not this writer's), while General Manekshaw was patiently waiting for the Himalayas' passes to close with snow to ensure that China would not be able to move its army south.

Gen. Azhar once spent a night at the Governor House Lahore. He was a guest of Gen. Attiq, the governor of Punjab. As the two met for breakfast the following morning, Gen. Attiq asked his visitor whether he had had a comfortable night. Azhar had not slept well; he had heard a lot of commotion at night from the room above his. And so he asked, "Who was staying in the room above mine?" An embarrassed Attiq reported that it was YK, enjoying the company of some women friends. The year was 1971, and East Pakistan was sinking fast. Gen. Hamid, YK's COAS, "a despised intriguer widely disliked in the army" according to Air Cdre. Sajad Haider, told his staff that any orders given by the president at night should be verified the following day.

An incident that had been reported by many later—but suppressed at the time—was YK urinating in the parking area of Persepolis, where he had gone to attend the 2,500 years' celebration of the Persian Empire. Apparently, he had too much to drink and was unable to control his bladder. He relieved himself behind a bush.

Back to the picture of YK—I often wonder what Majid Nizami of *Nawaiwaqt* was thinking. He was carrying the legacy of his legendary brother Hameed Nizami. *Nawaiwaqt* was the most prestigious Urdu newspaper in the country that claimed—and probably still does—not to be afraid of telling the truth to the despot; perhaps he got carried away. It is hard to imagine that Nizami could exceed this folly. But this was precisely what he did; years later, he was to confer the title of *Mard-e-Hur*—whatever that means—on Zardari, one of the most despised and corrupt politicians of Pakistan.

As I think about it, *Nawaiwaqt* was not the only newspaper that misled the nation in those troubled times. There were many others too who joined the bandwagon. *Urdu Digest*, a popular magazine of its time, published a moving article by Altaf Hasan Qureshi, *Mohabbat ka zamzam beh raha hey*. The whole nation was swept by hysteria of patriotism, misled by the print media and the government-controlled radio and TV.

Here is another mind-boggling thing: YK was often described as an outstanding officer. Yet there was not much evidence to support it. Here is an excerpt from *Flight of the Falcon*, written by a real defender of Pakistan, Air Cdre. Sajad Haider; the first paragraph is about the war of 1965 while the next concerns 1971:

> Unfortunately, back on the ground, "Op Gibraltar" petered out, resulting in total failure, while "Grand Slam" came to a scratching halt. Major Gen. Yahya Khan, the commander of 7 Div who had replaced Maj Gen. Akhtar Malik did not launch the grand finale against Akhnur, on the flimsy pretext that Gen. Musa was not happy with the command communication system. His better and more valid excuse could have been that he neither had been associated with Akhtar Malik's planning of the "Grand Slam" nor was he familiar with the terrain.
>
> PAF was almost intact after flying over 3,000 operational missions and was ready for the blitzkrieg by Tikka Khan's 2nd Corps. A paralyzed President (read YK) and his inept coterie ware waiting for the American Pacific fleet to stop the Indians. YK successfully prevented a historic joint operation in the making which could have turned the tables and saved us from humiliation.

The Doctor From The East

But YK was too preoccupied with the likes of Noori. While the young men were laying down their lives for Pakistan—among them a young major Shabbir Sharif, from this writer's home district—the Romeo General was busy "conquering the fort of *Chataur.*" It is a myth also that YK handed over power to Bhutto voluntarily after the fall of Dhaka. He was forced to do it once made aware of the impending coup at Mangla Garrison.

The most revealing account of YK's activities has been written by Chaudhary Sardar, SP police, special branch, Rawalpindi, whose responsibilities included security of the president. Here is his narrative:

> The President House was then quite a place, with all kinds of people. The president was a drunkard and a womanizer. . . . Then there were the pimps and prostitutes, some of whom enjoyed very high status. Aqleem Akhtar Rani, Mrs. K. N. Hosain and Laila Muzaffar were at the top. There were hordes of other ill-reputed but attractive women, smoking, drinking and dancing all over the place. The police constabulary used to call the President House the *Kanjar Khana*, the Army GHQ the *Dangar Khana* . . . In Karachi, Rani told the interrogators, the Shah of Iran, on a state visit, was getting late for his departure but the President would not come out of his bedroom in the Governor House. A very serious protocol problem had arisen but nobody could enter his bedroom. Gen. Ishaq, M.S. to the President, requested Rani to go in and bring him out. When she entered the room, she claims that the most famous female singer of the country was performing oral. . .on YK. Even Rani found it abhorring. She helped the President dress up and brought him out. . . . Yahya had several women to relax with . . . one evening he went to the residence of Mrs. K. N. Hosain, widely known as "Black Beauty." . . . The President remained there for three days and nights without being available to anybody. On the fourth day, he took Mrs. Hosain with him, lodged her in the State Guest House and permanently employed her as an interior decorator. Her husband was appointed

> as ambassador to Switzerland . . . when asked later whey YK had stayed at her house for three days, she said she had been teaching him Bengali music!

After the fall of Dhaka, YK declared on TV that the war would continue on the western front after "a temporary setback on the Eastern Sector," as he put it. But the following day, he accepted a unilateral cease-fire announced by India. The reality had finally dawned on him. Having lost half the country, YK was now getting ready to announce a new constitution; *the defender* was making himself available to continue as president. Our nation should be eternally grateful to those courageous army officers at Mangla who, at great personal risk, helped us get rid of YK. They were the unsung heroes of Pakistan.

Before leaving for Dhaka in March 1971, on that fateful meeting with Mujib—a meeting that effectively sealed the fate of East Pakistan—the following conversation took place between YK and Sardar Yousaf Chandio, a member of National Assembly. The narrator is again, Chaudhary Sardar, who heard it from a DSP on duty, the venue a lake near Karachi and the event duck shooting:

> YOUSAF: Sain, what will happen now? The elections have thrown up a swine [Mujib] on one side and a hound [Bhutto] on the other.

> YK: Bachoo, don't worry and just see the *tamasha*. I shall throw such a bait that either the swine will finish the hound or the hound will kill the swine. The lion will destroy both of them.

Some of YK's proclamations remind one of an interesting character from the American Civil War. Before the Battle of Chancellorsville, Gen. Hooker—who was commanding the army of the North—made a boisterous statement. "My plans are perfect. May God have mercy on General Lee [his opposing general], for I will have none." The following day, Hooker had suffered a crushing defeat and was relieved of command by Lincoln. YK, we are told, had been an instructor at Staff

College Quetta. One wonders if he had taken the trouble of reading the chapter on the American Civil War.

After Tikka Khan's military action in March 1971, millions of refugees crossed into West Bengal. Precisely in those times, what was *the defender* doing? Read on; the narrator is Chaudhary Sardar:

> YK continued to indulge in his merrymaking. With one of his favorite women by his side, he would be out every night for a pleasure drive on the roads of Rawalpindi and Islamabad, duly escorted by my security guards. Sometimes he would stand up in his open-top car and deeply kiss the woman, in full view of the police escort following him. The armed guards resented intensely such behavior of the head of a Muslim state . . . YK's abhorrent public display of debauchery was reported to IG Police; his response, "The President is burdened with so many serious problems and needs some relaxation." Some relaxation!

YK's sympathizers often blame his advisers for having misled him. But who chose them? It was not that sane advice was not given; indeed, it was but was simply ignored. There were upright, well-informed people who begged him not to postpone the NA session at Dhaka. On February 27, 1971, Gen. Yaqub and Admiral Ahsan—who were serving in East Pakistan—told him that it would be most unwise to postpone the NA session. "A few weeks earlier, S. M. Ahsan had courageously refused to order Pakistani troops to open fire on striking Bengalis. He was replaced by Yaqoob who too rejected genocidal orders," writes Stanley Wolpert. They were stunned when YK, surrounded by his whiskey group, brushed aside their pleas.

A letter by Podgorny, President of USSR, that had suggested political settlement in East Pakistan was unwisely ignored. *The defender* was in a hurry to "let loose his tigers" on Bengalis, oblivious to how bleak the circumstances were in East Pakistan. Intoxicated by power and surrounded by sycophants, YK once boasted that his war machine was better than India's. And so Gen. Yaqub was recalled from East Pakistan, demoted, and retired from service. Years later, he was to distinguish himself as Pakistan's ambassador in Washington.

And who was sent by YK to defend East Pakistan at that critical moment? Gen. Niazi. His first question to Gen. Khadim Raja, who had come to receive him at Dhaka Airport, was "How many women do you have ready for me?" Just a few months later, Niazi was seen tamely handing over his revolver to Gen. Aurora; they had been course mates once. Years later, Niazi had the audacity to say that he was the most decorated general in the history of the world; he also compared himself to Gen. Rommel and Tariq ibn Ziyad in an interview; there, you have another *defender of Pakistan*.

Now fast-forward to 1972—YK was in protective custody in Banni Bangla, a rest house near Kharian, and was being escorted to a Sihala Rest House to appear before the Hammod-ur-Rahman Commission, by Sardar, who has left this account for posterity:

> YK refused to travel back by helicopter and insisted on going by road . . . I was not prepared for that as it involved a great security risk . . . YK insisted on knowing the reason it was risky to travel by road. "Because people might lynch you." I said. "Why people should be against me?" asked YK. "Because of defeat in East Pakistan." YK response to this is one for the ages: "Am I a pariah? Did I touch the private parts of somebody's female ass?"

The actual statement was in Punjabi and presumably more colorful. YK had his way, and they started by road. At the Sihala railroad crossing, the car had to stop. YK was recognized by passersby, who started to throw stones on the car.

> YK was ashen faced and totally shaken up as if death was coming to him. Having seen his reaction, I offered to take him to Raja Bazar. He was trembling by now; so much for the brave soldier . . . finally, he was begging me to take him to Banni rest house where he came up with another request; he wanted to be shifted to Abbotabad. On being asked, why, YK said. "I do not like this place as it is full of jackals and they howl too much at night." "A good company, Sir." I replied.

The day after the fall of Dhaka, Roedad Khan—MD of PTV—called on Nurul Amin, the VP. This was what Roedad wrote in his memoirs:

> I had never seen Nurul Amin, a true Pakistani and a great patriot, in such an angry mood. He had been trying in vain to meet the President for two days. I contacted YK on the green line and arranged a meeting that very evening. YK asked me to accompany Nurul Amin to the President House. When we got there, Gen Hamid was already there and they were all—you guessed it—having drinks. Nurul Amin burst out and told the President, "So Dhaka has fallen and East Pakistan is gone, and you are enjoying whisky" . . . YK put the entire blame on Mujib. It was one of the most painful meetings I have ever attended.

There is yet another picture of *the defender* that some would recall. YK is sitting next to Bhutto. Ghulam Ishaq is placing a document on the table for his signature. YK's facial expression personifies dejection, humiliation, and all. How far the mighty had fallen!

References: *Ganjay Farishtay* by Manto; *Flight of the Falcon* by Sajad Haider; *The Ultimate Crime* by Ch. Sardar; *Zulfi Bhutto of Pakistan* by Stanley Wolpert; *Pakistan-A Drean Gone Sour* by Roedad Khan

Zulfiqar Ali Bokhari: The Man for All Seasons

The other day, after finishing his autobiography, this writer made a list of those whom ZAB had befriended: Faiz Ahmad Faiz, Abul Kalam Azad, Nazar-ul-Islam, Charag Hasan Hasrat, Josh Malihabadi, John Gielgud, Prithviraj Kapoor, Balraj Sahni, Satyajit Ray, George Orwell, E. M. Forster, T. S. Eliot, Lord Willingdon, Majaz, Rafiq Ghaznavi, Diwan Singh Maftoon, and Kh. Hasan Nizami. This read like a who's who of the Indian subcontinent and Britain.

ZAB was multitalented—a respectable musician, a good actor, an excellent director, and a superb administrator. He was a good poet too. Faiz is on record that when he would come up with a new verse, there were only six people to whom he would recite it to get their approval; ZAB was on that list. But one thing that remains ZAB's legacy is Radio Pakistan. It is no exaggeration to say that ZAB was to Radio Pakistan what Shah Jahan was to Taj Mahal or Leonardo da Vinci to *Mona Lisa*. He had been associated with radio before partition, along with his illustrious brother, Patras Bokhari. The association of two Bokhari brothers with radio had allowed someone to quip that BBC in India had become *Bokhari Brothers Corporation*. While Patras returned to Government College Lahore after partition and then left for UN as Pakistan's permanent representative, ZAB was made DG of Pak Broadcasting Corporation, which he renamed Radio Pakistan.

Pakistan had only three radio stations in 1947: Lahore, Peshawar, and Dhaka. ZAB went to extraordinary lengths to develop Radio Pakistan. The Second World War had just ended; he sent his engineers and technicians abroad and procured the necessary radio equipment at throwaway prices from the junkyards. He would personally interview the staff being hired. There have been many stories of his forays into the less desirable areas to find the artists for radio. By the early '60s, Radio Pakistan was in excellent shape that compared favorably with the best in the world. As our generation was growing up, radio was king. ZAB had retired by then, but his beloved Radio Pakistan was being run by those whom he had recruited and trained.

ZAB had a busy and eventful public life. Naturally, there were controversies and professional jealousies. There were arrogant politicians and bureaucrats to deal with. But through it all, he kept going with his single-minded devotion to Radio Pakistan.

Bade Ghulam Ali Khan had left Pakistan back in the '50s. There have been all kinds of stories about his move to India. ZAB has, for once, put the record straight; arguably the greatest classical singer of his generation, Khan Sb was not so great when it came to monetary issues. For his radio program, he demanded three thousand rupees, an astronomical amount back then. ZAB tried to reason with him. But Khan Sb had convinced himself of the greener pastures across the eastern border. What transpired for him later in India is another story.

Agha Nasir was hired by ZAB for radio but later moved on to PTV and eventually became its MD. Agha Nasir reports that ZAB had an impressive and dominating personality—tall, of fair color, elegant, always well dressed, and eloquent to a fault. With a commanding voice and faultless pronunciation, he would spellbind his audience. Late actor Mohammad Ali was once asked from where he had learned his impressive dialogue delivery. "ZAB" was his answer.

Punctual to a fault and a hard taskmaster, ZAB led by example. His subordinates had to be on their toes, for he expected nothing less than perfection. He could be harsh at times and, while always appreciated their hard work, allowed only a few in his inner circle. He was a workaholic, ate and slept very little, and lived life with a remarkable discipline. He entertained his friends late into the night at his house. These were mostly literary gatherings where poetry, music, literature, and sometimes current affairs were discussed. At the end, ZAB would drop everyone at their residence in his own car. Since he was an early riser too, it left little time for sleep. Despite that, he would turn up for work the following morning on time, looking fresh.

Ustad Bundu Khan, one of the finest violinists of his generation, used to work at Karachi Radio. There is an interesting story about him. The radio van used to pick him up from home. Along the way, it also picked up a famous Maulana who used to recite Koran to begin the morning radio transmission. This Maulana was not happy to be in the company of a violinist and lodged a complaint with the secretary of information, who spoke to ZAB. ZAB promised to look into this but did nothing. Sometime later, the secretary asked if the issue had been addressed. "Yes, I have tendered an apology," he said.

"But Maulana is still traveling with Bundu Khan," said the surprised bureaucrat.

"Bundu Khan is the one who deserved and got the apology," explained ZAB. "Bundu Khan is only one of a kind and indispensable to radio while Maulana can be easily replaced." While this episode shows the arrogance of our religious elite, it also illustrates the extent to which ZAB respected the staff at Radio Pakistan.

Prof. Mirza Saeed was a respected scholar. He used to deliver lectures from AIR, Delhi, before 1947. He had moved to Karachi after partition. ZAB had great regard for him and used to visit him. On one of his visits, ZAB brought along Fielden, the former DG of AIR.

The Doctor From The East

Fielden was an admirer of Professor Saeed too. Back in the '50s, fear of communism was widespread. Fielden asked whether Pakistan was at risk of becoming a communist state. "No, but it is at risk of becoming a theocracy," said Professor Saeed.

After retirement from radio, ZAB continued to live in Karachi. Patras, his elder brother, had died years earlier. Still in good health, he tried to work in PTV, but times had changed and, being essentially a man of radio, soon gave up. Late into his life, he remained in demand for *marsiya* reading, for which he had no peer. ZAB died quietly in Karachi in 1975. It is not known what he thought of the changing world of broadcasting where radio had essentially been pushed into a distant second place behind the TV juggernaut.

During his life time, PTV had recorded a detailed interview of ZAB, to be shown after his death. The day arrived in 1975. Many in PTV, including Agha Nasir, were admirers of ZAB. A memorable and well-deserved tribute was paid to the father of Radio Pakistan. Those who watched it realized on that day the enormous contributions made by the late broadcaster. The following day, however, Agha Nasir received a strange phone call. It had come from the PM's office. It conveyed the PM's displeasure at the program that "made it look like as if a head of state had died." Apparently, the inflated ego of the Oxford and Berkeley educated PM had been bruised. Aghast, Agha Nasir—a PTV employee—apologized to the PM. "How could I tell them that ZAB was indeed the king of broadcasting?" he writes with sadness.

ZAB was multilingual. He was fluent in Pashto, Hindko, Punjabi, Bengali, English, and Urdu. While Persian was not listed as one of the languages that he spoke, his autobiography has numerous references to poetry of Hafiz and Sa'di. Clearly, he had a good understanding of Persian too.

ZAB was not afraid to stand up to higher-ups. Pir Ali Muhammad Rashdi, arrogant to the core, was the minister of information. In a meeting with ZAB, he began to criticize Radio Pakistan. "Nothing is right. Programs are of poor quality."

"May I have a pen and paper?" demanded ZAB.

"What for?" asked an irritated minister.

"So that I may be able to jot down your brilliant ideas about how to immediately improve our very mediocre programs," said ZAB. Rashdi, a snob, may have realized then that in ZAB he had met more than his match.

At the height of the Second World War, ZAB and Leslie Howard (Vivien Leigh's love interest in *Gone with the Wind*) were sent to Portugal. ZAB was then working for BBC while Howard was there to entertain the British troops. Their return military plane had only one available seat, reserved for ZAB. Howard had an urgent shooting schedule in London, and ZAB allowed Howard to take that seat. The plane was shot down by Germans. ZAB survived to mourn the loss of a dear friend.

On September 11, 1948, Quaid-e-Azam died. Radio Pakistan made arrangements to do the live broadcast of the funeral procession. Among the three spots chosen, the first was given to Agha Ashraf and the second to Sadiq Ahmad—both were renowned broadcasters. The last one, right at the burial ground was taken by ZAB himself. The young nation was overwhelmed with grief. ZAB was aware of the enormous responsibility. He called on decades of experience gained by working with Agha Hashar and, with giants of BBC like Fielden and John Gielgud, rose to the challenge. His command of Urdu and mastery of the verse were at full display. Those who heard that broadcast were unanimous that ZAB had exceeded all expectations. There was hardly anyone who did not break down. "That may have been the finest day of his professional life," writes Hameed Naseem, a colleague at Radio Pakistan. "On that day, ZAB was seen as a giant, un-matched, unique, one of a kind broadcaster . . . I would have been honored to kiss his feet that day."

Back in 1520, Robert Whittington had called Sir Thomas More a man for all seasons. There has been hardly anyone in Pakistan who excelled in so many disciplines and deserved this title except ZAB. One would have expected that a genius like him would be well remembered by the current generation. It is sad that he is not. Such are the times that we live in. *Baqi rahe naam Allah ka.*

References: *Sarguzasht* by ZA Bokhari; *Gumshuda Log* by Agha nasir; *Namumkin Ki Justajoo* by Hamid Nasim

Index

A

Abbasid caliphate, 7, 86
Abd ar-Rahman, 7
Abdul Hamid Adam, 23
Abu Abdullah, 6
Abu Sa'id, 86
Ahmad, Usman, 199–202
Ahmad III, 3
Akbar the Great, 24, 105
Akhtar, Hameed, 92, 97, 101, 168–70
Al-Andalus, 6–10
alcoholism, 21–24, 97
Alhambra, 9
Almohads, 8
Almoravid Dynasty, 8
Anand, Dev, 60, 62–63, 143
Anwar, Raja, 41, 148, 150, 155–57
Ara, Shamim, 175–78
Arif, K. M., 37, 41, 209
Asma Begum, 58
Atatürk. *See* Kemal, Mustafa
Averroës. *See* Ibn-Rushd
Azad, Abul Kalam, 24, 28, 93
Azam, Chaudhry, 156

B

Banu, Saira, 58, 145

Bashir, Ahmad, 102, 104, 138
Batalvi, Ashiq, 22, 138–40, 145
Batalvi, Ijaz, 136–37, 195
Battle of Tours, 7
Bers, Sofia, 111, 114
Best, George, 23
Bhagat Singh, 26–29, 51, 79, 102, 154
Bhutto, Begum Nusrat, 36, 41–42, 155
Bhutto, Mumtaz, 37
Bhutto, Murtaza, 156
Bhutto, Zulfikar Ali, 5, 23–24, 30–43, 49, 53, 65, 71–73, 125, 132–33, 135, 148, 150, 155–56, 183, 187, 195, 208–9, 215–16, 219, 221, 223
Bilawal Zardari, 30, 39
Biswas, Anil, 95, 120–21, 196, 198
Bokhari, Patras, 17, 20, 139, 164, 195, 221, 223
Bokhari, Zulfikar Ali, 220–24
Bonaparte, Napoléon, 79, 112, 140, 144, 155, 182–83, 203–6
Borh Bungalow, 130
Bridges of Madison County, 142
Brontë, Anne, 44, 46
Brontë sisters, xiii, 44–48, 56, 117
Bugti, Ahmed Nawaz, 35

C

Charlesworth, Richard, 184
Chaudhary (sardar), 32, 38, 215–17
Childhood (Tolstoy), 111
Churchill, Winston, 12, 82, 108
courage, 83, 97, 153, 157

D

Dada Amir Haidar, 49–53
Dalai Camp, 35
Daniyal (son of Akbar the Great), 24
death, 2–3, 14, 16, 18–19, 22–26, 39, 46, 53, 59, 62, 83, 89, 103, 110, 114, 116, 119, 121, 123, 129, 136, 138, 141, 143–45, 152–53, 155–56, 166, 171, 174–75, 178, 218, 223
Death of Ivan Ilyich, The (Tolstoy), 136
Dehlavi, Mumtaz Jehan. *See* Madhubala (actress)
Do Bihga Zamin, 17
Dutt, Guru, 57, 143
duty, 38, 75, 153, 211, 216

E

Edward VIII, 144
elections, 38, 65, 68, 70, 132, 165, 183, 216

F

father, 64–69

G

Galip (Turkish politician), 15
Gallipoli, 12
Gandhi, 18, 29, 68, 114, 167
Gardezi, Kaswar, 33
Garm Hava, 18
Gascoigne, Pal, 23
Ghulam Mustafa, 43
Granada, 6, 8–9, 89–90
Guevara, Che, 155
Gujranwala, 60
Gul Hassan, 37, 41, 73, 186
Gunga Jumna, 56–57, 59

H

Hadji-Murad, 79–84, 155
Hadji-Murad (Tolstoy), 111
Haider, Sajad, 70–73, 213–14, 219
Hasan, Khalid, 31, 34, 39, 43, 59, 123, 158, 187, 212
Hashr, Agha, 22
Hasrat, Charag Hasan, 22–23
Henry VIII, 153
Hussain, Syed, 51, 145–46

I

Ibn Battuta, 85–90
Ibn Juzayy, 85, 89
Ibn Juzzay, 9
Ibn-Khaldūn, 9
ibn Nasr (founder of Granada), 8
Ibn-Rushd, 9, 74
Iftikhar Tari, 35
Inayat Begum, 146
infatuation, 63, 142, 193
insensitivity, 208
Iqbal (poet), 20, 22, 67, 91, 139, 145, 165
Islamic Spain, 7, 9–10
Ismet İnönü, 13–14

J

Jahangir (Mogul governor), 24
Jane Eyre (Brontë, C.), 45, 47
Janissaries, 1–4, 182
Jaywant, Nalini, 57
Jinnah, Fatima, 132, 161
Josh Malihabadi, 22–23, 91–93, 220
journals, 38

Journey to Disillusionment, A (Mazari), 33
Jungle Book, The (Kipling), 105

K

Kasuri, Ahmad Raza, 32, 43
Kasuri, Mohammad Ahmad, 26, 31
Kaushal, Kamini, 58
Keats (poet), 145
Kemal, Mustafa, 11–15, 24
Kennedy, Edward, 24
Kennedy, Jacqueline, 135
Khan, Imran, 79, 184
Khan, Tikka, 37, 41, 72, 183, 214, 217
Khan, Yahya, 40, 72, 132–33, 178, 186–87, 207, 212–19
Khan, Yusuf. *See* Kumar, Dilip
Khanum, Farida, 189
Khuro, Ayub, 35
Khurshid Anwar, 20, 100–104, 122, 190
Kim (Kipling), 108
Kinross, Lord, 1, 3, 5
Kipling, Rudyard, xiii, 105–9
Kumar, Dilip, 17, 47, 55–59, 117, 119, 144, 187

L

Laila, Runa, 189
Latife (wife of Mustafa Kemal), 12
Lenin, 112
love, 28, 61–62, 75, 97, 101, 105–6, 108–9, 117, 142–46, 151, 175, 187, 193, 201
Ludhianvi, Sahir, 92, 97, 119, 121, 143, 168–71

M

Madhubala (actress), 57–58, 116–19, 144, 171, 176, 180
Madinat al-Zahra, 9

Mahmood, Talat, 21, 120, 122–23, 172, 174, 196–98
Mahmud II, 3–5
Majaz, Asrar ul Haq, 21–22, 91
Malik, Akhtar, 41, 72, 214
Malik, Nasrullah, 147–48, 150–51
Malik Asad, 134
Malik Meraj Khalid, 35
Malik Muzaffar, 134
Manto, Saadat Hasan, 21, 58, 114, 184, 187, 189–90, 199, 213
Man Who Would Be King, The (Kipling), 107
Masih, Parvez, 156
Masroor, Hajra, 44, 48, 169
Mazari, Sherbaz, 33, 35–36
Meeraji (poet), 75, 136–37
Mian Abbas, 208
Mian Tufail, 33
Mirza, Humayun, 126–28
Mirza, Iskander, 30, 124–28, 131
Mirza, Nahid Iskander, 124–29
Mohammad, Nazar, 188
More, Thomas, 153–54, 157, 224
Muhammad Hakim, 24
Muhammad ibn Tughluq, 87–88
Mukesh, Nitin, 123
Mukesh (singer), 95, 120–23, 197–98
Mulkane, Joe, 51
Murad (Ottoman sultan), 1–2, 24
Musa ibn Nusayr, 6, 89, 137, 140, 144, 189, 214

N

Nawab Amir Mohammad Khan (Nawab of Kalabagh), 130–35
Nehru, Jawaharlal, 19, 27, 29, 36, 59, 92–93, 145, 149, 167
newspapers, 28, 38, 45, 58, 109, 214
Ney (French marshal), 155, 203
Niazi, Kausar, 24

Niazi, Nahid, 37, 72, 101, 183, 190, 218
Nizami, Feroz, 188

O

Orhan (Ottoman sultan), 87
Osman (Ottoman sultan), 1, 3, 87
Ottoman Centuries, The (Kinross), 1, 3
Ottoman Empire, 1–3, 11, 13–14, 87

P

Pakistan, 4–5, 13, 18, 31, 41, 70, 92, 131–35, 163–66, 188, 211, 213, 216–17, 221, 223
Pasha, Anwar Kamal, 137, 184–85

Q

Qadir, Manzoor, 140
Qateel Shifai, 101–2, 170, 172–73, 177, 190
Quaid-e-Azam, 68, 158–62, 167, 187, 212, 224
Qureshi, Wahid, 155–56

R

Rafiuddin (colonel), 40–43
Rahim, J. A., 34, 37, 72–73, 209
Rai, Lajpat, 27, 51
Rana, Mukhtar, 33
Rashid, Noon Meem, 60, 137, 184
Rashid, Pervaiz, 184
Rashid, Rao, 37
Raza, Salim, 172–74
Reconquista, 8, 89
Rihlah (Ibn Battuta), 9, 85–87, 89–90
Rizvi, Shaukat, 143–44, 187–89
Ruttie (wife of Quaid-e-Azam), 158–62

S

Sahni, Balraj, 17–20, 27–29
Saigal, K. L., 23, 69, 95–99, 120, 123, 196
Salam, Abdus, 20, 74–77, 193–94
Sardar, Hassan, 184
Shah Jahan, 144, 221
Shamil (imam), 79–81, 83, 155
Sharma, Kidar, 60, 95–99, 117, 119
Shirani, Akhtar, 22, 145
Shuja, Hakim Ahmad, 137–38, 176
Singh, Khushwant, 20, 24, 138, 140–41, 209
Siraj (professor), 143, 192–95
Sirajuddin (professor), 192, 194
Sondhi, Urmila, 75, 192–95
Suleiman (king of Mali), 89
Süleyman the Magnificent, 182
Sultana, Nighat, 189
Suraiya (actress), 60–63, 143

T

Tariq ibn Ziyad, 6, 218
Tenant of Wildfell Hall (Brontë, A.), 45–46
time, 208–9
Tiwana, Khizer Hayat, 75, 164
Tiwana, Umar Hayat, 164
Tolstoy, Leo, 79, 110–15, 136, 140, 155
travel, 208
truth, 70, 73, 96, 107, 122, 147, 191, 209, 214

U

Ultimate Crime, The (Chaudhary), 32
Ulyanov, Vladimir. *See* Lenin
Umayyad caliphate, 6–7, 9

W

War and Peace (Tolstoy), 111–12
Waterloo, 140, 155, 182, 203–6
Wellington, Duke of, 59, 140, 182, 203–6
work, xiv, 9, 13, 15, 23, 31, 44–45, 50, 53, 55, 75, 89, 100–101, 103, 115, 121, 129, 138, 150, 159–60, 177, 185, 197–98, 208–10, 222–23
Wuthering Heights (Brontë, E.), 45–46

Z

Zaidi, Mustafa, 69, 92, 143
Zia Sarhadi, 17
Zia-ul-Haq, 5, 33, 37, 41, 43, 65, 70–71, 73, 156, 209

Printed in the United States
By Bookmasters